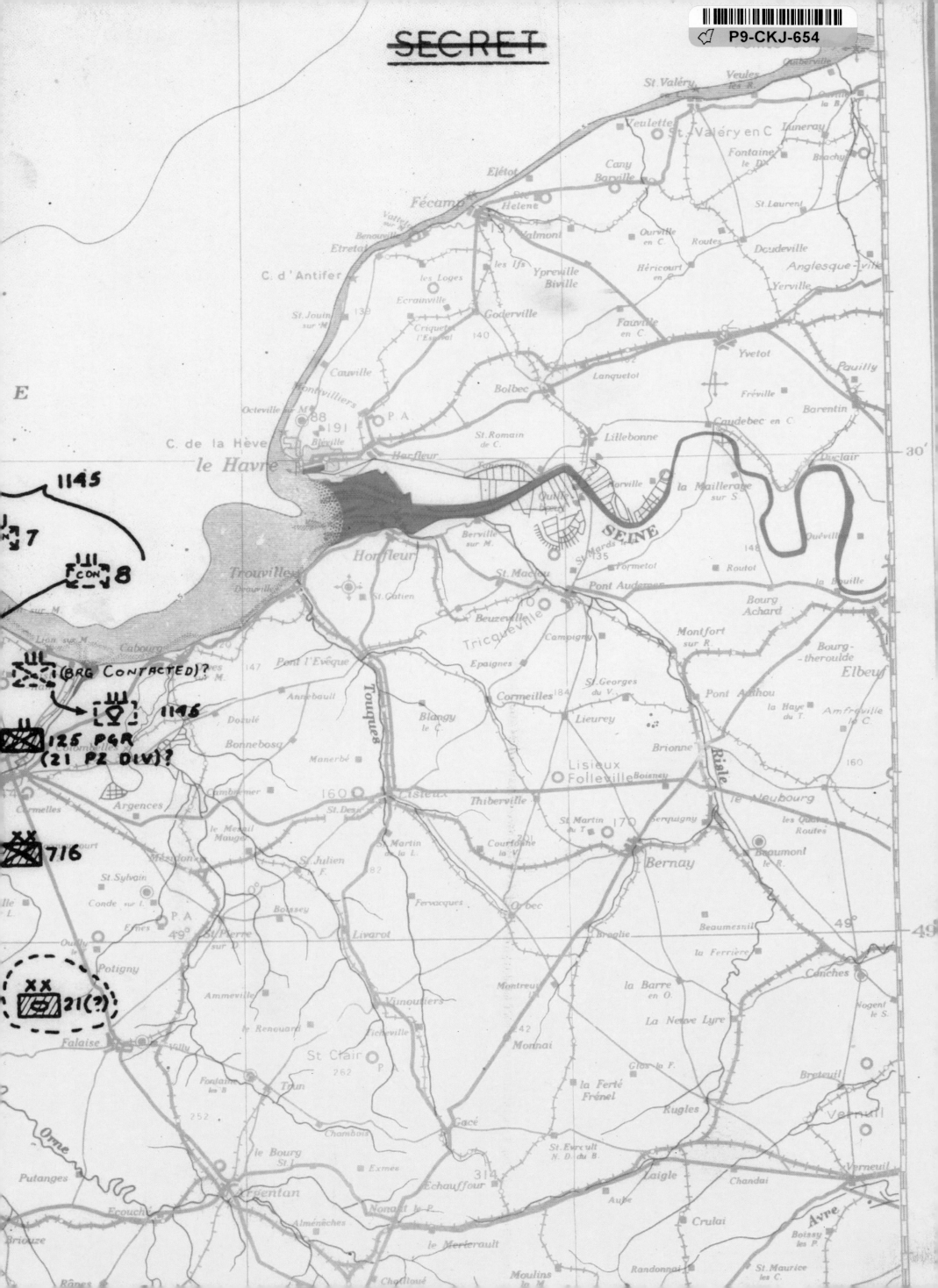

U.S. ARMY ATLAS
of the European Theater in
WORLD WAR II

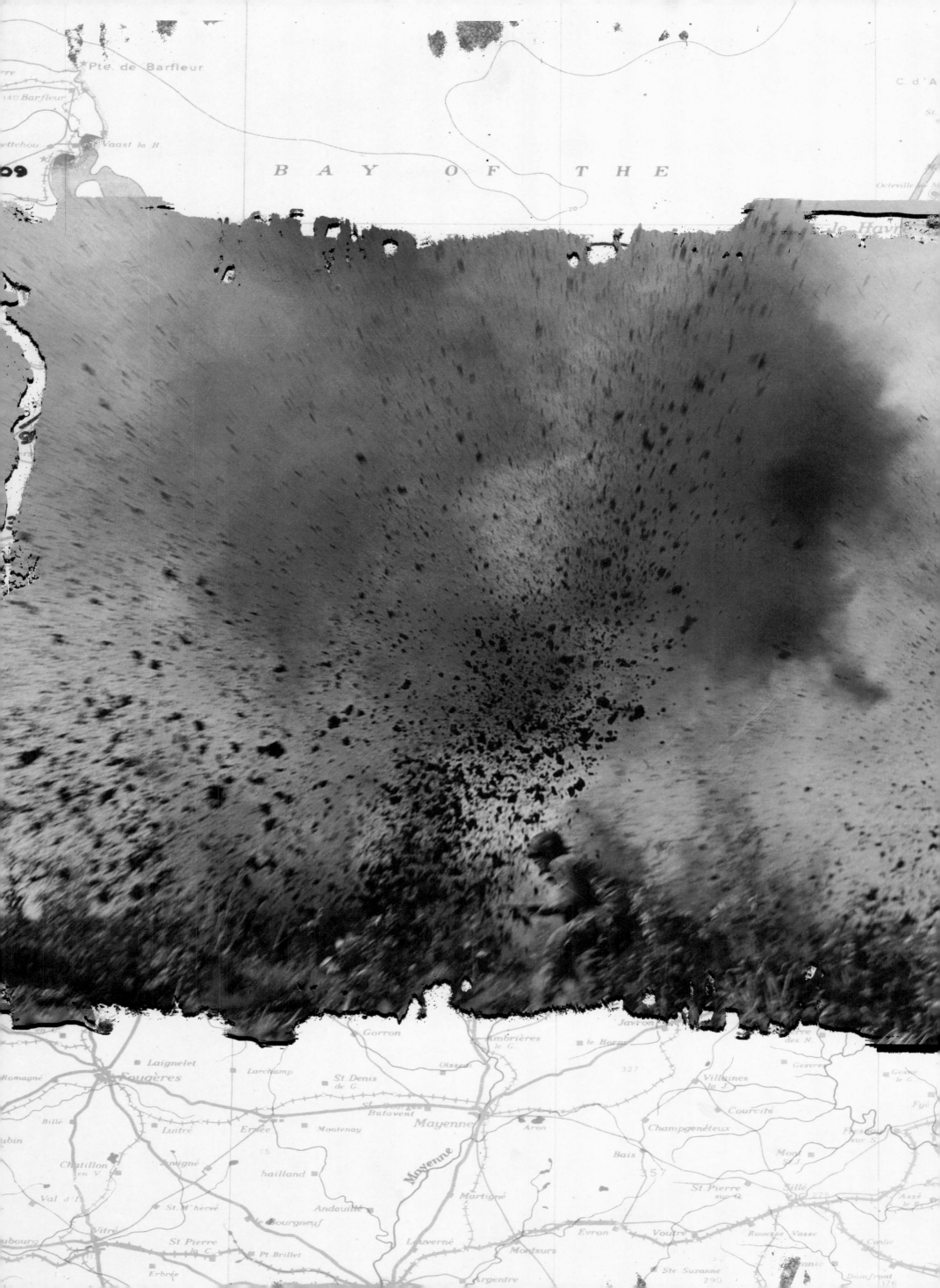

U.S. ARMY ATLAS
of the European Theater in
WORLD WAR II

Edited and with an Introduction by
Donald L. Gilmore

BARNES & NOBLE BOOKS

NEW YORK

ISBN 0-7607-5214-1

Digital imaging by Christopher Bain
Digital reproduction by Bright Arts Graphics, Singapore
Printed and bound in China by SNP Excel

1 3 5 7 9 10 8 6 4 2

HALF-TITLE PAGE: *An American soldier, Private Margerum, walks
through a deceptively peaceful forest near Bastogne, Belgium, December
27, 1944. Ironically, some of the most violent fighting of World War II
was being fought within a few short miles of this tranquil scene, where
tanks dueled and the men could no longer feel their fingers or feet
because of debilitating frostbite. It was one of the coldest winters
on record for the region.* **TITLE PAGE, LEFT:** *Two American paratroopers scurry through horrendous artillery fire near Arnhem, the
Netherlands, in late September 1944 as part of Operation MARKET-
GARDEN. Poor planning and execution by the Allies, commanded by
Field Marshal Bernard Montgomery, led to a military debacle at
Nimjegen and Arnhem that slowed down the Allied advance toward
Germany.* **TITLE PAGE, RIGHT:** *An American soldier stands guard in
front of an off-limits building in La Haye-du-Puits, France, after the
town's capture by the U.S. 79th Infantry Division. The village, at the
base of two hills manned by German artillery, was captured after a
fierce engagement. Later, a British officer remarked to the Americans,
"You were the chaps at La Haye-du-Puits, weren't you? We heard
you had a piece of cake over there—a bloody piece of cake it was."*
RIGHT: *Members of Headquarters, 134th Infantry, 35th Division,
sort through maps before distributing them to Allied units in the
St. Lô, France, sector of the front, July 1944. Aided by good terrain
maps, well-organized and mechanized Allied forces broke out of their
Normandy lodgment and drove the Germans before them in the Allied
version of blitzkrieg warfare.* **CONTENTS PAGE:** *An American soldier
observes the Remagen Bridge, sited at the midway point between
Koblenz and Cologne, from high atop the bank of the Rhine River in
spring 1945. The taking of the bridge on March 7, 1945, marked the
beginning of the end for the armies of the Third Reich because it allowed
the Allies to cross the Rhine in force and establish a presence on the
east side of the river. In a decisive thrust, the 9th Armored Division
charged across the bridge before the Germans could destroy it
(though they did manage to damage it). Once the bridge was in
American hands, the Germans tried to bomb it from the sky, but the
raids were unsuccessful. A planned attempt to blow up the bridge
using German frogmen proved pointless as the weakened structure
finally collapsed on its own on March 17. With a rending metallic
shriek, the structure fell into the Rhine at roughly 1500, local time,
injuring nearly one hundred of the engineers working on it and killing
twenty-eight others. By then, a pontoon bridge had already been
completed, giving the Allies a strong foothold in Germany.*

PHOTO CREDITS

Collection of Dennis Giangreco: pp. 4–5

Corbis: pp. 10–11 top, p. 10 bottom, p. 63 bottom, p. 115 bottom,
p. 116 bottom, pp. 132–133 top, p. 133 bottom, p. 147 bottom,
p. 162 bottom, p. 163 bottom, p. 164 bottom; © Bettmann, p. 3;
© Hulton-Deutsch Collection, pp. 2–3, p. 61 top and bottom,
p. 64 top, p. 117 bottom, p. 118 top and bottom, p. 164 top;
© Pfc. Donald R. Ornitz, p. 1

Imperial War Museum: p. 132 bottom

National Archives: p. 7, p. 11 bottom, pp. 40–41 top, p. 40 bottom,
p. 41 bottom, pp. 62–63 top, p. 62 bottom, p. 64 bottom, p. 115 top,
p. 116–117 top, p. 145, pp.146–147 top, p. 146 bottom, pp. 162–163 top

Contents

NOTE: The numbers shown in parentheses after the map titles refer to the maps' designations in the Center of Military History's original U.S. Army in World War II volumes.

The Siegfried Line Campaign 116

The Ardennes: Battle of the Bulge 132

The Riviera to the Rhine 146

The Last Offensive 162

Introduction

Overview

When historical military campaigns are studied, discussed, or written about, maps are essential in understanding the story. Words have always proven relatively poor tools when describing complex spatial relationships, such as in depicting military operations. For that reason, since earliest times, maps have been used by strategists to provide an explicit description of land areas, especially sites where combat operations have occurred, are occurring, or will occur. Military commanders have used everything from hand-drawn sketches to elaborate topographical maps to direct their field operations. And, after wars have been fought, equally illuminating maps have been used to inform ordinary readers, students, and historians concerning armed encounters.

After World War II, the U.S. Army sought to create a record of its military operations in several series of books. Professional historians, cartographers, and other staff at the U.S. Army Center of Military History (CMH) accomplished the task, including a ten-volume series titled "The U.S. Army in World War II: The European Theater." In this series, CMH drew on a multitude of records and recollections to compile perhaps the most comprehensive and objective chronicle of the European war. Hundreds of maps, including oversized foldouts, were included in the text of the series as visual aids, representing some of the best U.S. military history maps ever produced.

The volume you are holding contains the latest version of these CMH maps, facsimiles of the originals enhanced by superior publishing production standards, the addition of contemporary photographs, and informative introductions to the atlas as a whole as well as to the individual campaigns. The maps are from the following volumes: *Cross-Channel Attack; Breakout and Pursuit; The Lorraine Campaign; The Siegfried Line Campaign; The Ardennes: Battle of the Bulge; The Riviera to the Rhine;* and *The Last Offensive.* The numbers shown in parentheses after the maps in the table of contents (mostly in Roman numerals, but in the case of The Riviera to the Rhine in Arabic numerals) refer to the maps' designations in the original CMH series.

Understanding the Atlas

The creation of modern, sophisticated military maps is a complex process that ultimately provides the reader with the tools necessary to visualize an area of ground vicariously, obtaining a fairly precise understanding of the landscape over which specific battles were fought. In a sense, such maps are "pictures" of the terrain, created in a stylized format that provides far more information than, for instance, a simple photograph ever could.

The information provided is fairly vast. The maps in this atlas provide scales, for example, showing the dimensions in miles. Also, the direction north is always located at the top of the page so that the viewer can quickly and easily determine the relative locations of the topographical features shown. Many of the maps have been furnished with contour intervals, series of lines simulating the elevation of the landscape on the maps. This allows readers to distinguish such land features as hills, mountains, valleys, and depressions—all of which are critical terrain features in a military campaign. Some of the maps differentiate elevations by showing them in varying hues. And, as you would expect, the maps in this atlas indicate cities, towns, forts, dams, rivers, oceans, marshes, railroads, highways, roads, and so on; on occasion, even individual houses, buildings, and other small objects are indicated.

Readers should always examine the legends (i.e., the information in the small boxes found in the corners of the maps) before attempting to understand the maps. The legends describe the meanings of the special symbols used in the body of the maps. The symbols are a sort of shorthand to help the viewer comprehend the elements of the situation being described. Symbols may be, for instance, dotted lines, showing a battle front line; a solid line with a comb-like appearance, indicating forward positions; or perhaps a bold arrow, demonstrating the movement and direction of an armored drive or deployment of troops. Symbols in blue show "friendly," or American-associated relationships, while those in red indicate "enemy," or German-associated relationships. Thus, a bold arrow in blue would indicate an American unit moving along "an axis of advance" (i.e., general directional thrust). A bold arrow in red shows an enemy unit in motion. Before studying any map, the legend should be read carefully for the precise meaning of the symbols used.

Readers without a military background should refer to the legend on page 9 for an overview of the basic military symbols, especially those specifying the various types of units. For instance, boxes with an X drawn through them are infantry units; those with an oval in the center are armor; those with a diagonal line drawn through the oval are reconnaissance units, and so on. Boxes with Xs atop them show the size of units: four Xs for an army, three Xs for a corps, two Xs for a division, and one X for a brigade or regiment. Platoons are marked by three black dots over a box, a section by two, and a squad by one. Unit numbers or designations are found on the right and left sides of boxes.

Another difficulty some readers may encounter while studying the maps is interpreting the abbreviations, acronyms, or other military terms. In this atlas, many words are abbreviated, for instance, "division" is shown as "div"; "infantry" as "inf"; "reconnaissance as "rcn"; and "objective" as "obj." And there are even more arcane abbreviations than these examples. It should also be noted that throughout the maps in this atlas, German units are italicized, with their names often translated into English equivalents (with a few exceptions for commonly known designations).

Finally, in order to better understand all the symbols as well as the abbreviations included in this atlas, readers may want to refer to any of several books on standard military notation. Alternatively, this information can be copied off the internet using an online search engine to look for the following terms: "standard military units, symbols" and "military abbreviations," respectively.

Using the Atlas

The maps in this atlas are intended as a visual aid in studying the battles and plans of World War II in relation to the European Theater of Operations of the U.S. Army. To help the reader put the CMH campaign maps included here into historical context, a brief description of events is provided before each series of maps.

Basic Military Map Symbols

Symbols within a rectangle indicate a military unit, within a triangle an observation post,
and within a circle a supply point.

MILITARY UNITS—IDENTIFICATION

Antiaircraft Artillery	Ordnance Department
Armored Command	Quartermaster Corps
Army Air Forces	Signal Corps
Artillery, except Antiaircraft and Coast Artillery	Tank Destroyer
Cavalry, Horse	Transportation Corps
Cavalry, Mechanized	Veterinary Corps
Chemical Warfare Service	
Coast Artillery	*Airborne units are designated by combining a gull wing symbol with the arm or service symbol:*
Engineers	Airborne Artillery
Infantry	Airborne Infantry
Medical Corps	

SIZE SYMBOLS

The following symbols placed either in boundary lines or above the rectangle, triangle, or circle inclosing
the identifying arm or service symbol indicate the size of military organization:

Squad	•
Section	••
Platoon	•••
Company, troop, battery, Air Force flight	I
Battalion, cavalry squadron, or Air Force squadron	II
Regiment or group; combat team (with abbreviation CT following identifying numeral)	III
Brigade, Combat Command of Armored Division, or Air Force Wing	X
Division or Command of an Air Force	XX
Corps or Air Force	XXX
Army	XXXX
Group of Armies	XXXXX

EXAMPLES

The letter or number to the left of the symbol indicates the unit designation; that to the right, the designation of the parent unit to which it belongs. Letters or numbers above or below boundary lines designate the units separated by the lines:

Company A, 137th Infantry

8th Field Artillery Battalion

Combat Command A, 1st Armored Division

Observation Post, 23d Infantry

Command Post, 5th Infantry Division

Boundary between 137th and 138th Infantry

WEAPONS

Machine gun	
Gun	
Gun battery	
Howitzer or Mortar	
Tank	
Self-propelled gun	

Cross Channel Attack

June 6–July 5, 1944

THESE MAPS ADDRESS PLANNING AND COMBAT FOR Operation OVERLORD—the invasion of Europe, June 1944—the largest amphibious military operation in history.

On June 6, 1944, after months of intensive preparation by millions of American, British, and Canadian troops, the Allies invaded "Fortress Europe," with 150,000 soldiers landing in Normandy the first day. General Dwight David Eisenhower was assigned Supreme Commander of Allied Expeditionary Forces, with General Bernard Montgomery serving as his combined Allied ground force commander. The target was the coastline between Orne Estuary and the southeastern end of Cotentin Peninsula.

On June 5, an overpowering aerial and naval bombardment began, and continued during the invasion, destroying much of the German coastal defenses and obliterating inland railroad and communications networks. Allied airborne and parachute infantry that had been dropped behind the lines further ravaged German defensive strong points and communications nodes. Meanwhile, more than 7,000 vessels were crossing the English Channel, preceded by 287 minesweepers. (German air power had, by this point, been largely extinguished.)

Reaching the beaches shortly after dawn, British Second Army landed on the eastern beaches—codenamed GOLD, JUNO, and SWORD, near Caen and Bayeux. U.S. First Army debarked on the right, between Cherbourg peninsula and St. Laurent—OMAHA BEACH—the site of the potent German 352d Division. Most of V Corps' tanks foundered in the surf, and the force met horrendous resistance in the form of withering fire from German installations along the coast, falling behind the rest of the invasion.

VII Corps, meanwhile, wheeled southwest, advanced inland, and captured Carentan, making a juncture with V Corps on June 14. The Germans around Cherbourg, fearing encirclement, began withdrawing from the peninsula on June 16. First Army, learning of the exodus, cut them off, sending the U.S. 9th Division to halt the German retreat on June 18. Meanwhile, VII Corps attacked and captured Cherbourg on June 27, seizing what would by September be one of the Allies' main dock facilities, a crucial link in the growing army's supply line.

LEFT: *American troops, after leaving the ramp of a Coast Guard landing craft, plunge into the English Channel on D-Day. The soldiers proceeded through the surf toward a beach explosively alive with bursting artillery rounds and zinging machine gun bullets. Their objective was the high cliffs above the beach, where German troops swarmed, ready to defend Axis-occupied France with their lives.* **OPPOSITE PAGE INSET:** *General Dwight D. Eisenhower briefs paratroopers before their assault on Normandy. "Full victory—nothing else!" he commanded, inspiring them with his fiery resolve and determination to defeat the Germans on the European mainland. Many of these same men would not long after lay down their lives for the cause of freedom in one of the most ambitious amphibious assaults in history.* **LEFT INSET:** *A U.S. paratrooper, weighted down by some seventy-five pounds of equipment, pulls himself aboard an aircraft. A parachute is fastened on his back, a reserve chute to his chest. His armaments, alone, consist of a light machine gun, carbine, grenades, ammunition, and a knife strapped to his right leg. In addition, he carries rations and necessary items for him to remain operative for forty-eight hours without further support.*

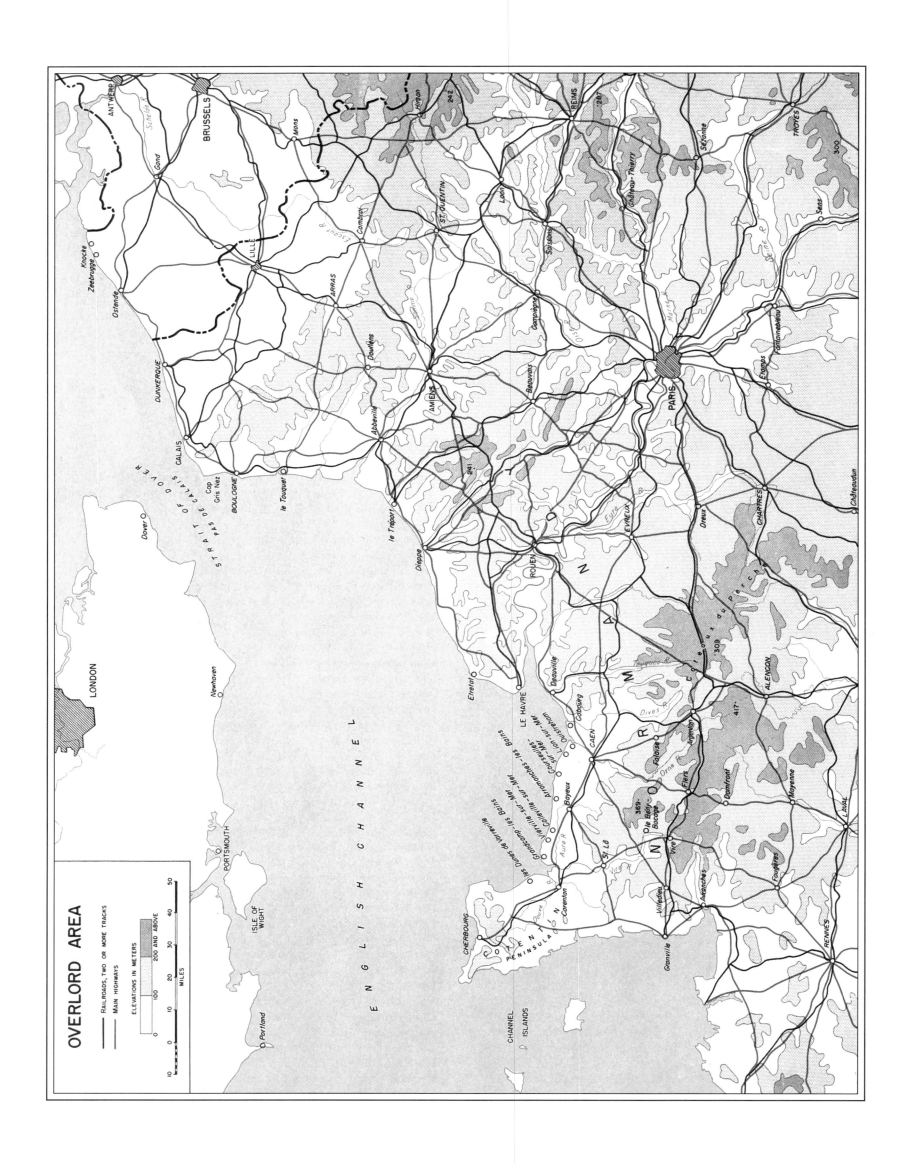

OVERLORD AREA

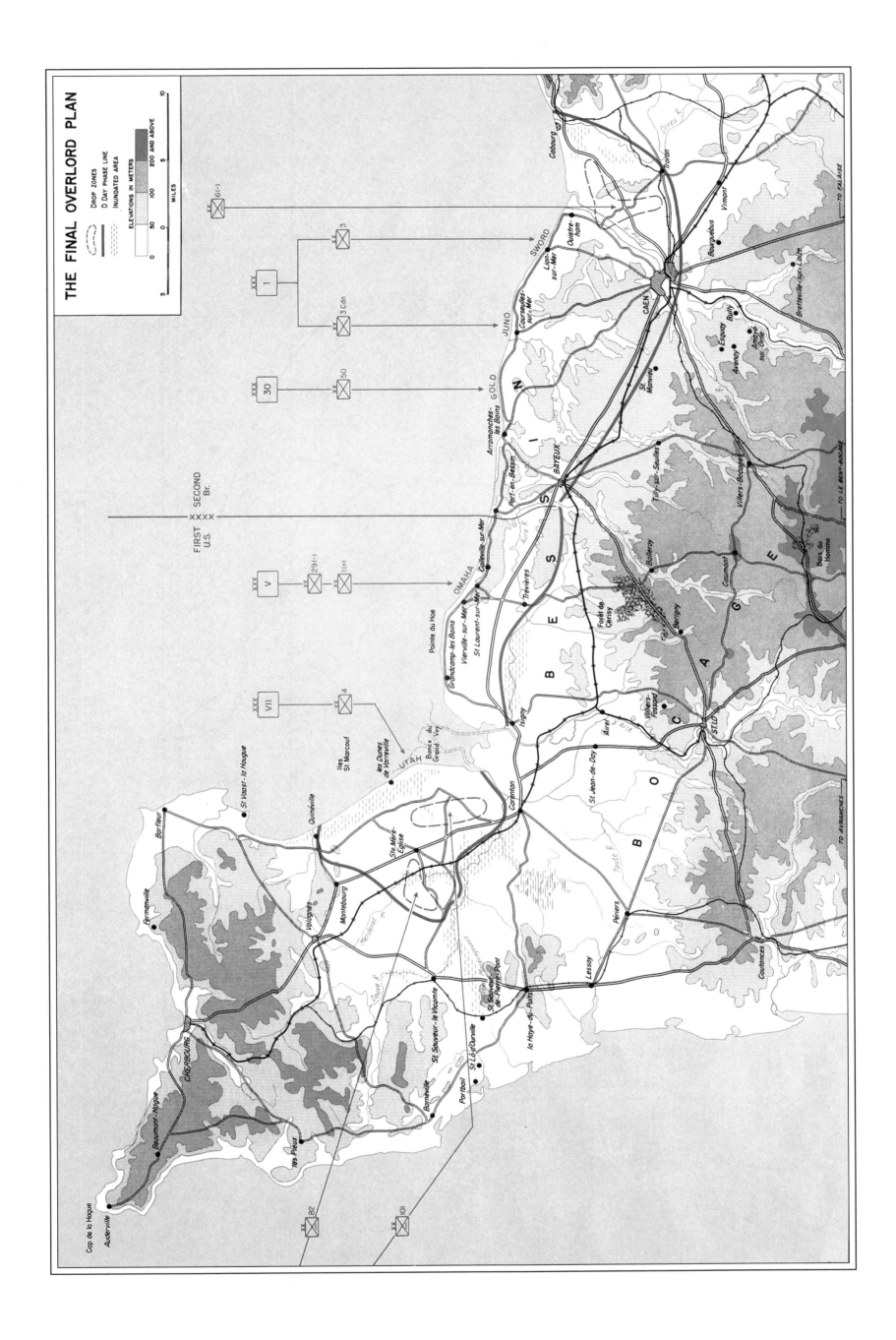

THE FINAL OVERLORD PLAN

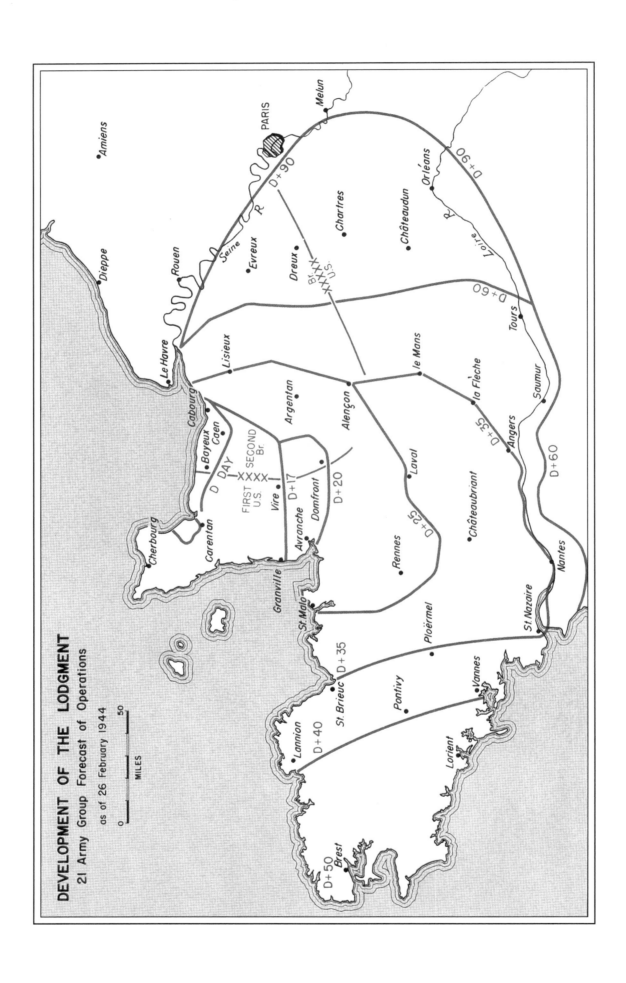

DEVELOPMENT OF THE LODGMENT
21 Army Group Forecast of Operations
as of 26 February 1944

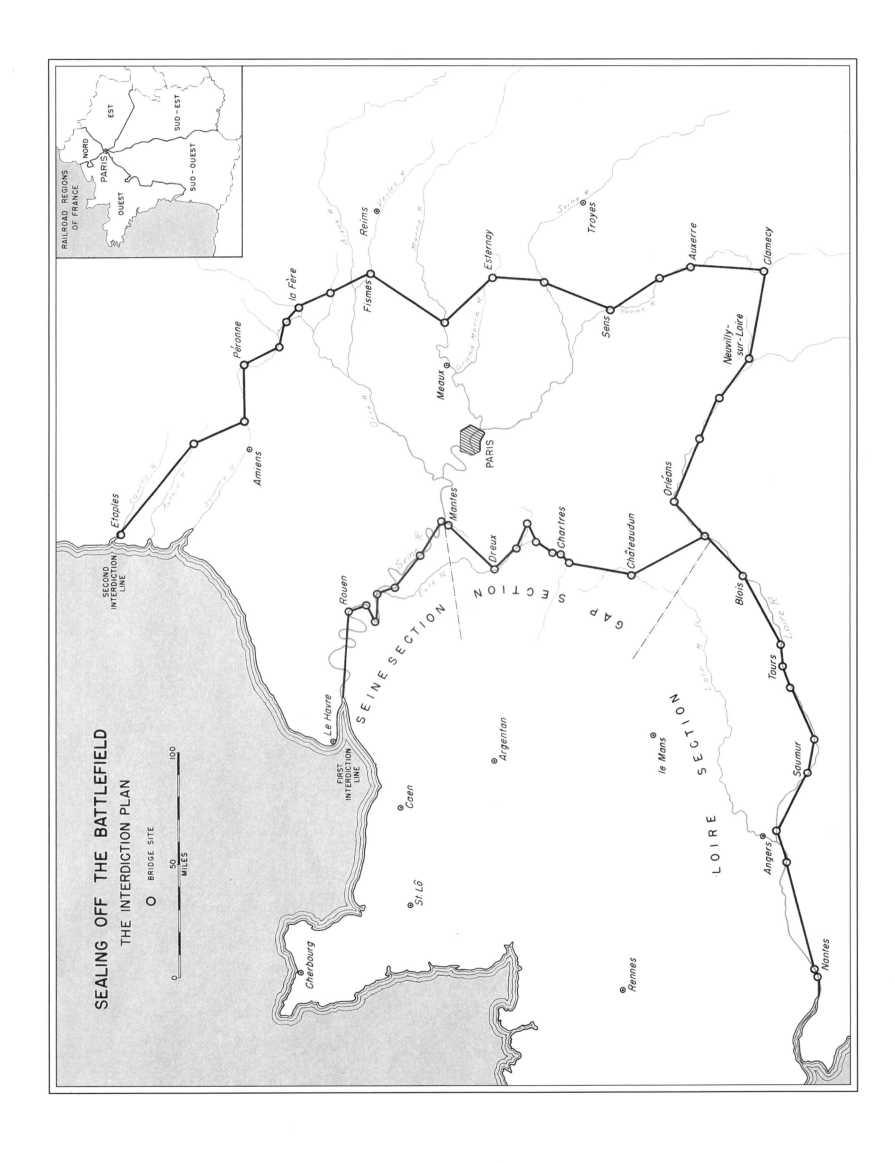

SEALING OFF THE BATTLEFIELD
THE INTERDICTION PLAN

○ BRIDGE SITE

MILES
0   50   100

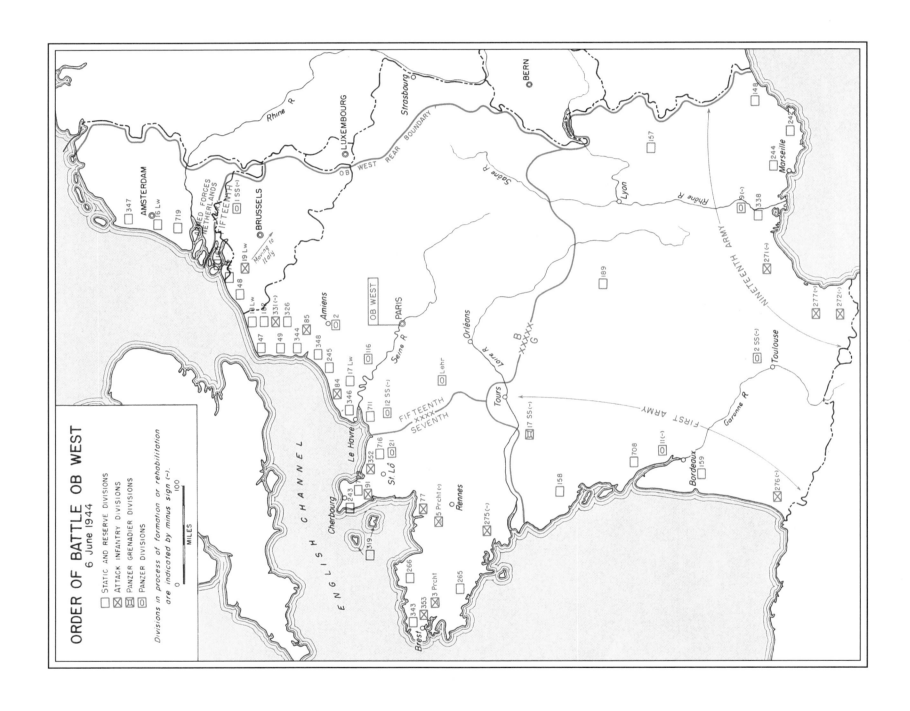

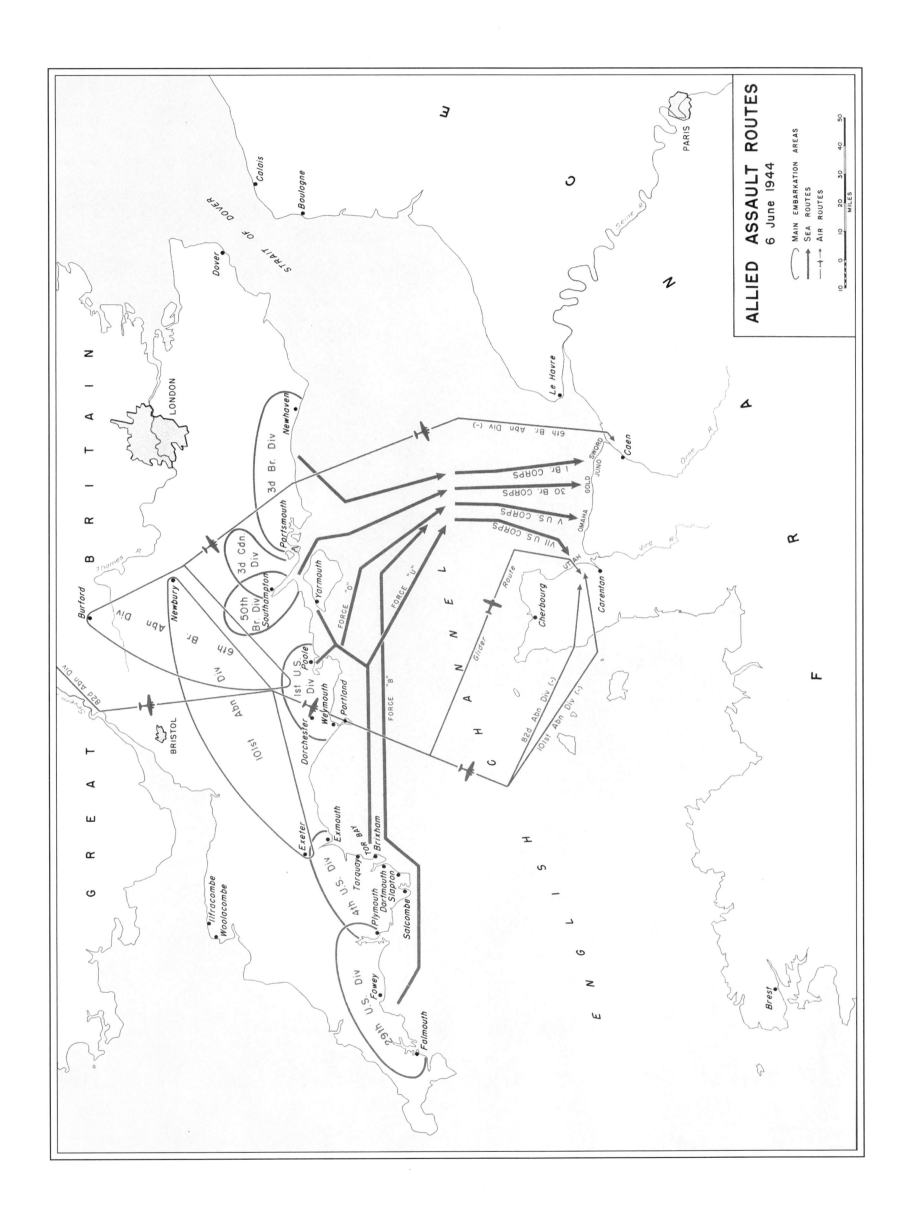

ALLIED ASSAULT ROUTES
6 June 1944

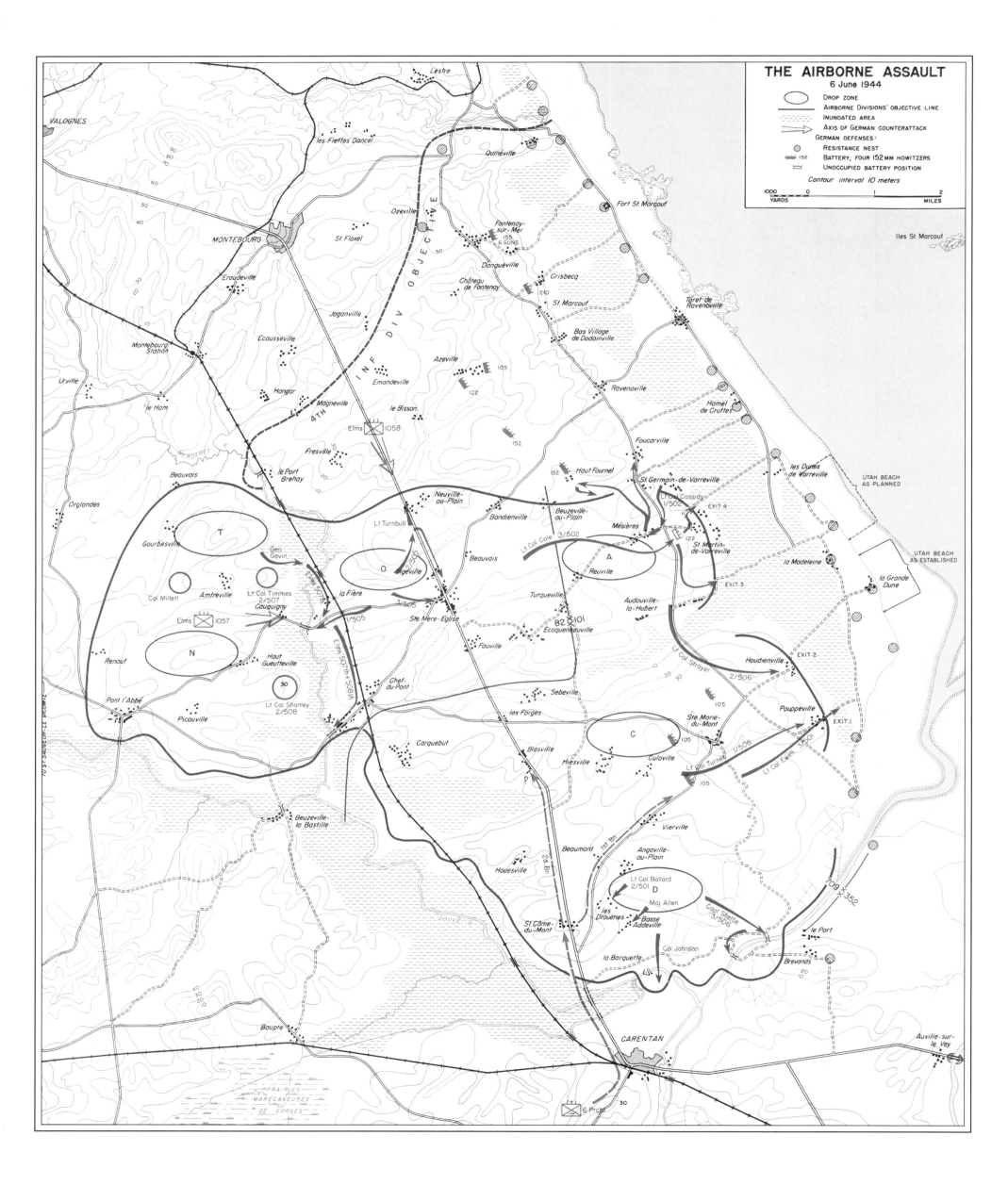

THE AIRBORNE ASSAULT
6 June 1944

⬭ DROP ZONE
── AIRBORNE DIVISIONS' OBJECTIVE LINE
‥‥ INUNDATED AREA
⟶ AXIS OF GERMAN COUNTERATTACK
GERMAN DEFENSES:
⬤ RESISTANCE NEST
⊣⊢152 BATTERY, FOUR 152 MM HOWITZERS
⊔ UNOCCUPIED BATTERY POSITION

Contour interval 10 meters

YARDS 1000   0   1   2 MILES

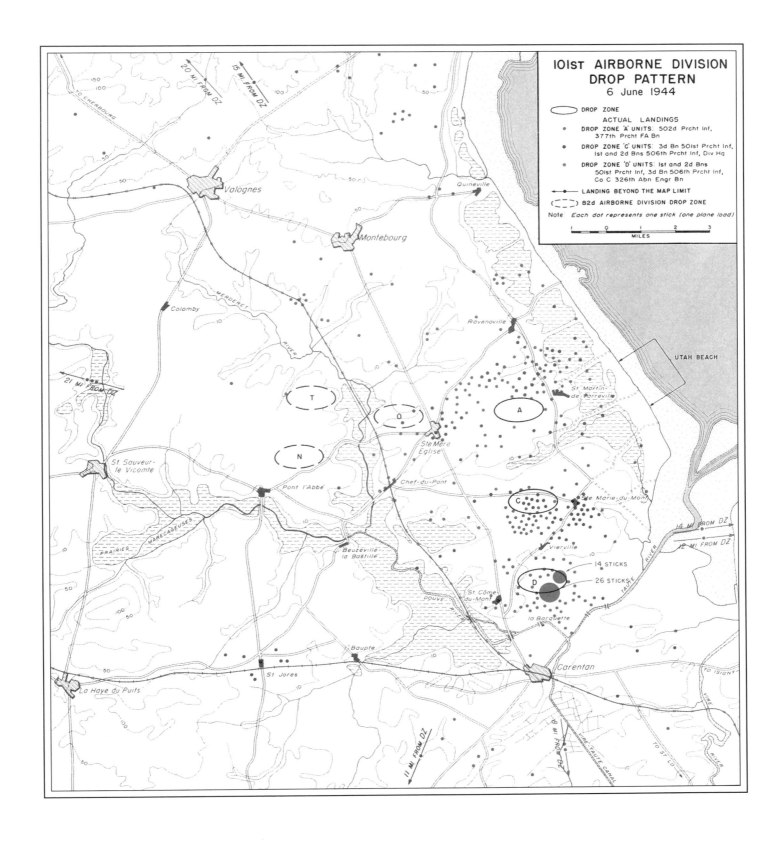

**IOIst AIRBORNE DIVISION
DROP PATTERN**
6 June 1944

⬭ DROP ZONE
ACTUAL LANDINGS
• DROP ZONE 'A' UNITS: 502d Prcht Inf,
377th Prcht FA Bn
• DROP ZONE 'C' UNITS: 3d Bn 50Ist Prcht Inf,
Ist and 2d Bns 506th Prcht Inf, Div Hq
• DROP ZONE 'D' UNITS: Ist and 2d Bns
50Ist Prcht Inf, 3d Bn 506th Prcht Inf,
Co C 326th Abn Engr Bn
⟵ LANDING BEYOND THE MAP LIMIT
(⬭) 82d AIRBORNE DIVISION DROP ZONE

Note: *Each dot represents one stick (one plane load)*

MILES

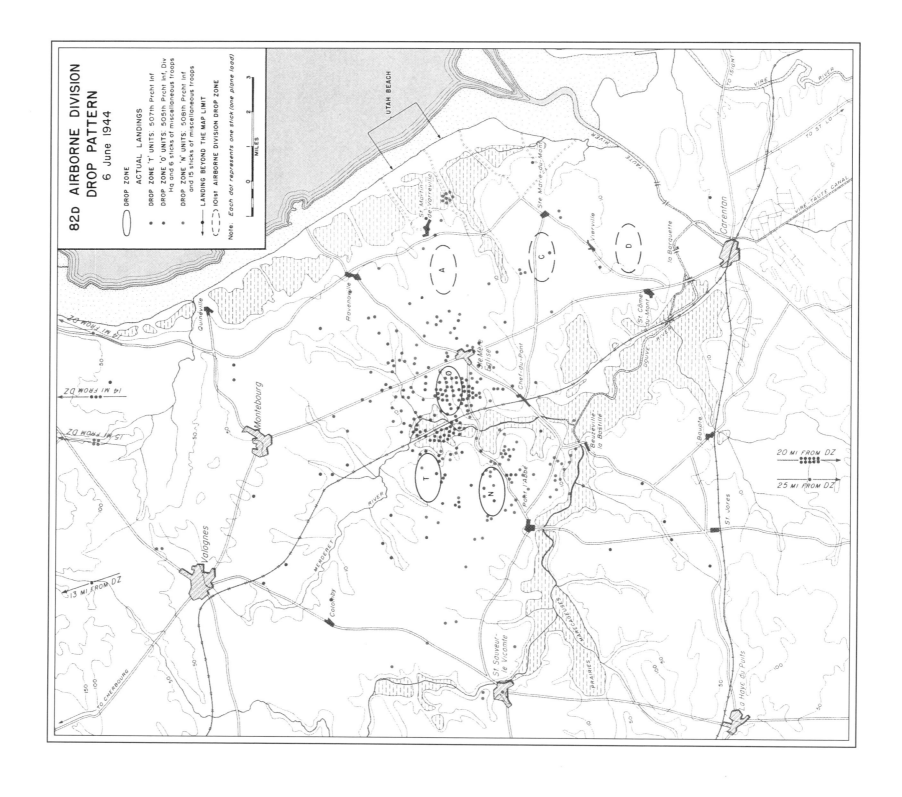

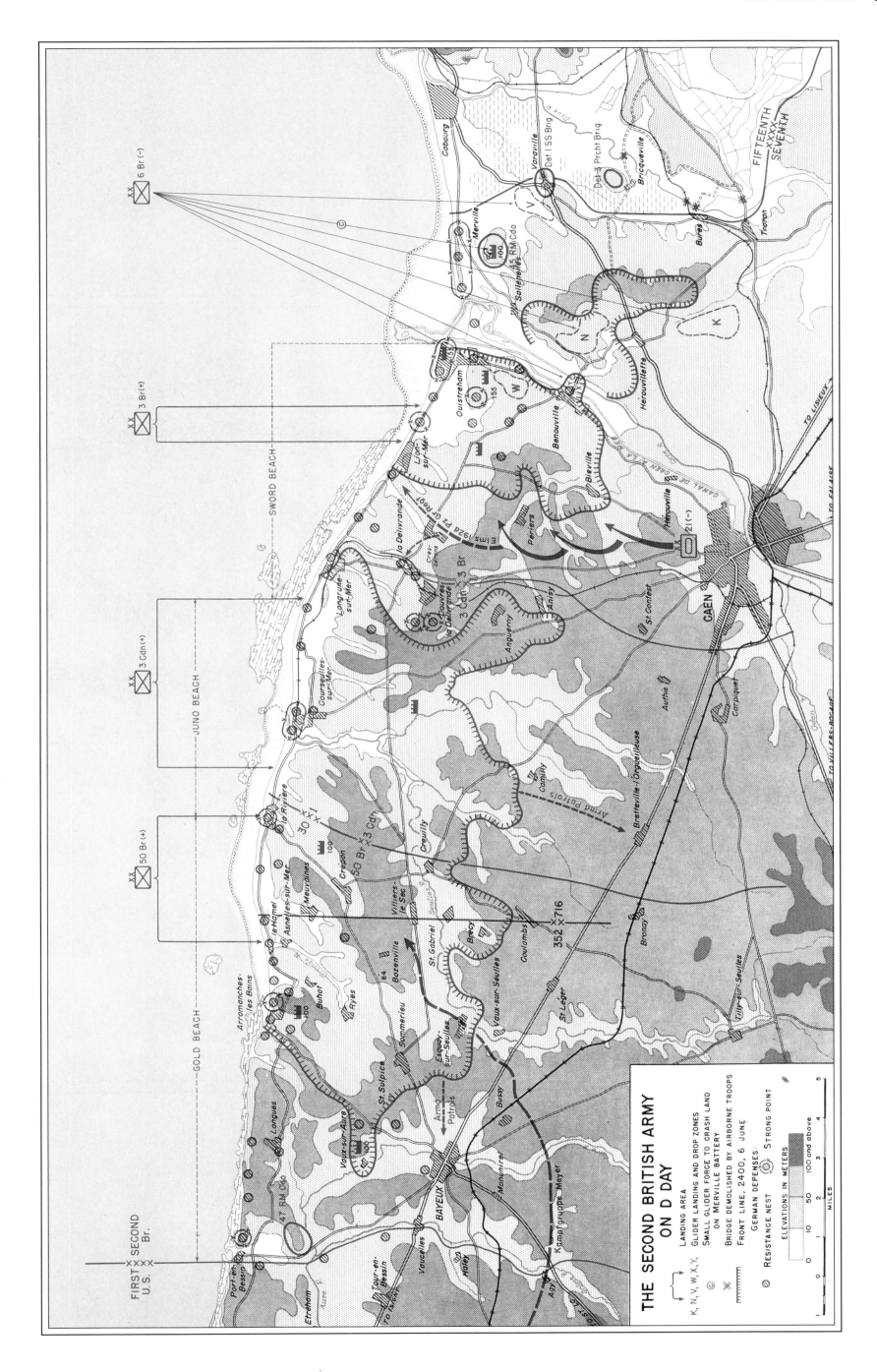

THE SECOND BRITISH ARMY
ON D DAY

K, N, V, W, X, Y,   LANDING AREA

          GLIDER LANDING AND DROP ZONES

◎   SMALL GLIDER FORCE TO CRASH LAND
         ON MERVILLE BATTERY

╳   BRIDGE DEMOLISHED BY AIRBORNE TROOPS

         FRONT LINE, 2400, 6 JUNE

         GERMAN DEFENSES

◎ RESISTANCE NEST   ✳ STRONG POINT

ELEVATIONS IN METERS

0   50   100 100 AND ABOVE

MILES

0   1   2   3   4   5

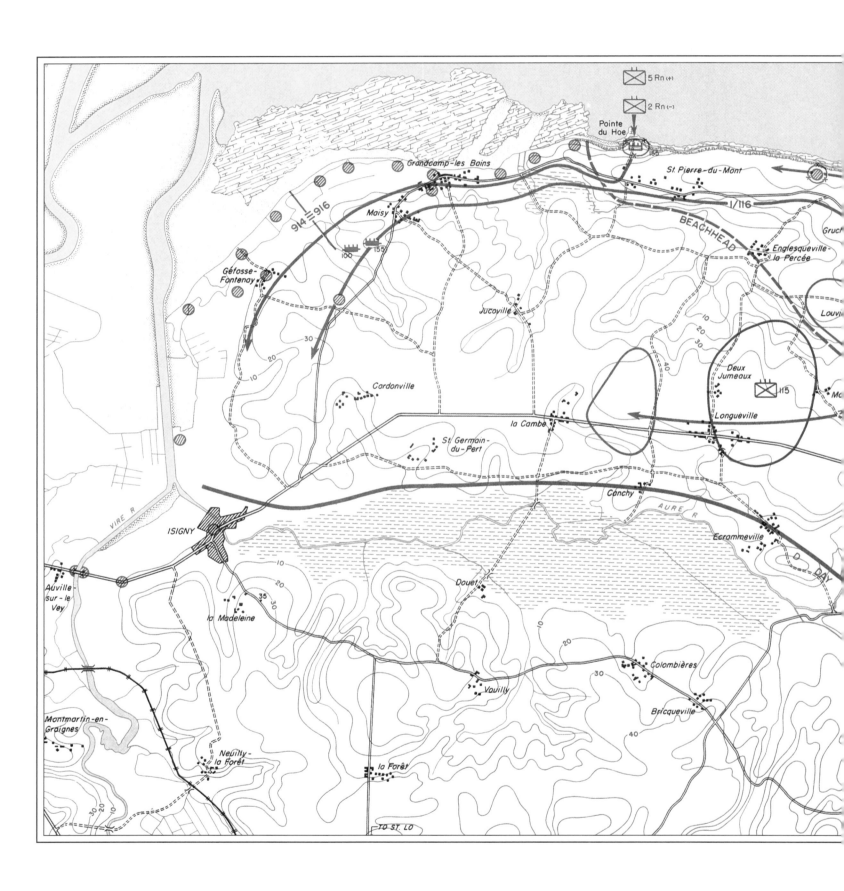

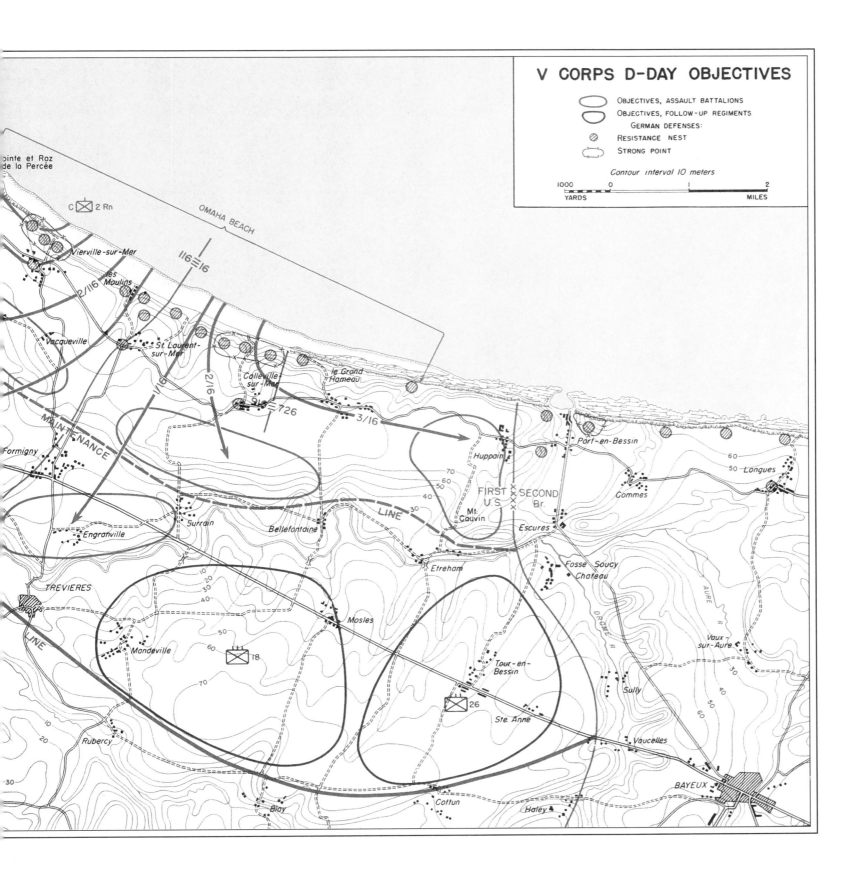

V CORPS D-DAY OBJECTIVES

OBJECTIVES, ASSAULT BATTALIONS
OBJECTIVES, FOLLOW-UP REGIMENTS
GERMAN DEFENSES:
RESISTANCE NEST
STRONG POINT

Contour interval 10 meters

1000 0 1 2
YARDS MILES

LEGEND

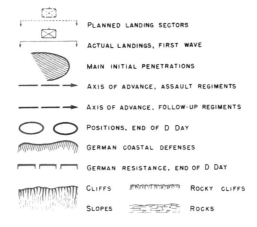

PLANNED LANDING SECTORS
ACTUAL LANDINGS, FIRST WAVE
MAIN INITIAL PENETRATIONS
AXIS OF ADVANCE, ASSAULT REGIMENTS
AXIS OF ADVANCE, FOLLOW-UP REGIMENTS
POSITIONS, END OF D DAY
GERMAN COASTAL DEFENSES
GERMAN RESISTANCE, END OF D DAY
CLIFFS   ROCKY CLIFFS
SLOPES   ROCKS

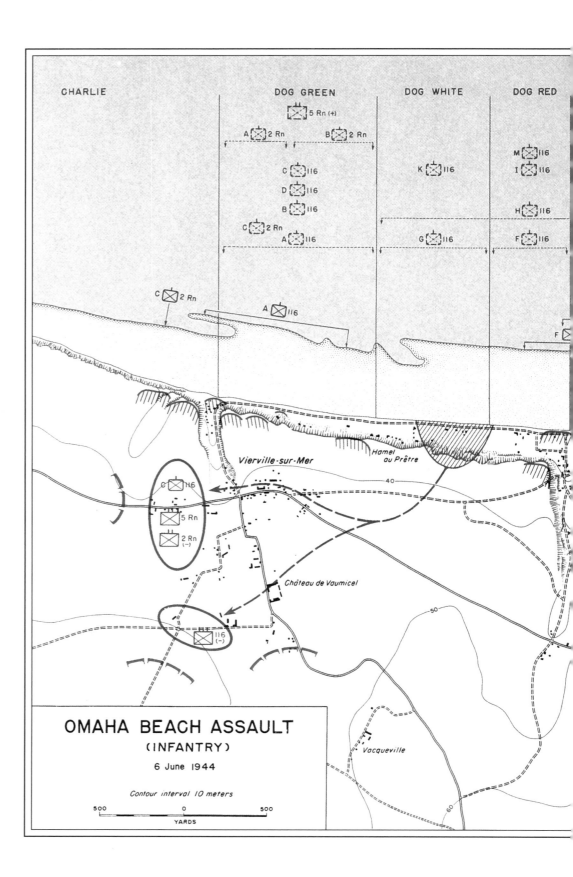

OMAHA BEACH ASSAULT
(INFANTRY)
6 June 1944

Contour interval 10 meters

500   0   500
YARDS

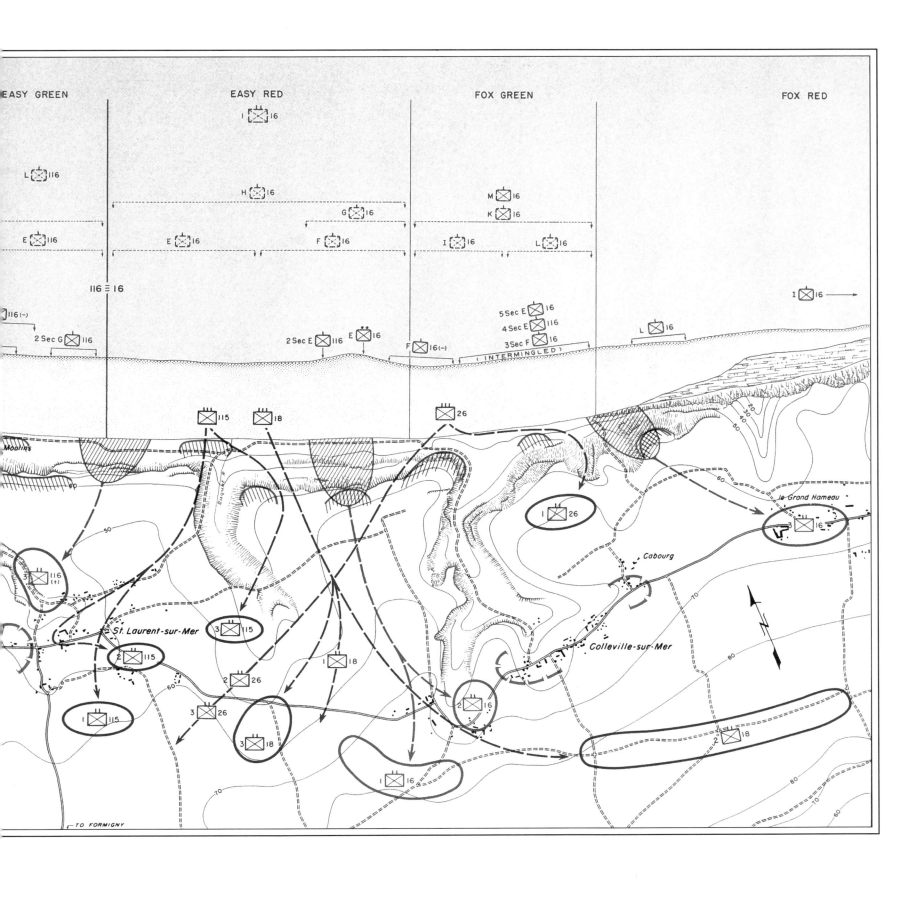

LEGEND

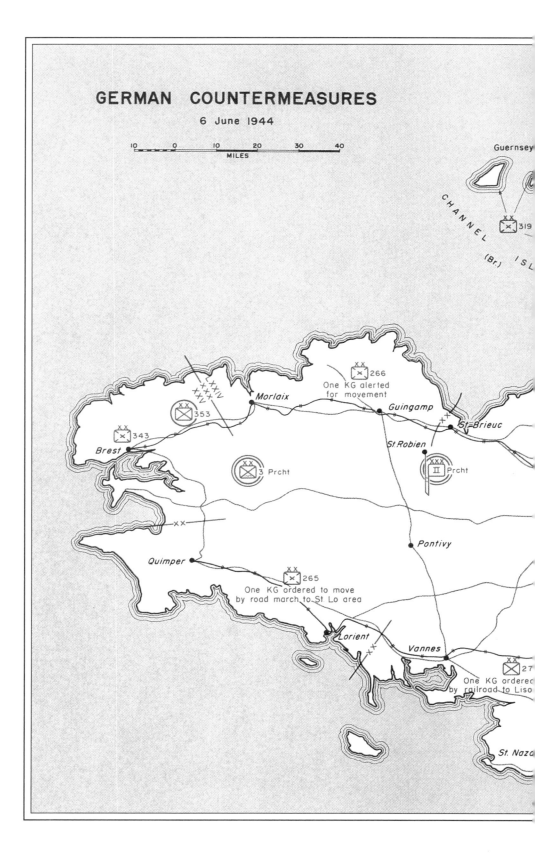

⊡	STATIC DIVISION
⊗	CORPS RESERVE
⊗	ARMY RESERVE
⊡	ARMY GROUP B RESERVE
⊡	OKW RESERVE
➤	DIRECTION OF MOVEMENT
KG	KAMPFGRUPPE
	MAIN RAILROADS
	HIGHWAYS

GERMAN COUNTERMEASURES

6 June 1944

10 0 10 20 30 40
MILES

Guernsey

CHANNEL (Br.) ISL

319

266
One KG alerted
for movement

Morlaix

Guingamp

St-Brieuc

St.Robien

353

II Prcht

343

Brest

3 Prcht

Pontivy

Quimper

265
One KG ordered to move
by road march to St Lo area

Lorient

Vannes

27
One KG ordered
by railroad to Liso

St.Naza

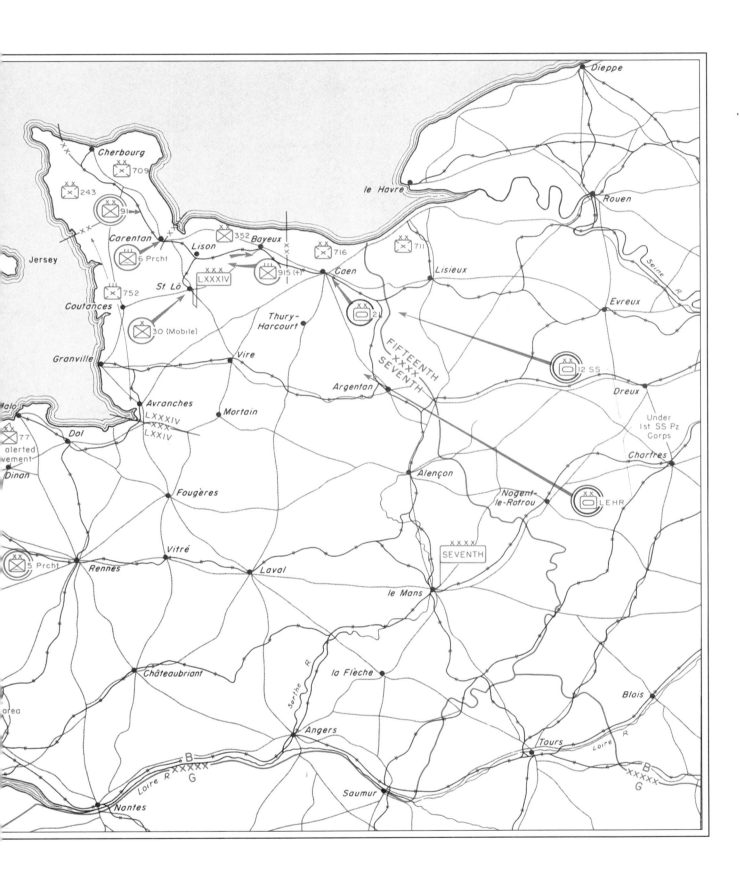

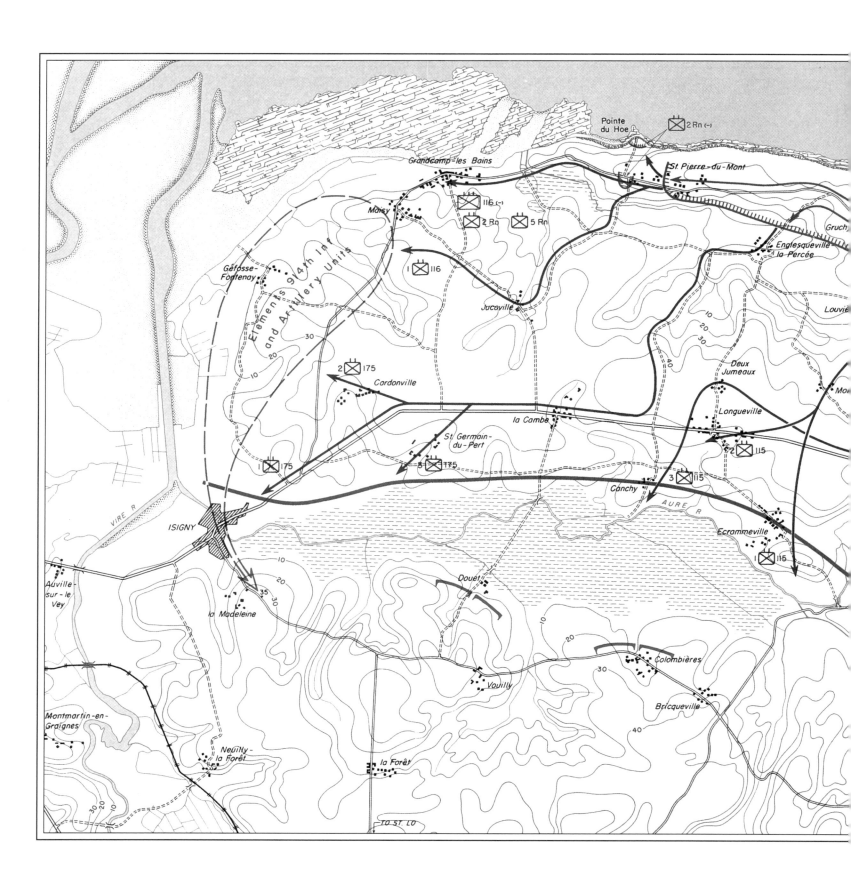

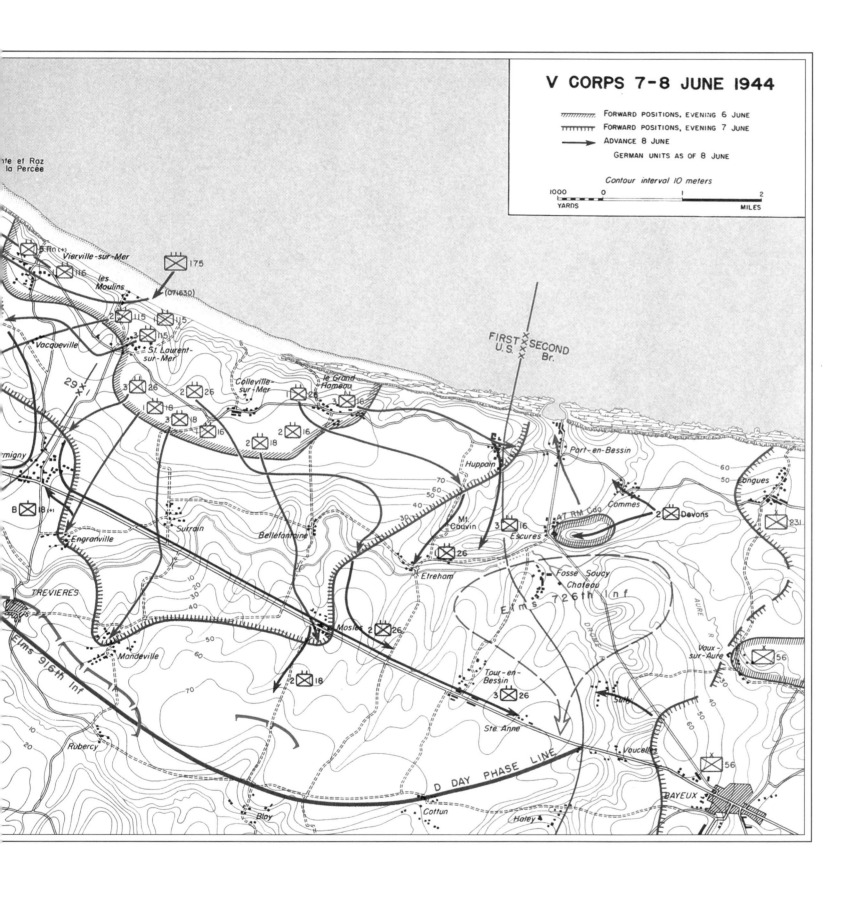

V CORPS 7-8 JUNE 1944

⫸⫸⫸⫸⫸	FORWARD POSITIONS, EVENING 6 JUNE
⟍⟍⟍⟍⟍	FORWARD POSITIONS, EVENING 7 JUNE
⟶	ADVANCE 8 JUNE
	GERMAN UNITS AS OF 8 JUNE

Contour interval 10 meters

1000 0 1 2
YARDS MILES

nte et Raz
lo Percée

Vierville-sur-Mer
5 Rn (+)
116
les Moulins
175
(071630)
2 115
115
Vacqueville
St. Laurent-
sur-Mer
Colleville-
sur-Mer
le Grand
Hameau
3 16
29
3 26
26
1 18
3 18
16
rmigny
2 18
16
70
60
50
Huppain
Port-en-Bessin
ongues
B 8 (+)
30
Mt.
Cauvin
3 16
Escures
AT RM Cdo
Commes
2 Devons
231
Suizrain
Bellefontaine
40
26
Engranville
Etreham
Fosse Soucy
Chateau
TREVIERES
10
30
40
726th Inf
Elms
AURE R.
Mosle
2 26
DRÔME R.
Vaux-
sur-Aure
56
Mandeville
60
50
Tour-en-
Bessin
Elms 916th Inf
70
2 18
3 26
Sully
40
Ste. Anne
10
Ruberoy
20
Voucelles
56
D DAY PHASE LINE
BAYEUX
Bloy
Cottun
Haley

FIRST SECOND
U.S. Br.

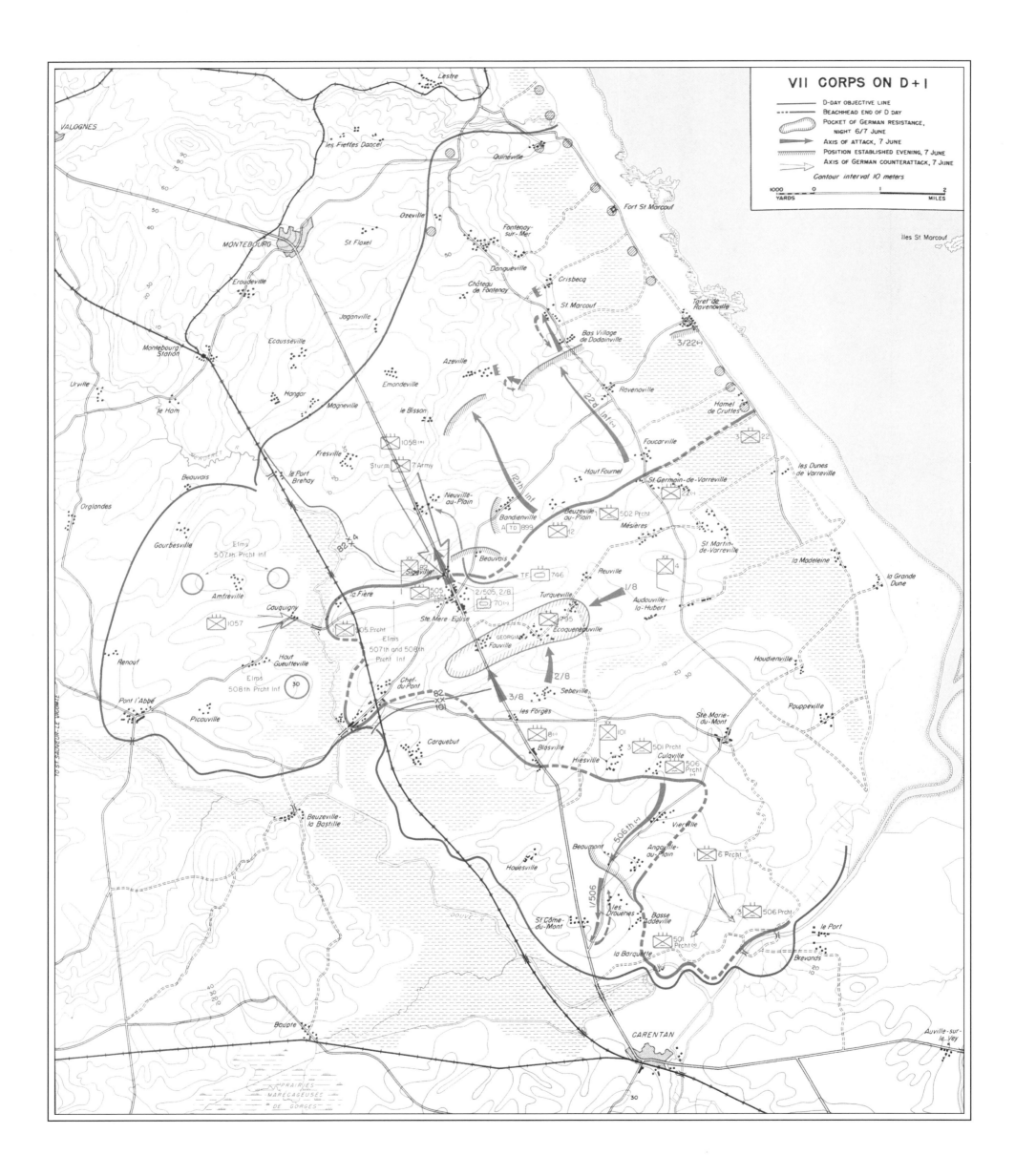

VII CORPS ON D+1

- — — — — D-DAY OBJECTIVE LINE
- ————— BEACHHEAD END OF D DAY
- POCKET OF GERMAN RESISTANCE, NIGHT 6/7 JUNE
- ————▶ AXIS OF ATTACK, 7 JUNE
- POSITION ESTABLISHED EVENING, 7 JUNE
- ——▷ AXIS OF GERMAN COUNTERATTACK, 7 JUNE

Contour interval 10 meters

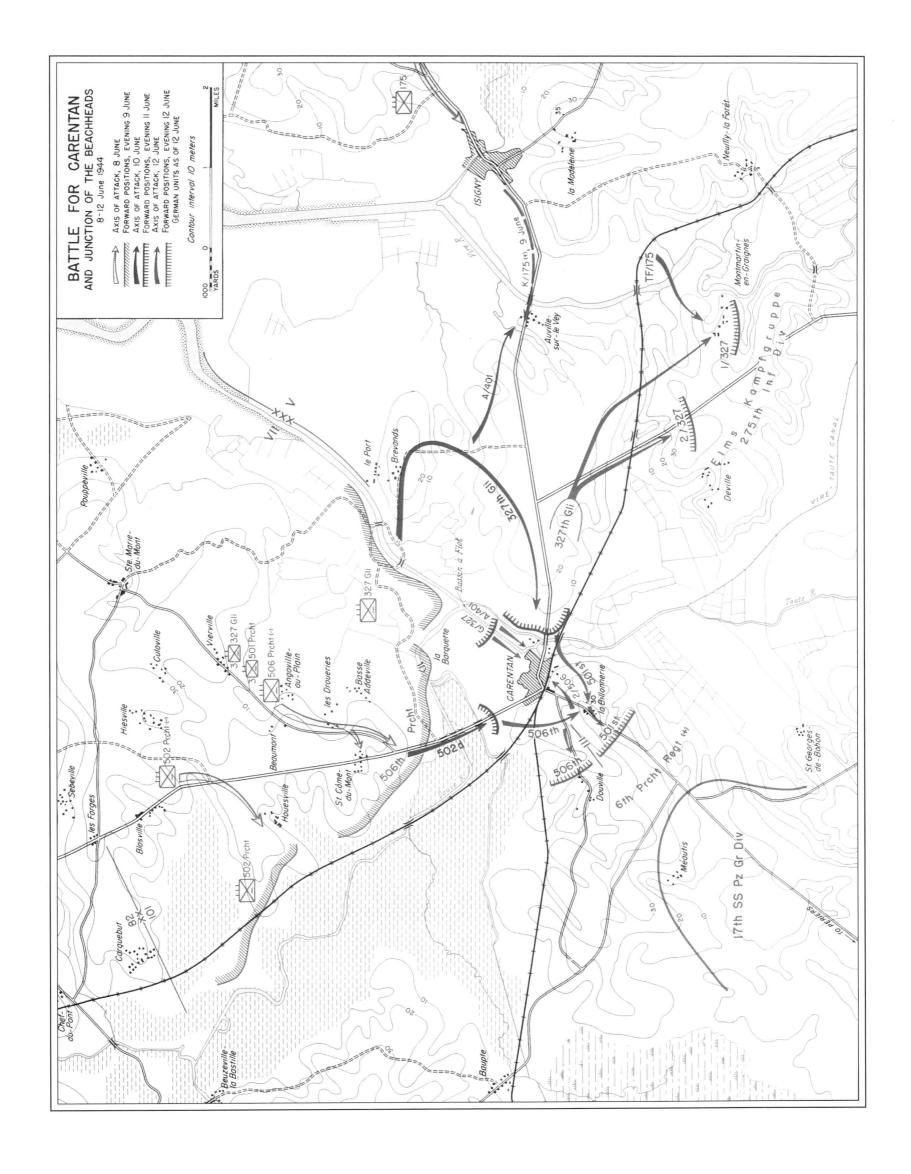

BATTLE FOR CARENTAN
AND JUNCTION OF THE BEACHHEADS
8–12 June 1944

Axis of attack, 8 June
Forward positions, evening 9 June
Axis of attack, 10 June
Forward positions, evening 11 June
Axis of attack, 12 June
Forward positions, evening 12 June
German units as of 12 June

Contour interval 10 meters

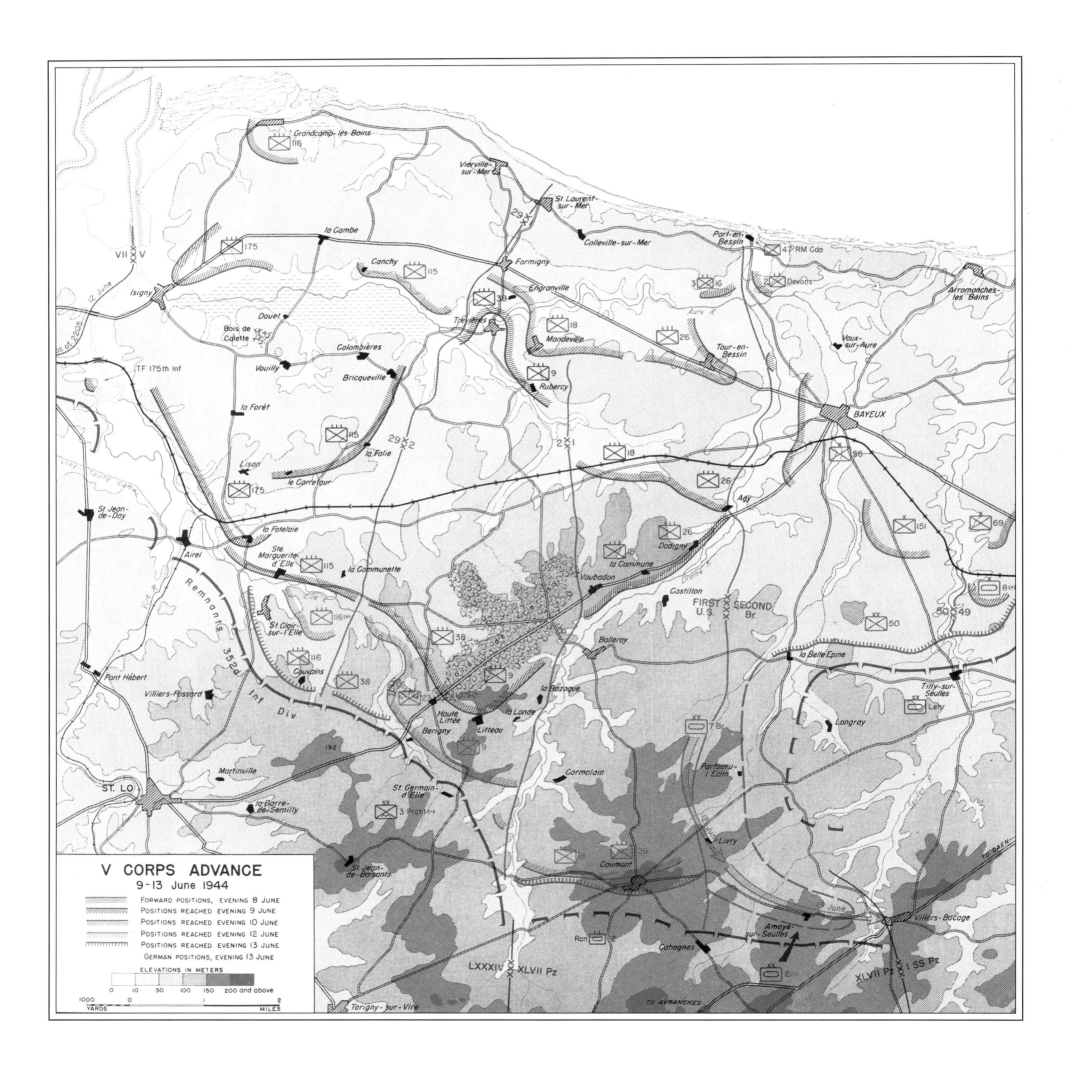

V CORPS ADVANCE
9-13 June 1944

Forward positions, evening 8 June
Positions reached evening 9 June
Positions reached evening 10 June
Positions reached evening 12 June
Positions reached evening 13 June
German positions, evening 13 June

ELEVATIONS IN METERS

0   10   50   100   150   200 and above

1000   0   1   2
YARDS   MILES

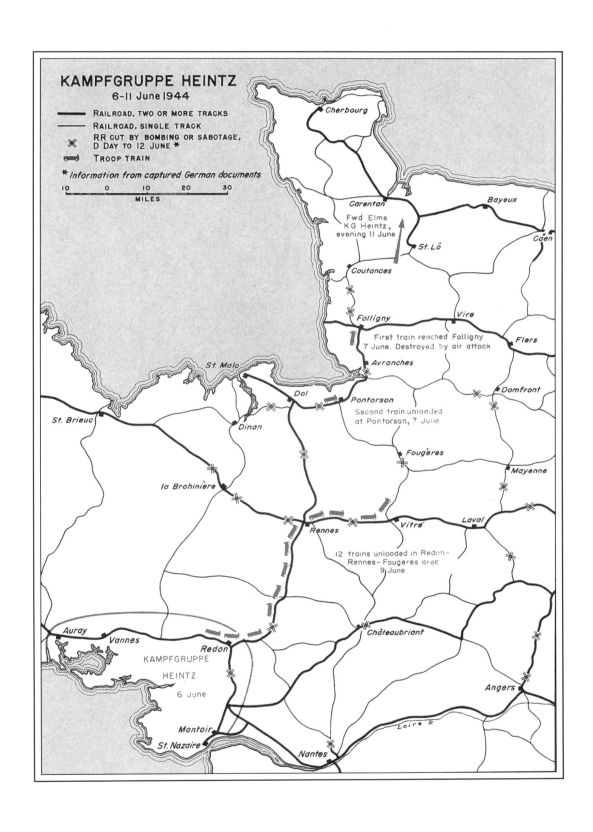

KAMPFGRUPPE HEINTZ
6-11 June 1944

RAILROAD, TWO OR MORE TRACKS
RAILROAD, SINGLE TRACK
RR CUT BY BOMBING OR SABOTAGE, D DAY TO 12 JUNE *
TROOP TRAIN

* Information from captured German documents

10 0 10 20 30
MILES

Cherbourg

Carentan
Fwd Elms KG Heintz, evening 11 June
St. Lô
Bayeux
Caen
Coutances

Folligny
Vire
Flers
First train reached Folligny 7 June. Destroyed by air attack

St. Malo
Avranches
Dol
Pontorson
Domfront
Second train unloaded at Pontorson, 7 June

St. Brieuc
Dinan
Fougères
Mayenne

la Brohinière
Rennes
Vitré
Laval
12 trains unloaded in Redon-Rennes-Fougères area 9 June

Auray
Vannes
Redon
Châteaubriant
KAMPFGRUPPE HEINTZ
6 June
Angers

Montoir
St. Nazaire
Nantes
Loire R

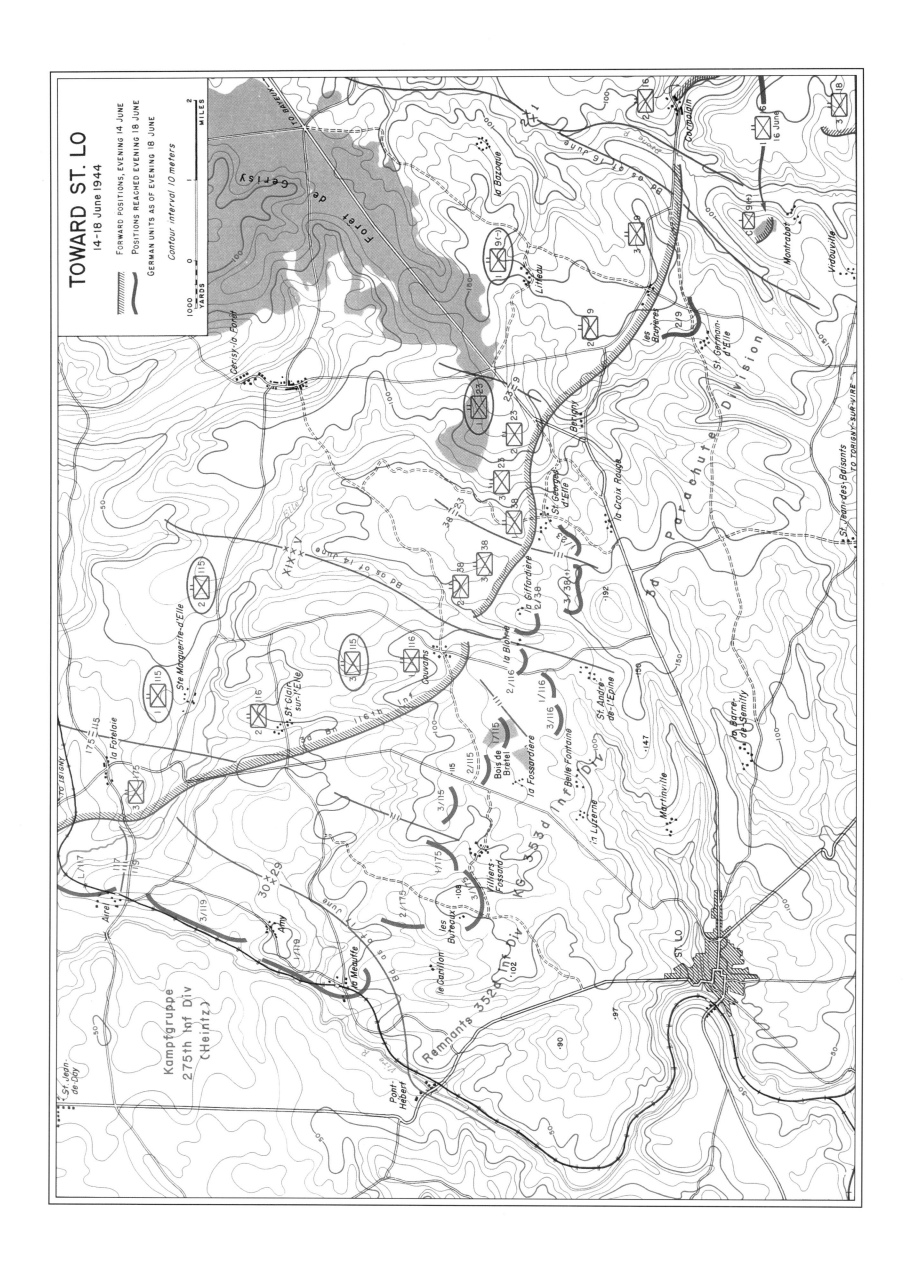

SECURING THE NORTH FLANK
8-14 June 1944

Forward positions, night 7/8 June
Forward positions, evening 10 June
Positions reached evening 12 June
Positions reached evening 14 June
Boundaries in green as of 2330, 12 June
Contour interval 10 meters

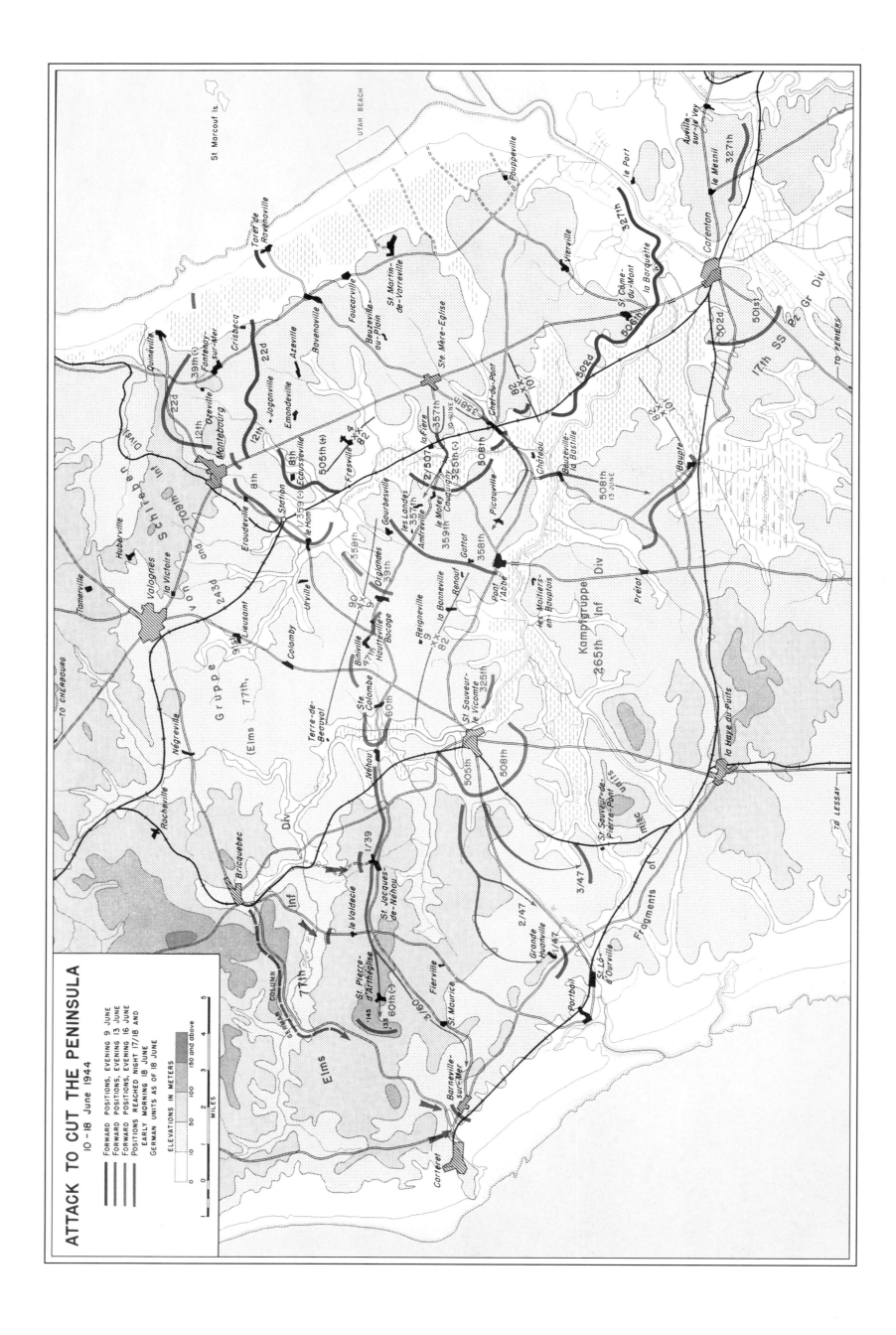

ATTACK TO CUT THE PENINSULA
10-18 June 1944

FORWARD POSITIONS, EVENING 9 JUNE
FORWARD POSITIONS, EVENING 13 JUNE
FORWARD POSITIONS, EVENING 16 JUNE
POSITIONS REACHED NIGHT 17/18 AND
EARLY MORNING 18 JUNE
GERMAN UNITS AS OF 18 JUNE

ELEVATIONS IN METERS

150 and above
100
50
10
0

MILES
0   1   2   3   4   5

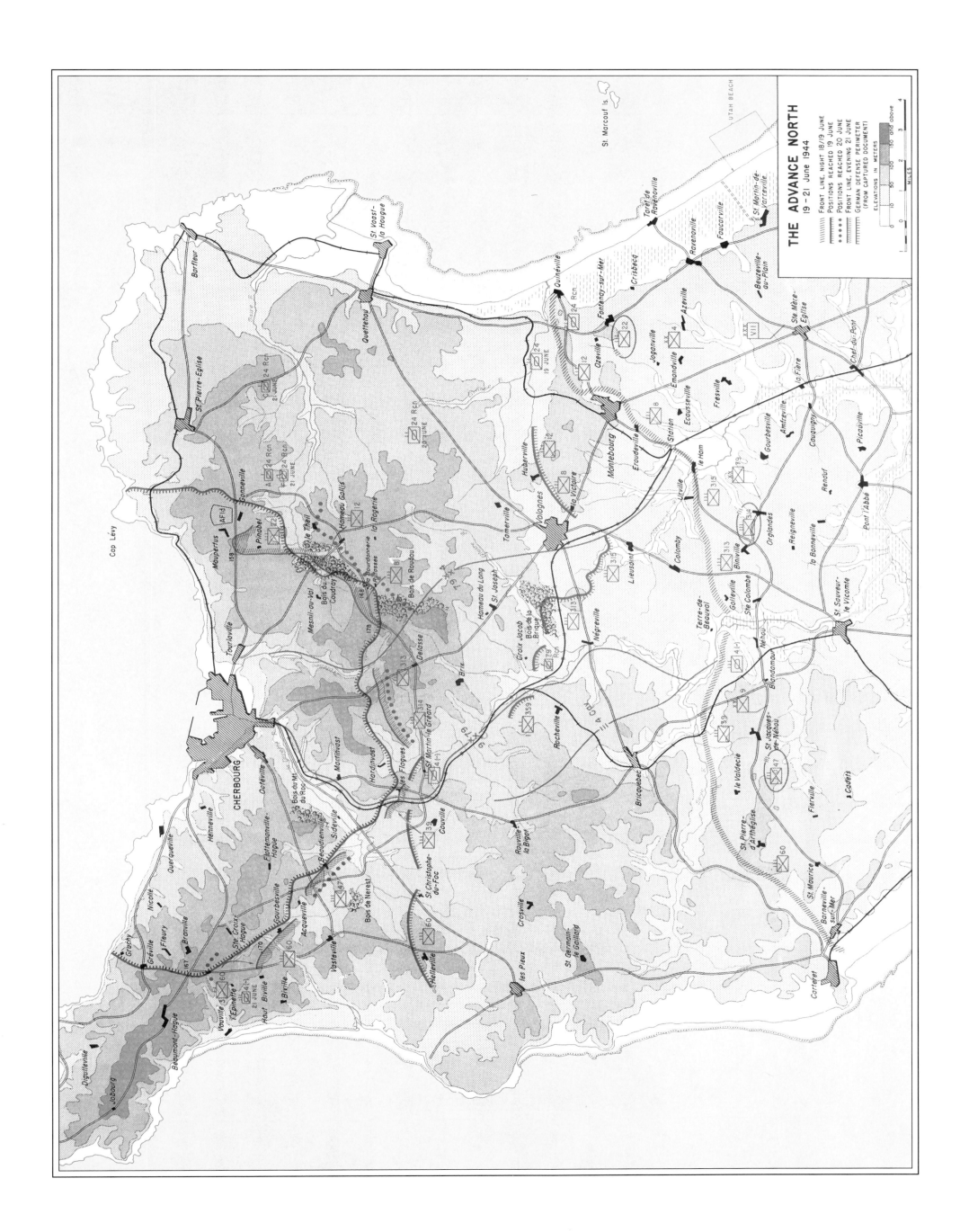

THE ADVANCE NORTH
19 – 21 June 1944

FRONT LINE, NIGHT 18/19 JUNE
POSITIONS REACHED 19 JUNE
POSITIONS REACHED 20 JUNE
FRONT LINE, EVENING 21 JUNE
GERMAN DEFENSE PERIMETER
(FROM CAPTURED DOCUMENT)

ELEVATIONS IN METERS

50   100   150 and above

MILES

Cap Lévy

BTRY HAMBURG 240

105

Maupertus

AFld

AA AA

AA AA AA

AA AA

Gonneville

Digosville

Tourlaville

Bourbourg 150

Fort des Flamands

CHERBOURG

Fort du Roule

Équeurdreville

Redoute des Fourches

Hameau du Tot

Querqueville

Hennuville

Tonneville

Nacqueville

AFld

Hainneville

le Theil

Bois du Coudray

Hameau Gallis

la Rogerie

Rufosses

Mesnil-au-Val

le Glacerie

Hameau Gringor

St. Sauveur

Octeville

Martinvast

Bois du Mt. du Roc

Tollevast

Hardinvast

St. Martin le Gréard

TO VALOGNES

79 XX 709

79 709

Sideville

Nouainville

Flottemanville-Hague

Beaudienville

Acqueville

Vasteville

Courbeville

Gréville-Hague

Gruchy

Fleury

Branville

Ste Croix-Hague

Hout Biville

Nr'Épinette

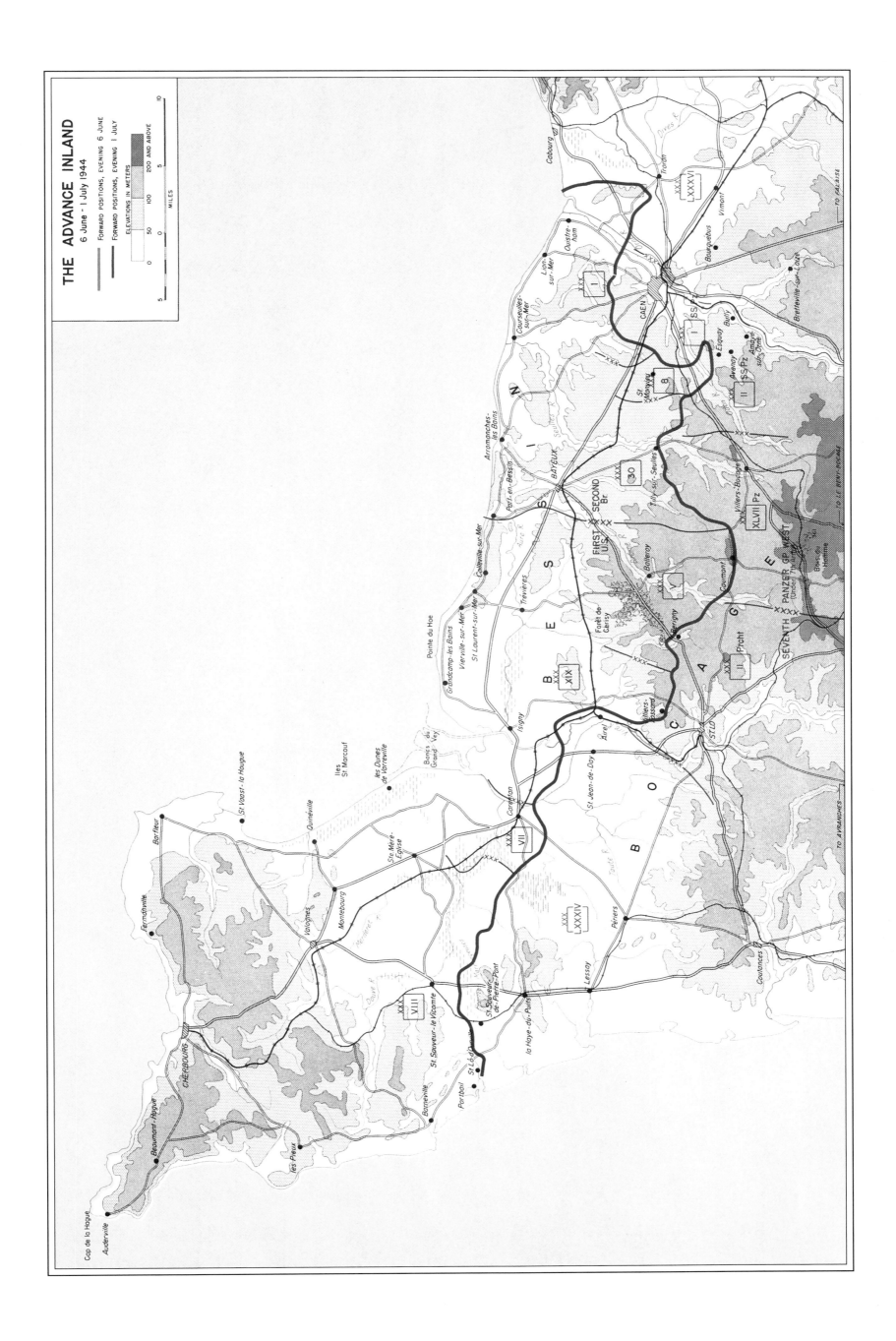

THE ADVANCE INLAND
6 June - 1 July 1944

FORWARD POSITIONS, EVENING 6 JUNE
FORWARD POSITIONS, EVENING 1 JULY

ELEVATIONS IN METERS

0   50   100   200 AND ABOVE

MILES
5   0   5   10

Breakout and Pursuit

July 2–August 25, 1944

ONCE THE ALLIES HAD SUCCESSFULLY ACHIEVED A hard-fought lodgment on the French mainland, they quickly realized it was only the beginning of their difficulties. Between D-Day and August 1, U.S. First Army would struggle to cross some of the most intimidating terrain any of the soldiers or officers had ever seen—as bad as Guadalcanal, Major General J. Lawton Collins described it.

While the British Second Army, on the Allies' left, moved steadily through rolling pastures and cultivated fields, U.S. First Army's fifty-mile arc of front was pocked with swamps and hilly fields surrounded by almost impenetrable hedgerows (natural walls of dirt and vegetation as much as four feet thick and fifteen feet high). Hitler ordered his troops to fiercely defend the area, called the Bocage, to slow the Allied advance.

Ultimately, through ingenuity and by adaptation, First Army was able to conquer the Bocage and open the way for a breakout beyond. One of the innovations that made the breakout possible was a tank specially designed to cut through the hedgerows. Called a "rhinoceros," such a tank was outfitted with a large cutting blade—fashioned from the metal beach obstacles—on its front that made it possible for the tank to burst through the mounds of dirt and trees, opening the way for infantry. First Army also developed clever tactics to root out the stubborn German infantry—which was supported by tanks, artillery, mortars, and machine guns—in the Bocage. By August 1, 100,000 Germans and the same number of Americans had died in this maze of defenses.

Once Allied troops had broken into open country, they began their dogged pursuit of the Wehrmacht. By July 25, the Allies had taken St. Lô and, by July 30, had advanced on Avranches, the passageway to Brittany. The British, meanwhile, pierced the German center at Caumont, approached Vire, and opened the way for an all-out attack on Brittany.

Eisenhower, on August 1, brought U.S. Third Army—under the command of Lieutenant General George S. Patton, Jr.—into the fight. Patton wielded some of the most powerful armor units in the U.S. Army. Third Army raced past Avranches and in one week charged 100 miles across the base of Brittany to the Bay of Biscay. The First Canadian Army followed up this advance by interdicting the road from Caen to Falaise. The Germans were stranded now in what was later called the "Argentan-Falaise Pocket." After a violent combined air and armor assault, the British and American forces captured 50,000 Germans and killed 10,000. The rest of the Wehrmacht narrowly escaped. Meanwhile, Paris fell on August 25 to the Second Free French Armored Division.

LEFT: *A 203mm mobile gun is hauled to the front near Brest, France. Guns like this, wielded by expert U.S. artillery units, crushed German resistance on all fronts. The gun was so effective, in fact, that the Germans grudgingly acknowledged their respect for what would prove one of America's most potent combat arms in World War II.* **OPPOSITE PAGE INSET:** *Lieutenant J.F. White and his crew of the 303d Bomb Group pose in formation next to their plane, Sweet Pea, a Boeing B-17 Flying Fortress. Though the U.S. Army Air Force suffered staggering losses in its night-and-day assaults on the Axis forces in France and Germany, the morale of the airmen remained high, as witnessed by the obvious esprit de corps exhibited by the men in this photo. Nor were the losses in vain: the bombing campaign against the German forces was devastatingly successful.* **LEFT INSET:** *A team of spirited artillerymen fire away with their howitzer at retreating Germans near Carentan, France. On June 14, after the initial landing in Normandy, the VII Corps and its artillery wheeled in a south-westerly direction, captured Carentan, and joined up with V Corps. By June 18, VII Corps had captured Cherbourg.*

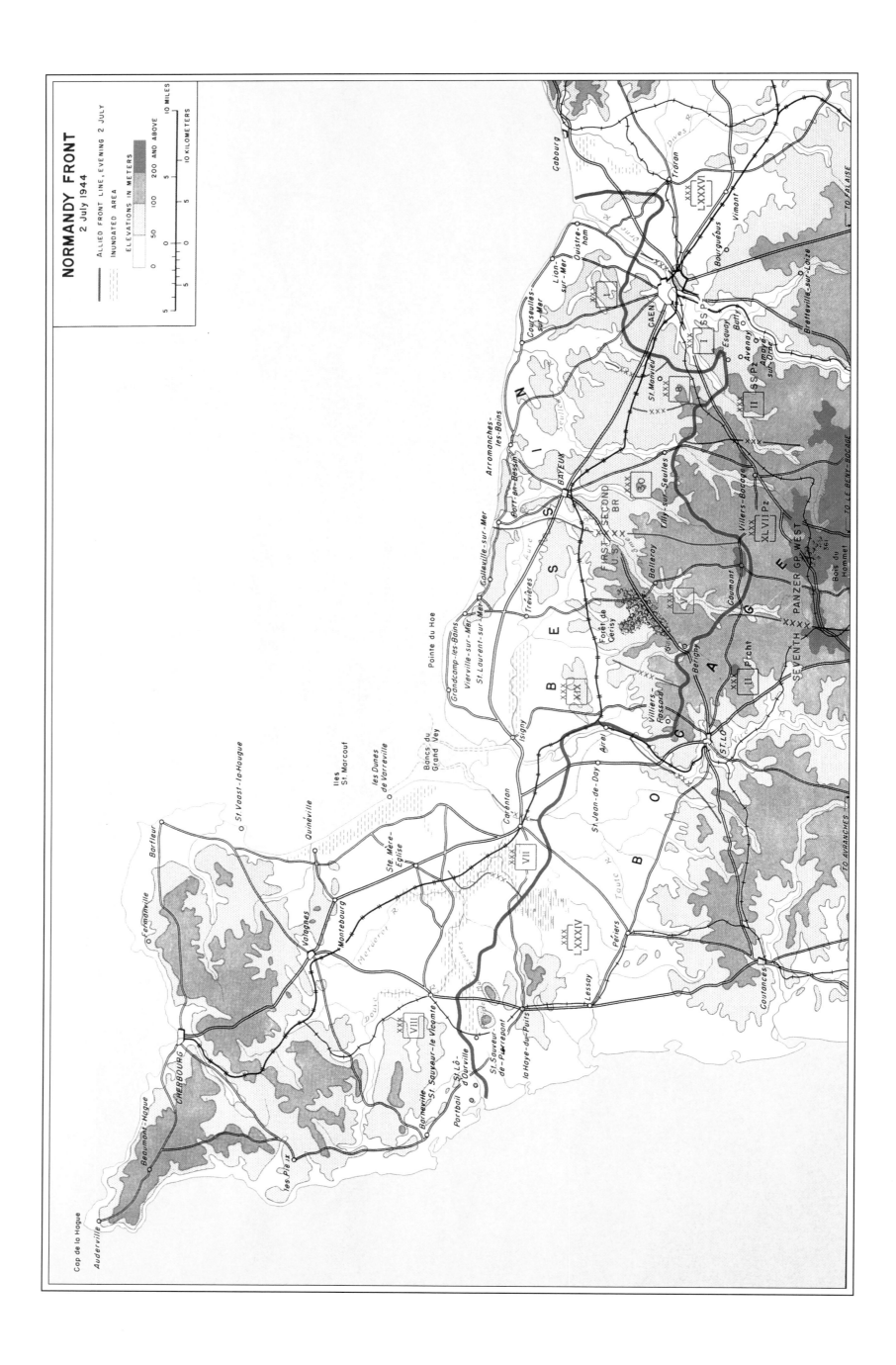

NORMANDY FRONT
2 July 1944

ALLIED FRONT LINE, EVENING 2 JULY
INUNDATED AREA
ELEVATIONS IN METERS

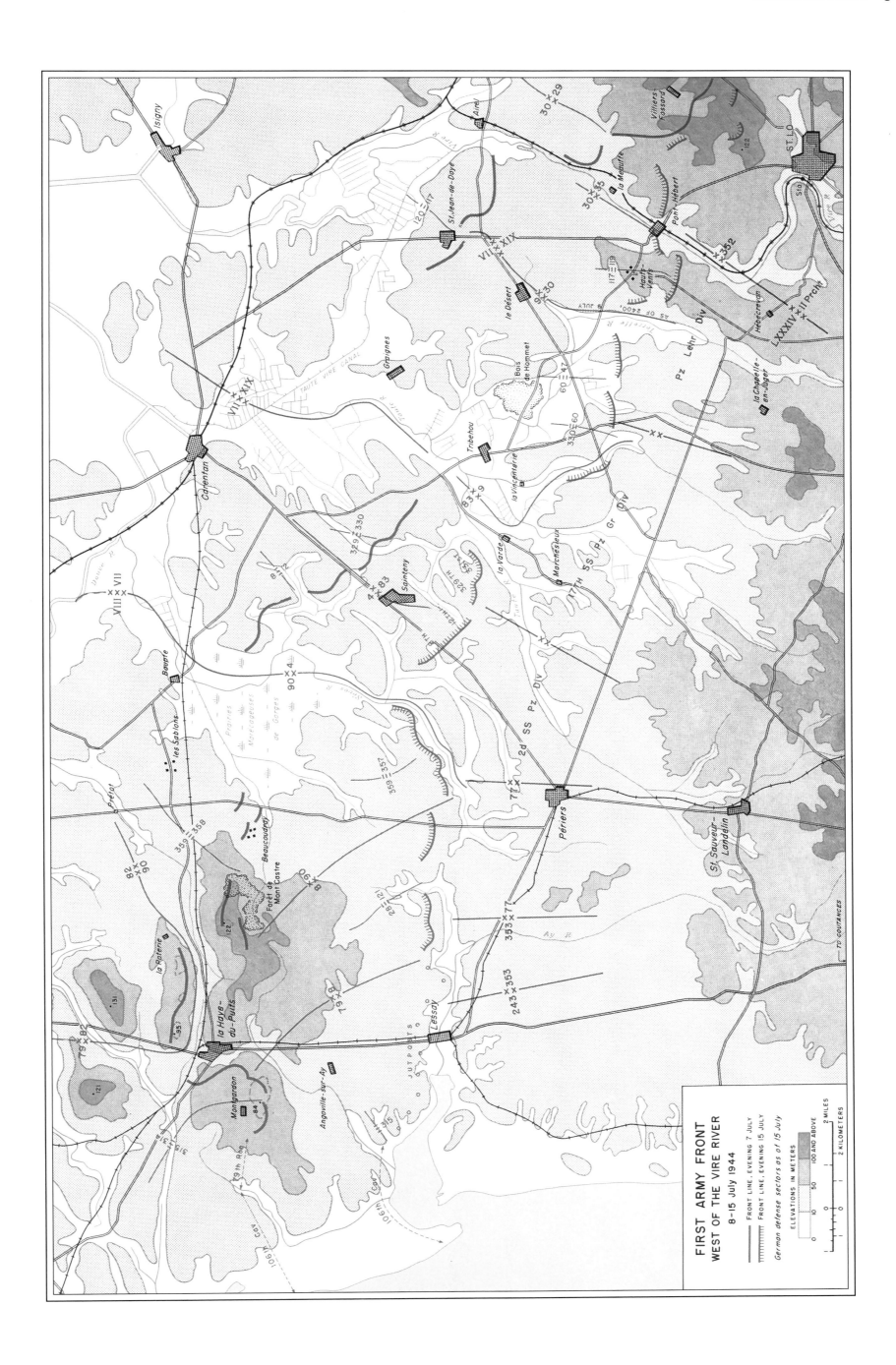

FIRST ARMY FRONT
WEST OF THE VIRE RIVER
8–15 July 1944

——— Front line, evening 7 July
——— Front line, evening 15 July
████ German defense sectors as of 15 July

ELEVATIONS IN METERS

░ 0
▒ 10
▒ 50
▓ 100 AND ABOVE

2 MILES
2 KILOMETERS

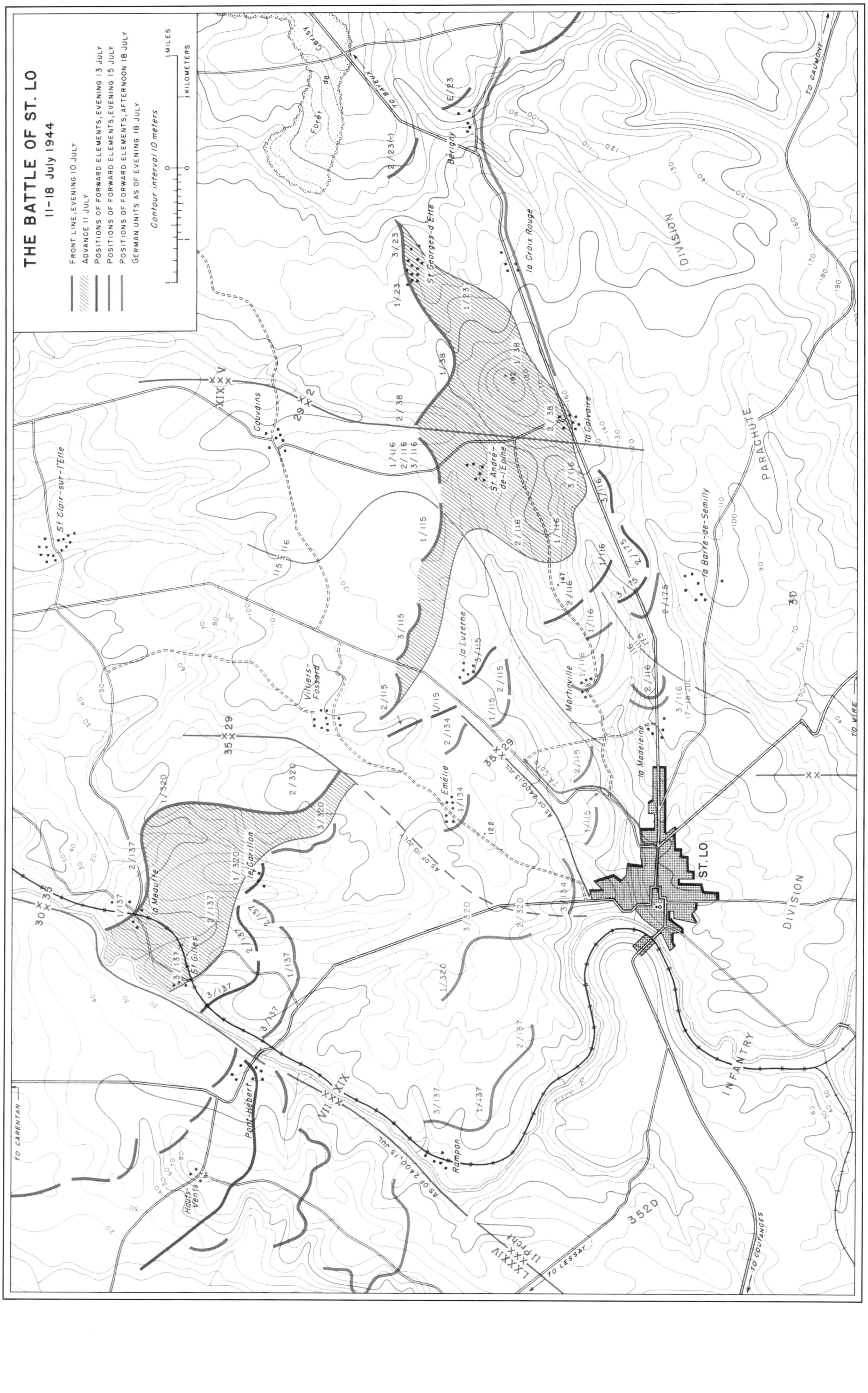

THE BATTLE OF ST. LO
11–18 July 1944

FRONT LINE,EVENING 10 JULY

ADVANCE 11 JULY

POSITIONS OF FORWARD ELEMENTS,EVENING 13 JULY

POSITIONS OF FORWARD ELEMENTS,EVENING 15 JULY

POSITIONS OF FORWARD ELEMENTS,AFTERNOON 18 JULY

GERMAN UNITS AS OF EVENING 18 JULY

Contour interval 10 meters

1 MILES

1 KILOMETERS

ST. LO

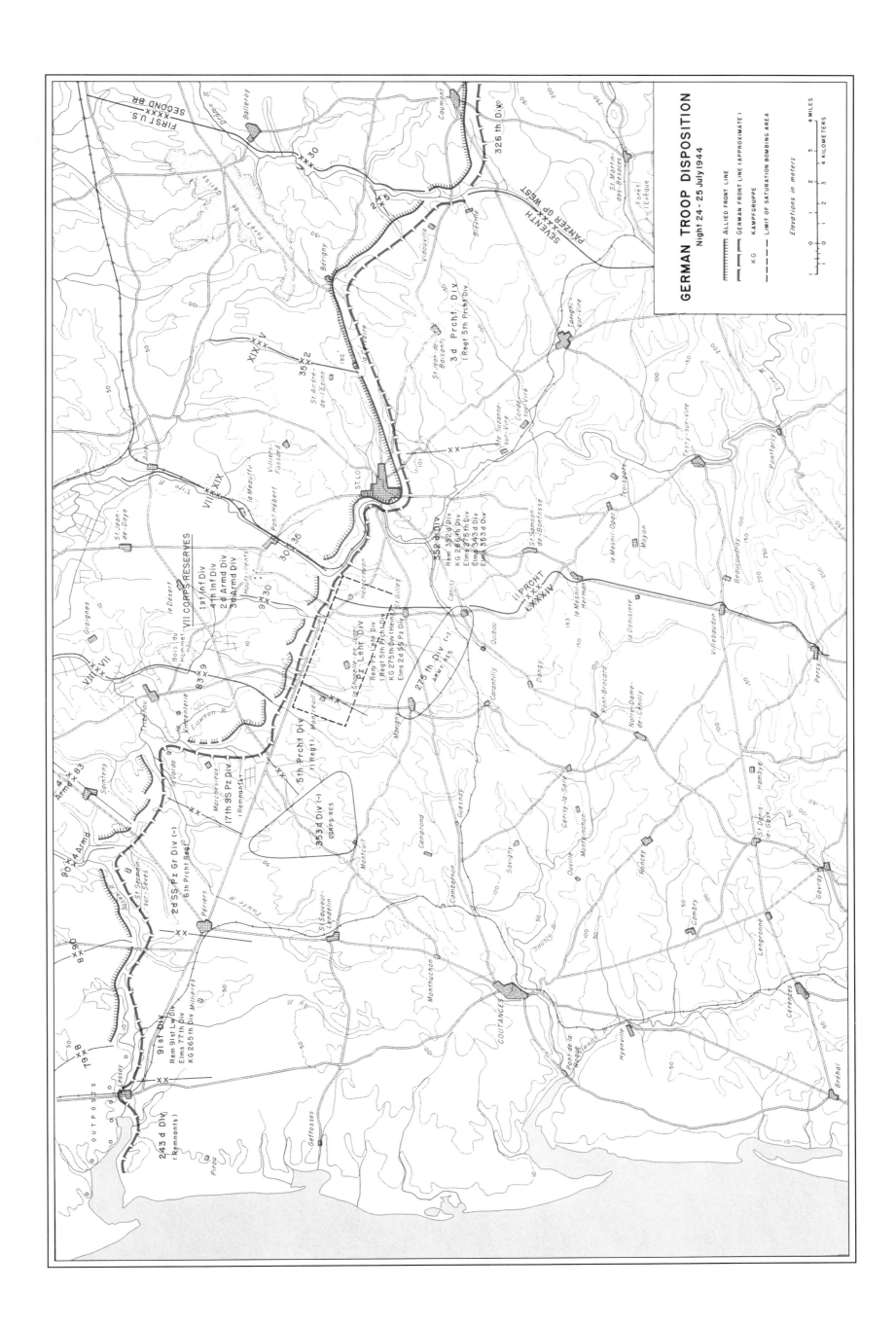

GERMAN TROOP DISPOSITION
Night 24–25 July 1944

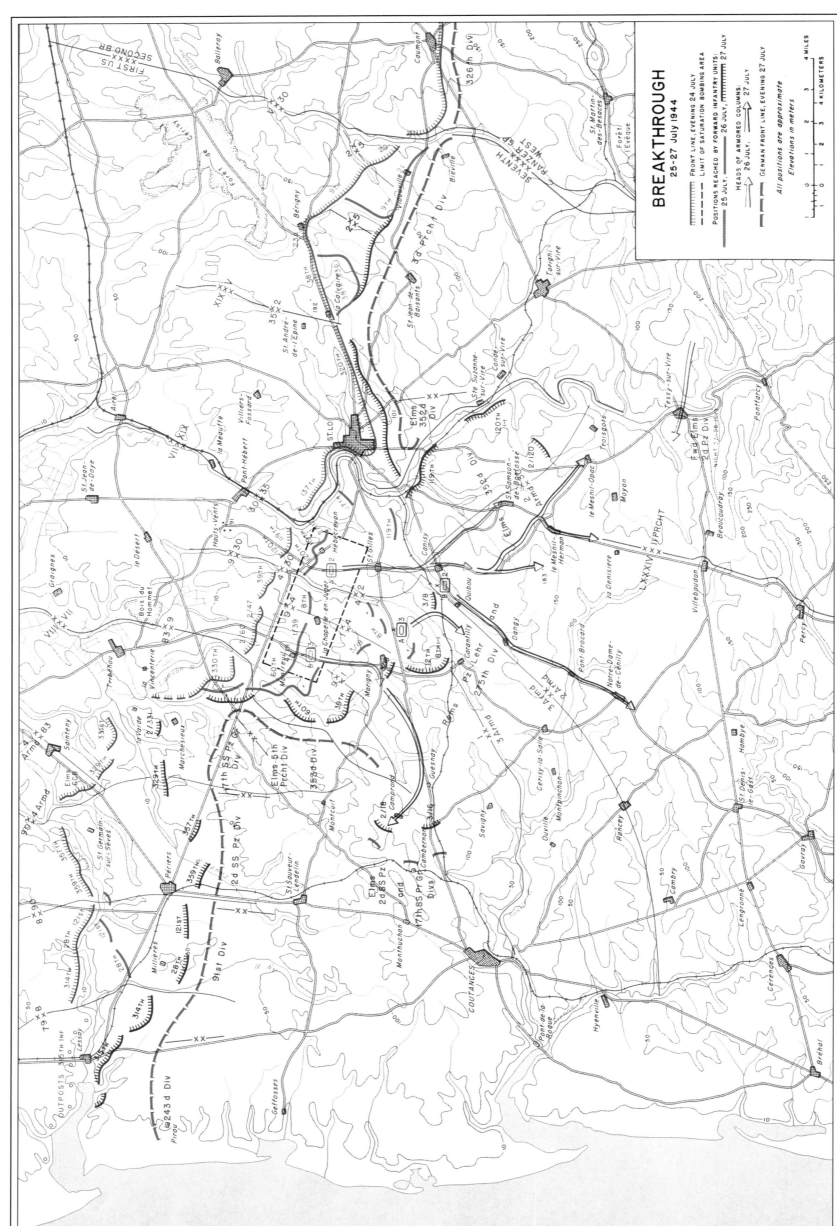

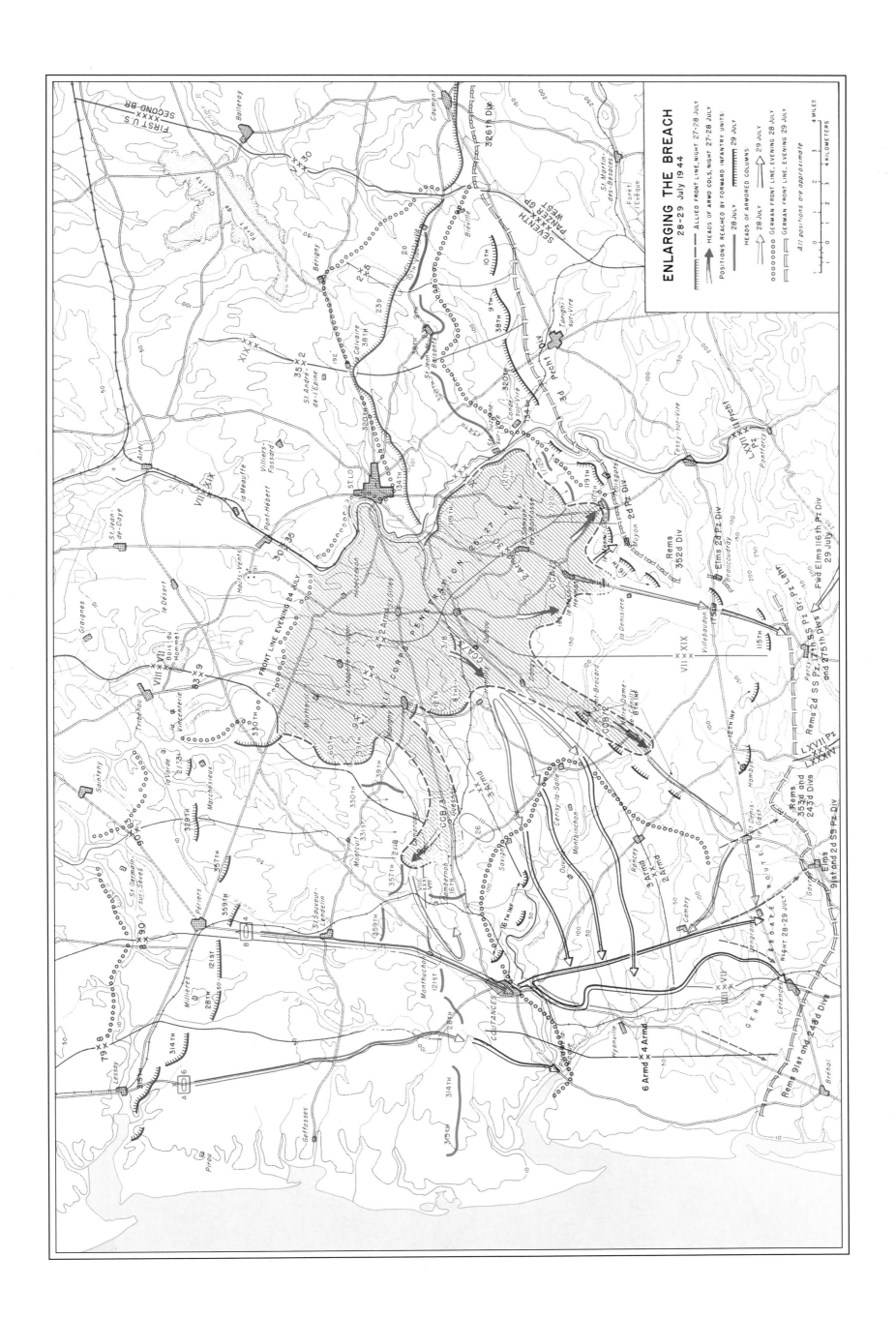

ENLARGING THE BREACH
28–29 July 1944

ALLIED FRONT LINE, NIGHT 27–28 JULY
HEADS OF ARMD COLS, NIGHT 27–28 JULY
POSITIONS REACHED BY FORWARD INFANTRY UNITS:
28 JULY
29 JULY
HEADS OF ARMORED COLUMNS:
28 JULY
29 JULY
GERMAN FRONT LINE, EVENING 28 JULY
GERMAN FRONT LINE, EVENING 29 JULY

All positions are approximate

0   1   2   3   4 MILES
0 1 2 3 4 KILOMETERS

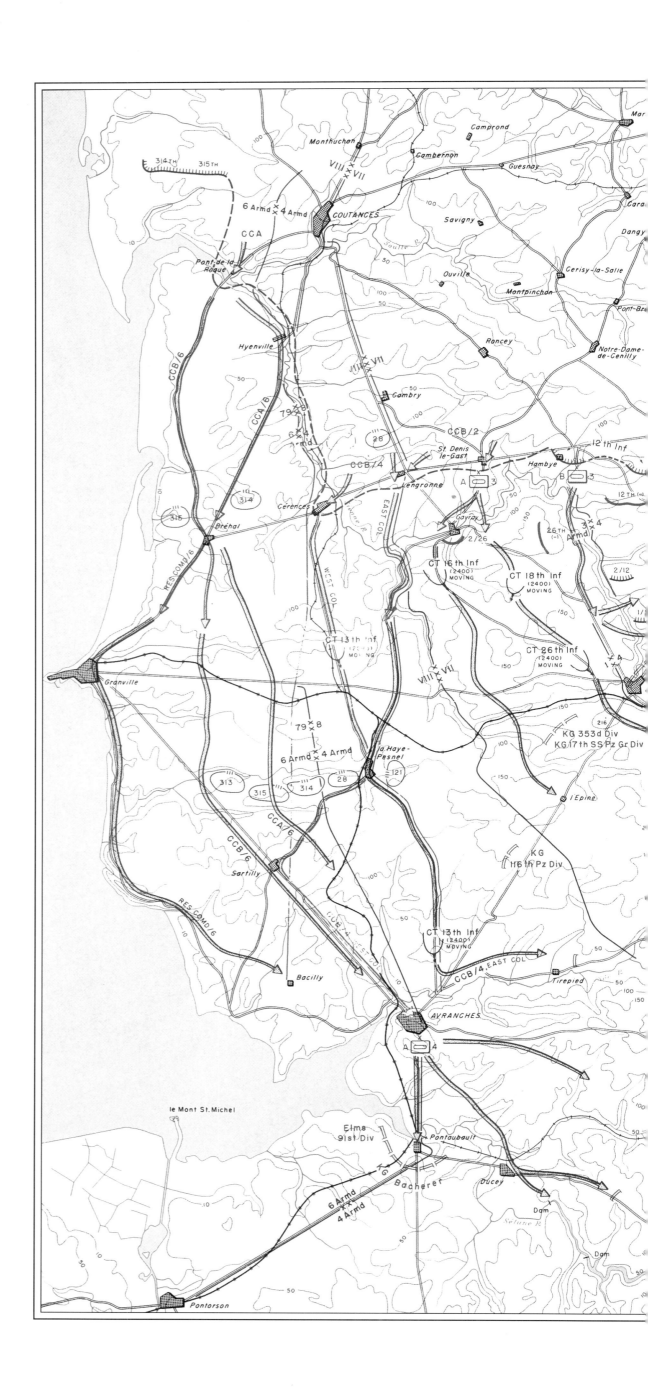

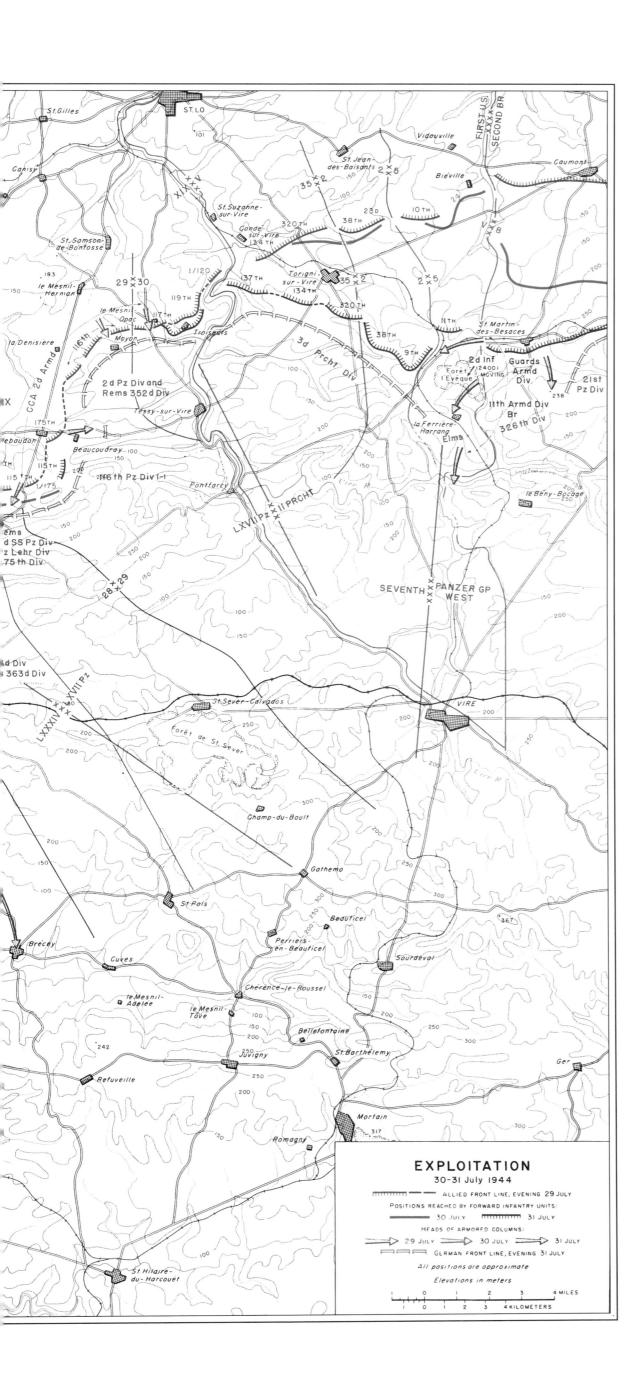

St. Gilles
ST. LO
Canisy
Vidouville
FIRST U.S.
SECOND BR
St.Jean-
des-Baisants
Bie'ville
Caumont
101
St.Suzanne-
sur-Vire
150
35 × 2
2 × 5
23 D
10 TH
St.Samson-
de-Bonfosse
Gonde-
sur-Vire
134 TH
320TH
38 TH
150
8
le Mesnil-
Herman
183
1/120
37 TH
134 TH
Torigni
sur-Vire
35 × 2
2 × 5
250
29 × 30
119TH
320 TH
11TH
St.Martin-
des-Besaces
le Mesnil-
Opac
117TH
Troisgots
38TH
250
21st
Pz Div
la.Denisiere
116th
Moyon
9TH
2d Inf
2400 I
MOVING
Guards
Armd
Div.
238
CCA 2d Armd
3d Prcht Div
150
2d Pz Div and
Rems 352d Div
Forêt
l'Eveque
11th Armd Div
Br
326th Div
175TH
Tessy-sur-Vire
150
la Ferrière-
Harrang
150
ebaudon
Beaucoudray
100
200
Elms
le Beny-Bocage
200
TH
115TH
115TH
1/175
116th Pz Div I-1
Pont Farcy
LXVII Pz II PRCHT
ems
d SS Pz Div
z Lehr Div
75th Div
200
150
28 × 29
SEVENTH   PANZER GP
WEST
150
d Div
363d Div
100
LXXVII Pz
150
St.Sever-Calvados
VIRE
200
200
200
LXXXIV
100
forêt de St.Sever
250
200
Champ-du-Boult
300
200
Gathemo
250
300
St.Pois
Beauficel
367
Brécey
Perriers-
en-Beauficel
Sourdeval
150
Cuves
le Mesnil-
Adelee
Chérence-le-Roussel
le Mesnil-
Tôve
100
Bellefontaine
250
300
200
150
242
550
Juvigny
St.Barthélemy
Ger
250
Refuveille
200
Mortain
317
Romagni

EXPLOITATION
30-31 July 1944

ALLIED FRONT LINE, EVENING 29 JULY
POSITIONS REACHED BY FORWARD INFANTRY UNITS:
30 JULY   31 JULY
HEADS OF ARMORED COLUMNS:
29 JULY   30 JULY   31 JULY
GERMAN FRONT LINE, EVENING 31 JULY
All positions are approximate
Elevations in meters

1   0   1   2   3   4 MILES
1   0   1   2   3   4 KILOMETERS

St.Hilaire-
du-Harcouet

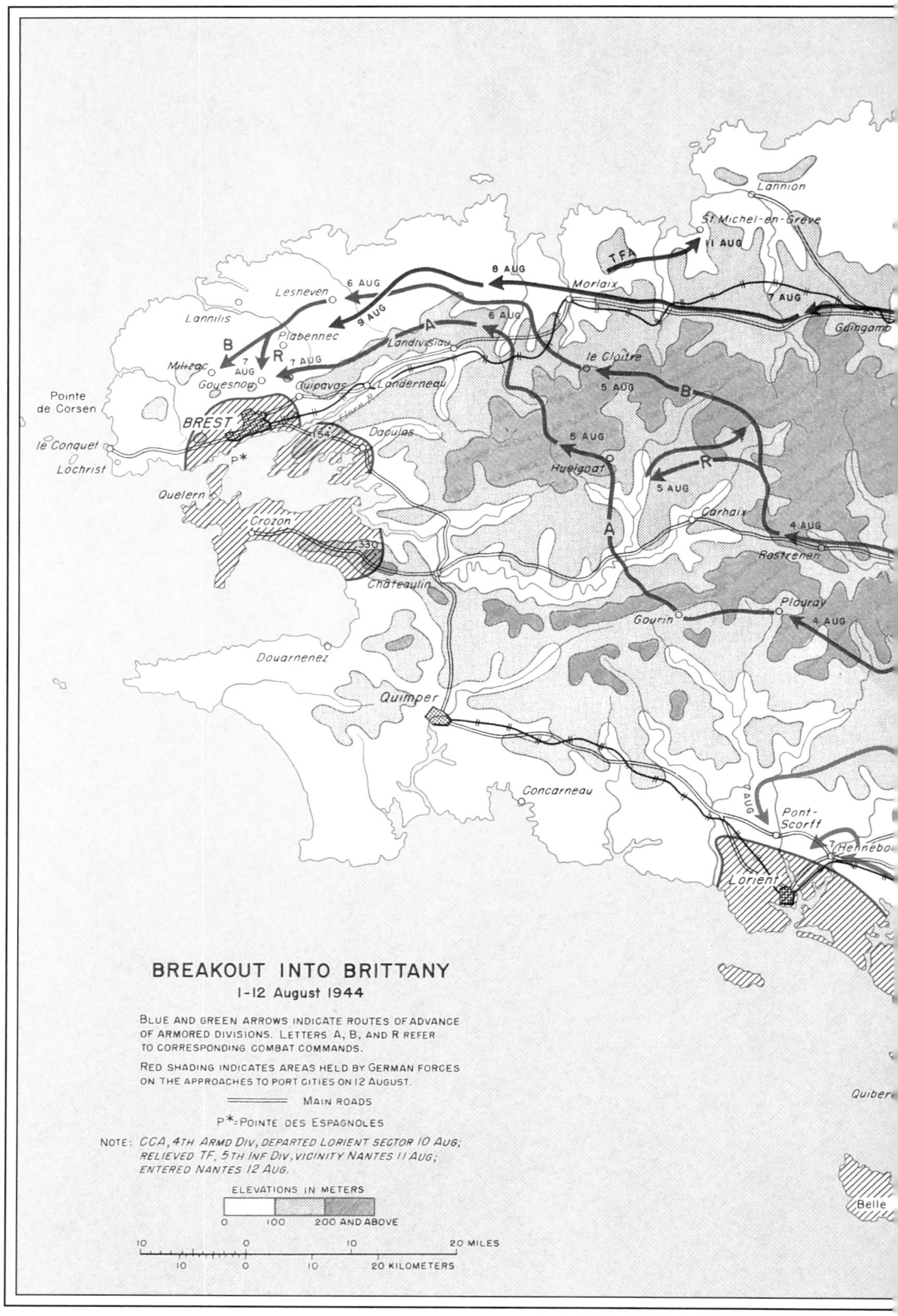

BREAKOUT INTO BRITTANY
1-12 August 1944

BLUE AND GREEN ARROWS INDICATE ROUTES OF ADVANCE
OF ARMORED DIVISIONS. LETTERS A, B, AND R REFER
TO CORRESPONDING COMBAT COMMANDS.

RED SHADING INDICATES AREAS HELD BY GERMAN FORCES
ON THE APPROACHES TO PORT CITIES ON 12 AUGUST.

========= MAIN ROADS

P*: POINTE DES ESPAGNOLES

NOTE: CCA, 4TH ARMD DIV, DEPARTED LORIENT SECTOR 10 AUG;
RELIEVED TF, 5TH INF DIV, VICINITY NANTES 11 AUG;
ENTERED NANTES 12 AUG.

ELEVATIONS IN METERS

| 0 | 100 | 200 AND ABOVE |

10   0   10   20 MILES

10   0   10   20 KILOMETERS

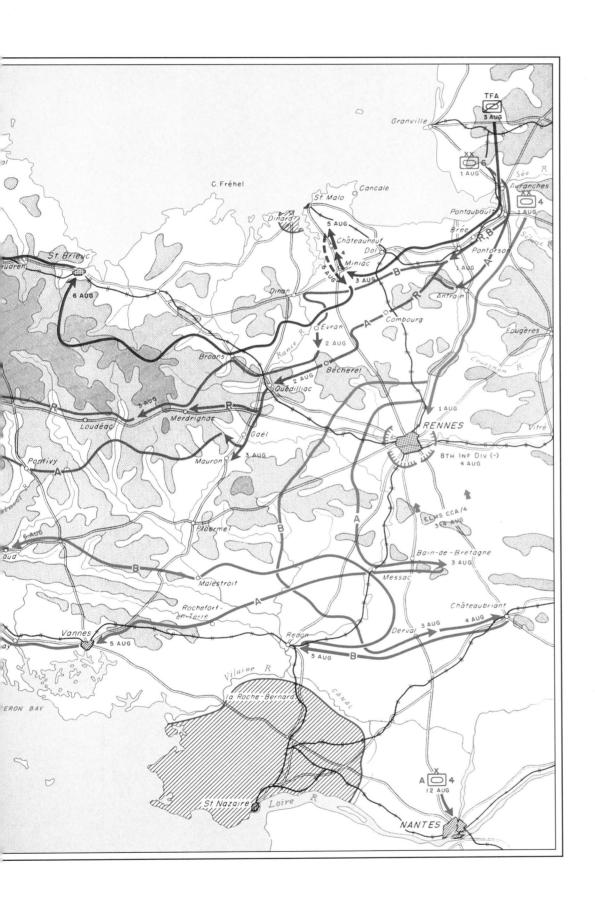

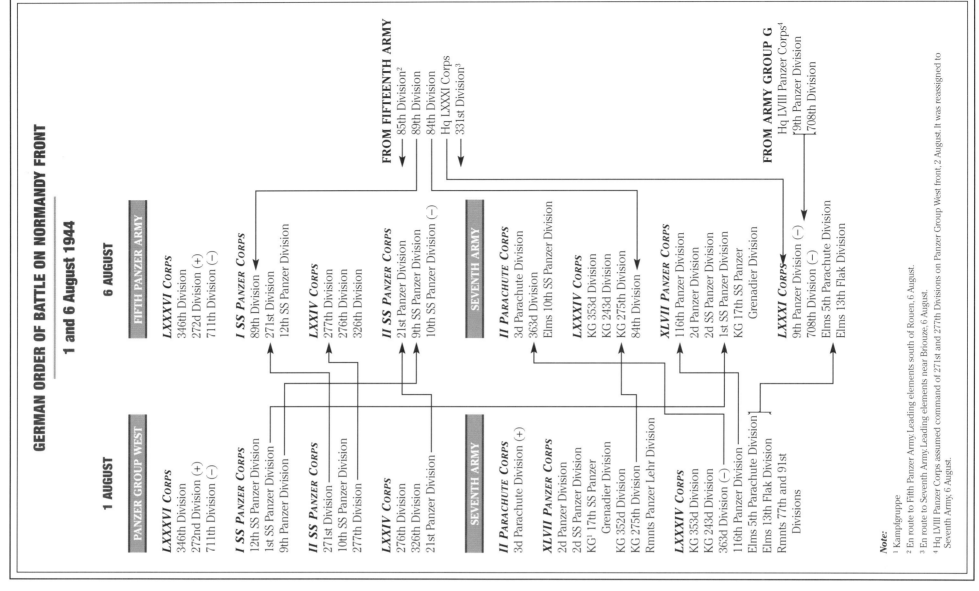

GERMAN ORDER OF BATTLE ON NORMANDY FRONT
1 and 6 August 1944

1 AUGUST

PANZER GROUP WEST

LXXXVI CORPS
346th Division
272nd Division (+)
711th Division (−)

I SS PANZER CORPS
12th SS Panzer Division
1st SS Panzer Division
9th Panzer Division

II SS PANZER CORPS
271st Division
10th SS Panzer Division
277th Division

LXXIV CORPS
276th Division
326th Division
21st Panzer Division

SEVENTH ARMY

II PARACHUTE CORPS
3d Parachute Division (+)

XLVII PANZER CORPS
2d Panzer Division
2d SS Panzer Division
KG[1] 17th SS Panzer
    Grenadier Division
KG 352d Division
KG 275th Division
Rmnts Panzer Lehr Division

LXXXIV CORPS
KG 353d Division
KG 243d Division
363d Division (−)
116th Panzer Division
Elms 5th Parachute Division
Elms 13th Flak Division
Rmnts 77th and 91st
    Divisions

6 AUGUST

FIFTH PANZER ARMY

LXXXVI CORPS
346th Division
272d Division (+)
711th Division (−)

I SS PANZER CORPS
89th Division
271st Division
12th SS Panzer Division

LXXIV CORPS
277th Division
276th Division
326th Division

II SS PANZER CORPS
21st Panzer Division
9th SS Panzer Division
10th SS Panzer Division (−)

SEVENTH ARMY

II PARACHUTE CORPS
3d Parachute Division
363d Division
Elms 10th SS Panzer Division

LXXXIV CORPS
KG 353d Division
KG 243d Division
KG 275th Division
84th Division

XLVII PANZER CORPS
116th Panzer Division
2d Panzer Division
2d SS Panzer Division
1st SS Panzer Division
KG 17th SS Panzer
    Grenadier Division

LXXXI CORPS
9th Panzer Division (−)
708th Division (−)
Elms 5th Parachute Division
Elms 13th Flak Division

FROM FIFTEENTH ARMY
→ 85th Division[2]
→ 89th Division
→ 84th Division
→ Hq LXXXI Corps
→ 331st Division[3]

FROM ARMY GROUP G
→ Hq LVIII Panzer Corps[4]
→ 9th Panzer Division
→ 708th Division

Note:

[1] Kampfgruppe

[2] En route to Fifth Panzer Army. Leading elements south of Rouen, 6 August.

[3] En route to Seventh Army. Leading elements near Briouze, 6 August.

[4] Hq LVIII Panzer Corps assumed command of 271st and 277th Divisions on Panzer Group West front, 2 August. It was reassigned to Seventh Army, 6 August.

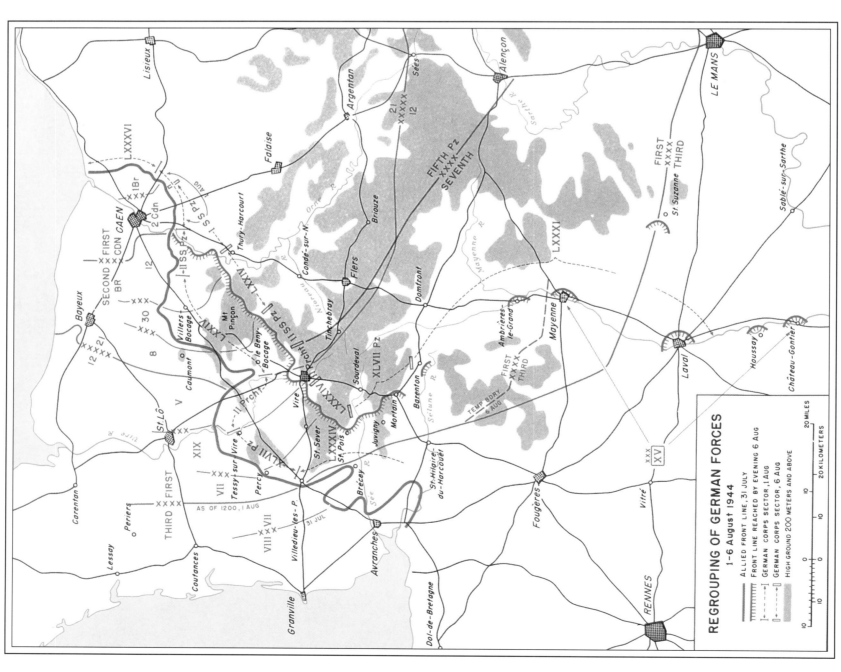

REGROUPING OF GERMAN FORCES
1–6 August 1944

— ALLIED FRONT LINE, 31 JULY
‒‒‒ FRONT LINE REACHED BY EVENING 6 AUG
[GERMAN CORPS SECTOR, 1 AUG
[GERMAN CORPS SECTOR, 6 AUG
▨ HIGH GROUND 200 METERS AND ABOVE

0   10   20 MILES
0   10   20 KILOMETERS

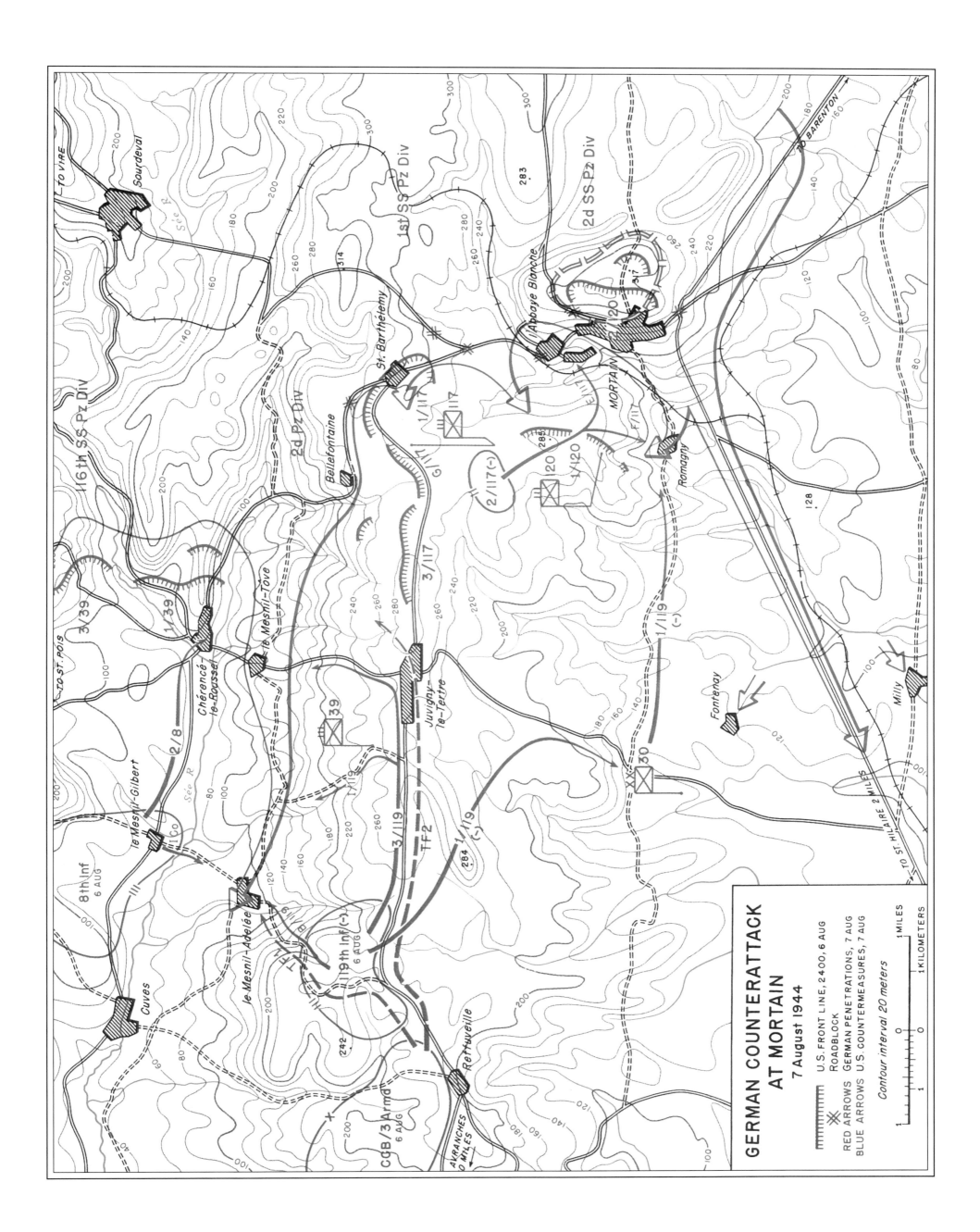

GERMAN COUNTERATTACK AT MORTAIN
7 August 1944

	U.S. FRONT LINE, 2400, 6 AUG
	ROADBLOCK
RED ARROWS	GERMAN PENETRATIONS, 7 AUG
BLUE ARROWS	U.S. COUNTERMEASURES, 7 AUG

Contour interval 20 meters

1 MILES
1 KILOMETERS

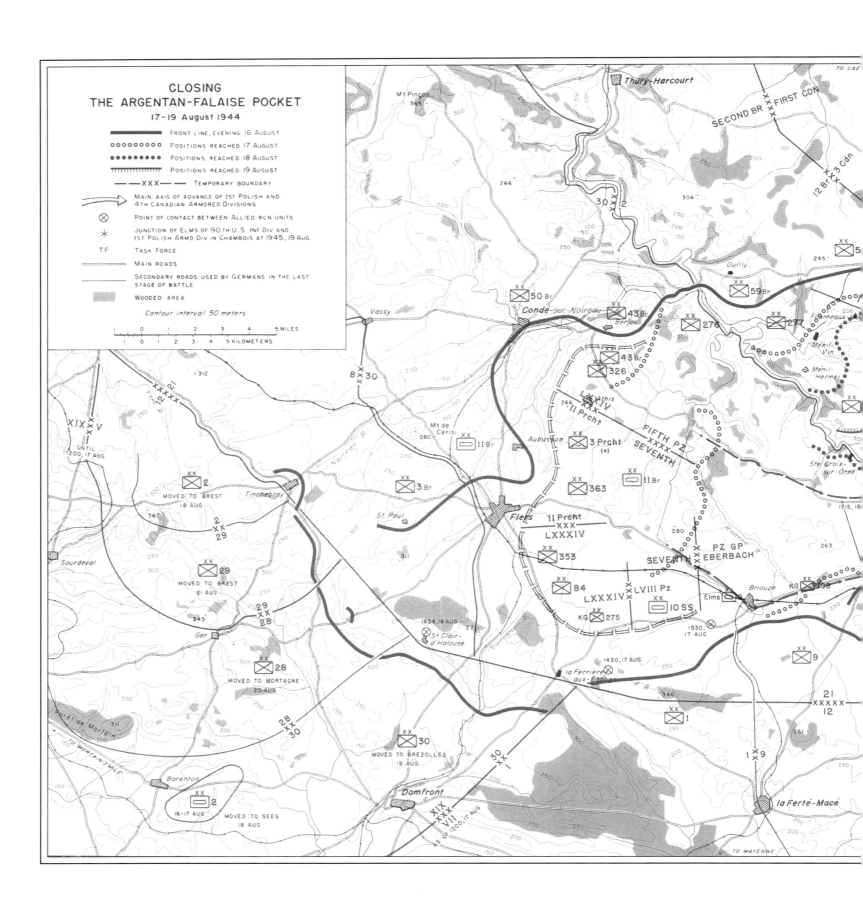

CLOSING
THE ARGENTAN-FALAISE POCKET
17-19 August 1944

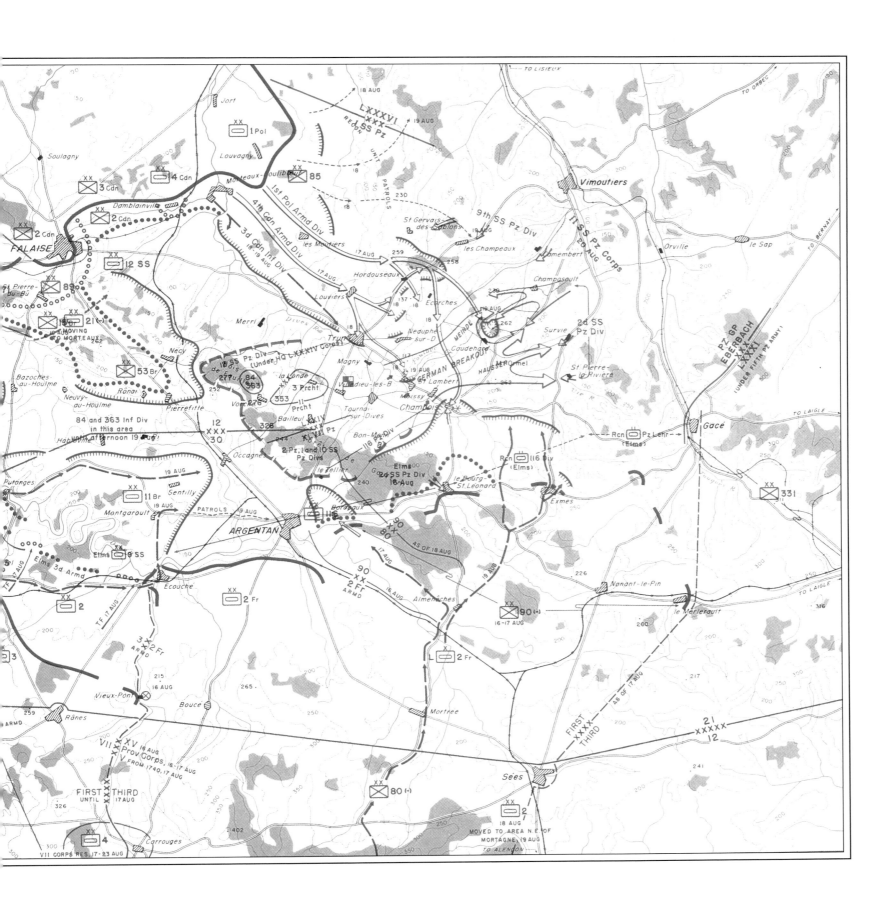

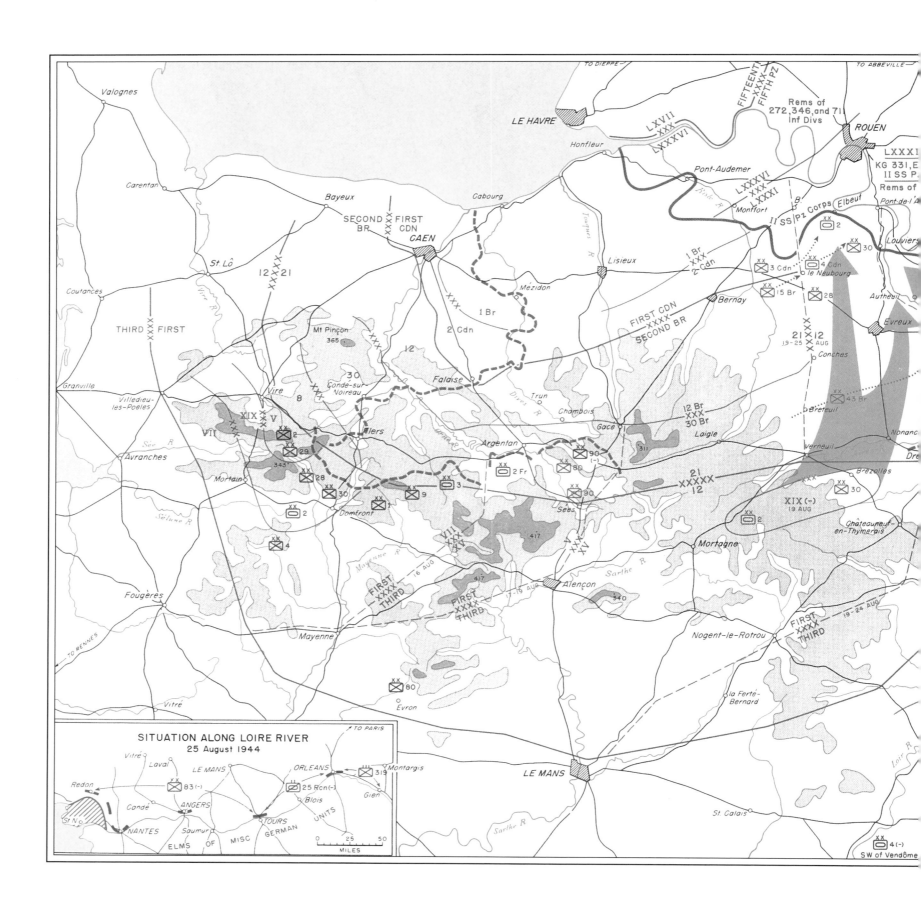

SITUATION ALONG LOIRE RIVER
25 August 1944

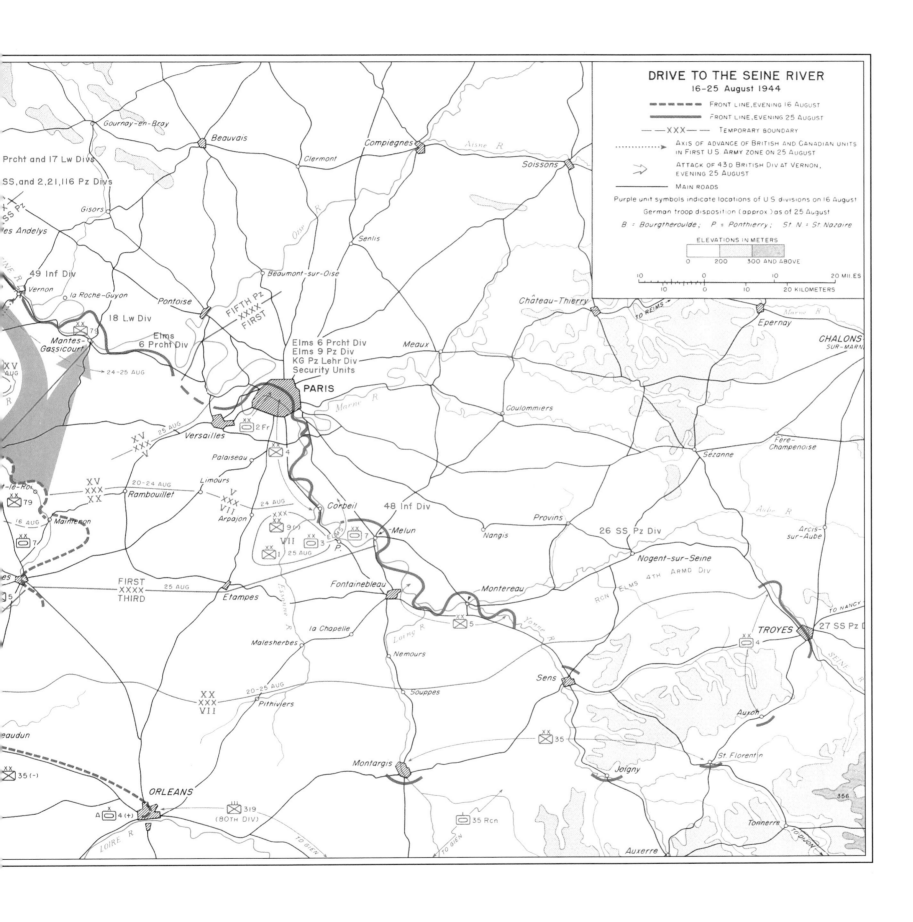

DRIVE TO THE SEINE RIVER
16-25 August 1944

———————— Front Line, Evening 16 August
━━━━━━━━━━ Front Line, Evening 25 August
— XXX — Temporary boundary
·········► Axis of advance of British and Canadian units in First U.S. Army zone on 25 August
→ Attack of 43d British Div at Vernon, evening 25 August
———————— Main roads

Purple unit symbols indicate locations of US divisions on 16 August

German troop disposition (approx.) as of 25 August

B = Bourgtheroulde;   P = Ponthierry;   St N = St. Nazaire

ELEVATIONS IN METERS
0   200   300 AND ABOVE

Prcht and 17 Lw Divs

SS, and 2,21,116 Pz Divs

Gisors

es Andelys

49 Inf Div

Vernon   la Roche-Guyon

18 Lw Div

Mantes-Gassicourt   Elms 6 Prcht Div

24-25 AUG

XV AUG

25 AUG

le-Ro

XV
XXX
V

XV
XXX
XX   Rambouillet   20-24 AUG

16 AUG

Mainten on

es

FIRST
XXXX   25 AUG
THIRD

35

35 (-)

eaudun

ORLEANS   319
(80TH DIV)

LOIRE R.

TO GIEN

Gournay-en-Bray   Beauvais   Clermont   Compiegnes   Aisne R.   Soissons

Senlis

Beaumont-sur-Oise

Pontoise   FIFTH PZ   XXXX   FIRST

Elms 6 Prcht Div   Meaux
Elms 9 Pz Div
KG Pz Lehr Div
Security Units

PARIS   Marne R.

2 Fr

Versailles   4

Palaiseau

Limours   Corbeil   48 Inf Div
Arpajon   9   Melun   Nangis

VII   3
P.
1   25 AUG

Fontainebleau   Montereau

Etampes   Essonne R.

la Chapelle   5

Malesherbes   Loing R.

Nemours

XX
XXX   20-25 AUG
VII   Pithiviers   Souppes

Montargis   Sens

Joigny

35   35 Rcn

Auxerre

Château-Thierry   Marne R.   Epernay

CHALONS
SUR-MARN

Coulommiers

Fère-Champenoise

Sézanne

Provins   Aube R.   Arcis-sur-Aube

26 SS Pz Div

Nogent-sur-Seine

Elms 4th Armd Div   TO NANCY

TROYES   27 SS Pz
4   SEINE R.

Auxon   TO REIMS

St Florentin

Tonnerre

TO REIMS

TO GIEN

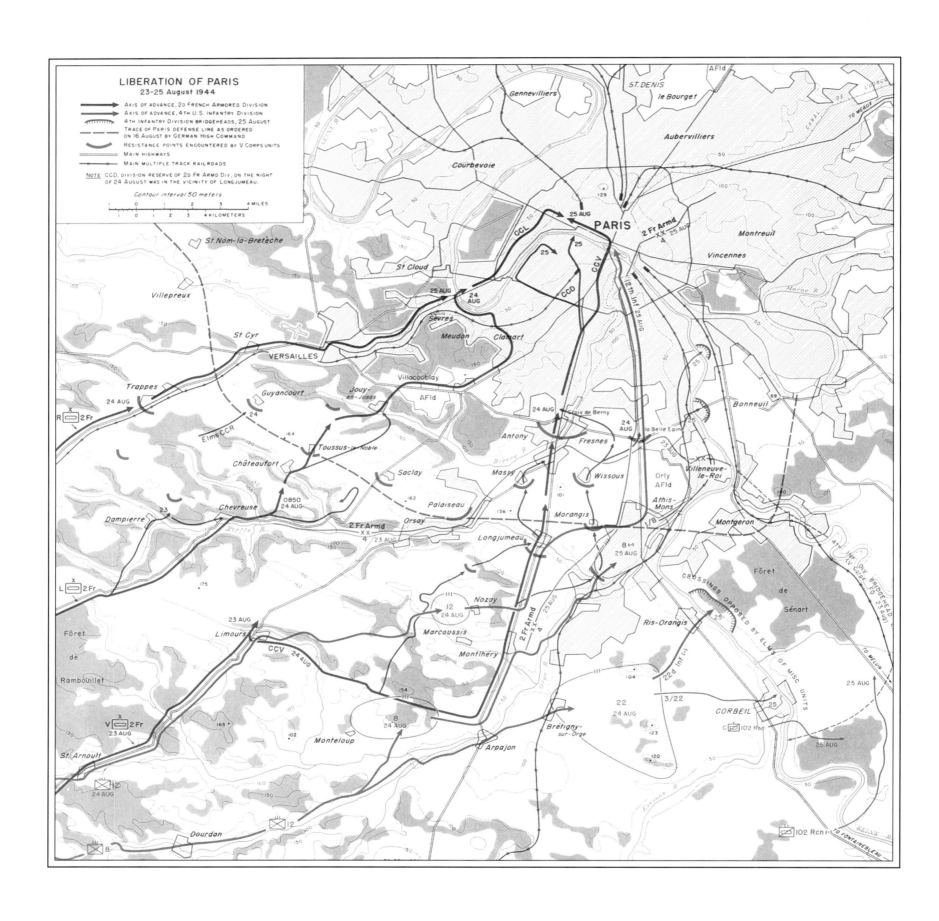

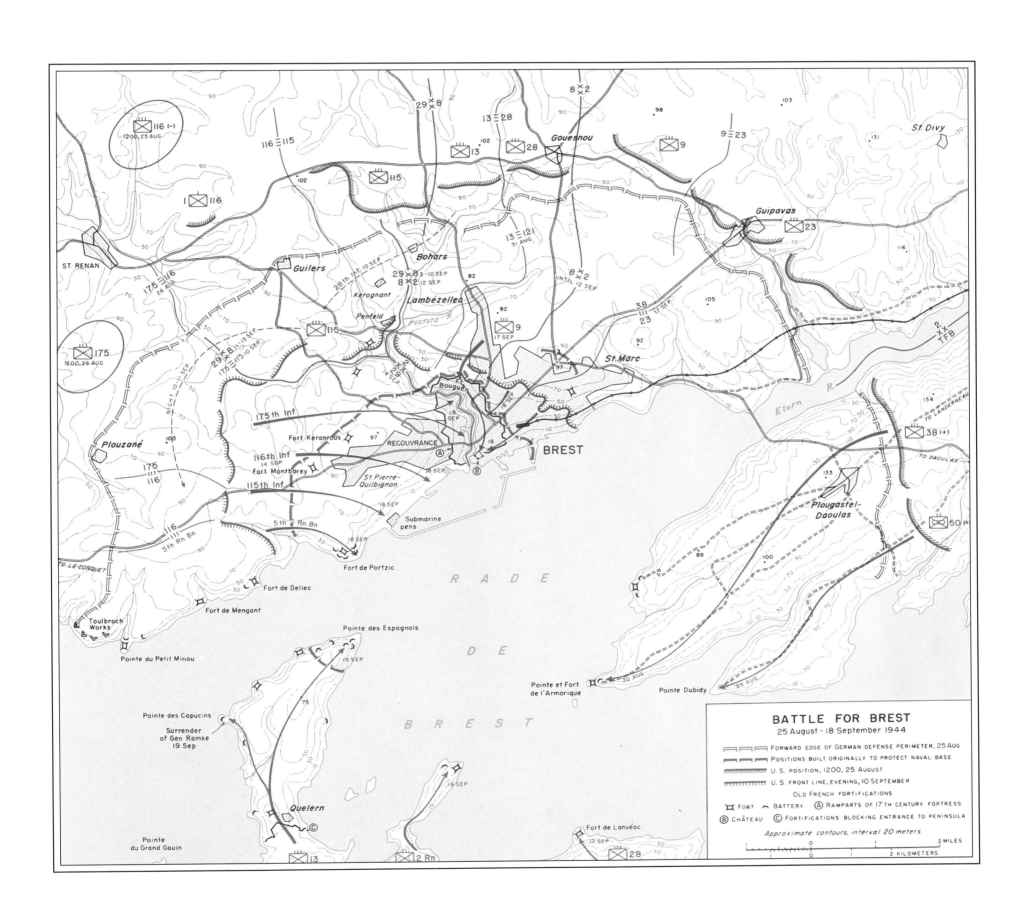

BATTLE FOR BREST
25 August - 18 September 1944

▭▭▭ FORWARD EDGE OF GERMAN DEFENSE PERIMETER, 25 AUG
▭▭▭ POSITIONS BUILT ORIGINALLY TO PROTECT NAVAL BASE
▭▭▭ U.S. POSITION, 1200, 25 AUGUST
▭▭▭ U.S. FRONT LINE, EVENING, 10 SEPTEMBER
OLD FRENCH FORTIFICATIONS
⊟ FORT ⌒ BATTERY Ⓐ RAMPARTS OF 17TH CENTURY FORTRESS
Ⓑ CHÂTEAU Ⓒ FORTIFICATIONS BLOCKING ENTRANCE TO PENINSULA
Approximate contours, interval 20 meters

2 MILES
2 KILOMETERS

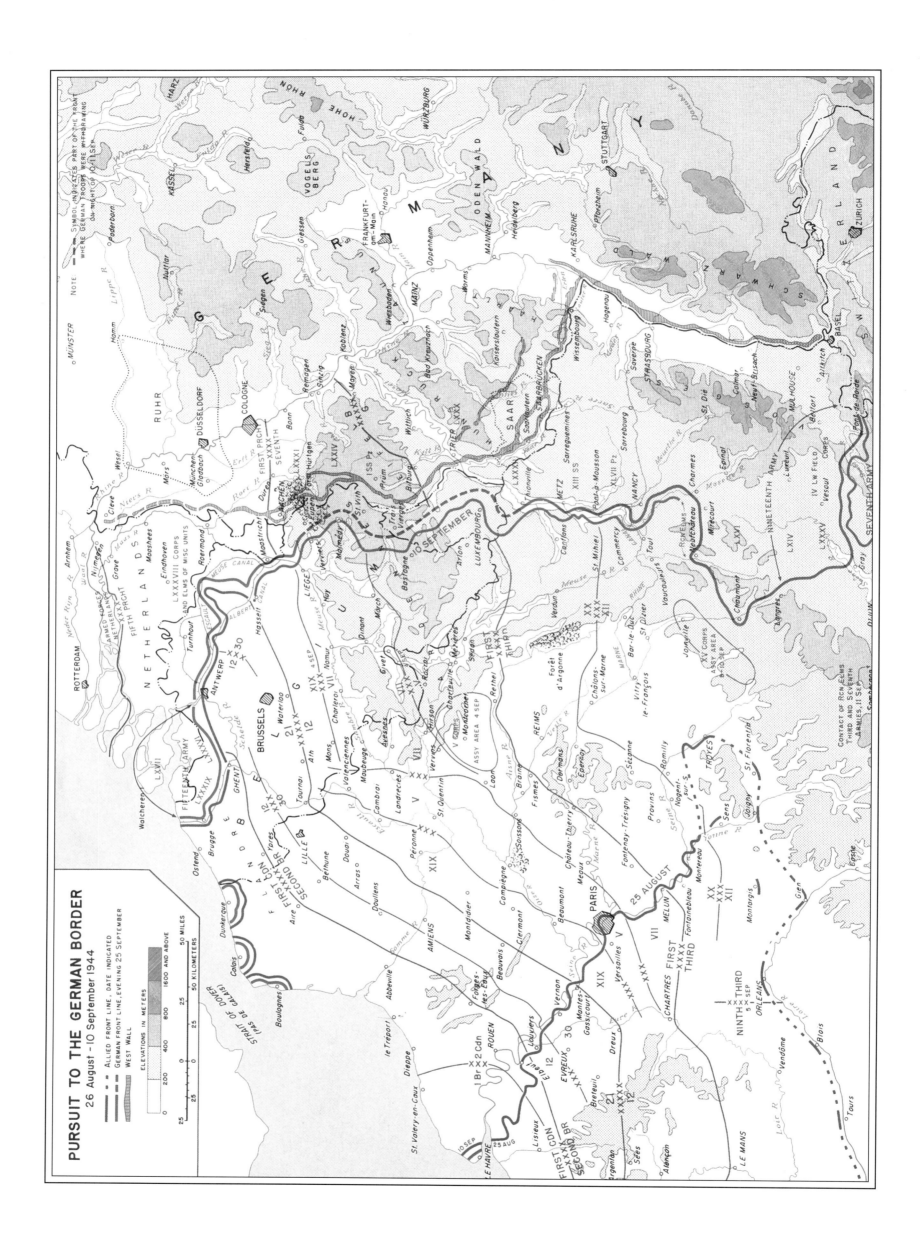

PURSUIT TO THE GERMAN BORDER
26 August – 10 September 1944

- - - - Allied front line, date indicated
━━━━ German front line, evening 25 September
West Wall

ELEVATIONS IN METERS

200   0   400   800   1600 AND ABOVE

0   25   50 MILES

0   25   50 KILOMETERS

NOTE ━ ━ SYMBOL INDICATES PART OF THE FRONT
WHERE GERMAN TROOPS WERE WITHDRAWING
OVERNIGHT OF 9/25 SEP.

ABOVE: *Two American paratroopers scurry through horrendous artillery fire near Arnhem, the Netherlands, in late September 1944 as part of Operation MARKET-GARDEN. Poor planning and execution by the Allies, commanded by Field Marshal Bernard Montgomery, led to a military debacle at Nimjegen and Arnhem that slowed down the Allied advance toward Germany.* **LEFT:** *Soldiers from General Omar Bradley's First Army approach a burning German Mark VI tank at Périers, France—a town fourteen miles west of St. Lô— during the Normandy invasion. The tank was part of German LXXXIV Corps' armor. The German Mark VI was superior in armor and firepower to American and British tanks, but suffered by comparison in other ways: it was generally underpowered, had transportation and repair weaknesses, and the turret traverse was slow. Nonetheless, it was a formidable weapon of war.*

The Lorraine Campaign

September 1–December 20, 1944

THESE MAPS FOLLOW U.S. THIRD ARMY'S PURSUIT of the Germans into Lorraine. Earlier, Third Army had advanced through France along a narrow corridor between the German Seventh Army and the ocean, turning the German flank in Normandy and roaring into the German rear. Patton's forces had driven south of the Loire River, then, north to join the British near Falaise, and finally, west into Brittany province, and east to the Seine River and Paris.

The Germans had collapsed before the Third's spearheading onslaught. When Third Army reached Lorraine, Patton's intelligence told him the way ahead was clear: the German defenses were a shambles. The problem for Third Army was that it had overextended its supply line (to depots at Cherbourg, over nearly 500 miles away), putting crippling strains on it. Supplies of gasoline and ammunition continued to shrink, and the army was forced to halt to replenish them. During the lull, the Germans were able to reinforce their troops and regroup.

Facing Third Army as it resumed the advance were numerous rivers, fortified towns, and other obstacles. Despite having put sufficient supplies in place, the Third became bogged down in grueling, costly assaults against a replenished German force fought over varied terrain. Unexpectedly, the campaign in Lorraine took three casualty-filled months to complete.

On September 5, XII Corps, commanded by Major General Manton S. Eddy, renewed the attack, sending the 35th Division to attack Nancy from the west, with the 4th Armored Division supporting it from the east across a Moselle River bridgehead. The attack failed miserably. On September 11, another assault was mounted across the Moselle south of Nancy, this time supported by an assault column from another bridgehead at Dieulouard. The combined attack met brutal fire, but due to a gallant follow-on strike led by Lieutenant Colonel Creighton Abrams, America's premier tanker, it succeeded in unhinging the German defenses, and Nancy fell on September 15.

But the relatively easy advances of the last couple of months were over. Manteuffel's LVIII Panzer Corps soon launched powerful counterattacks against the American positions around Nancy before falling back. Finally, after a brutal battle at Grémecey, Third Army regained its initiative.

In the north, Major General Walton Walker's XX Corps was ordered to take Metz and commenced an attack on September 7. Again, the Americans met fierce German resistance, and the fortress was not captured until November 21. In early December, XX Corps crossed the Saar River at Saarlautern and engaged tank obstacles, barbed wire entanglements, pillboxes, and fortified buildings. Third Army found itself in a different kind of war.

LEFT: *American infantrymen fight their way house-to-house as they enter the outskirts of Brest, France. Port cities like Brest, bypassed by U.S. forces as they pushed deep into France and reached the threshold of Germany, finally suffered overwhelming air, sea, and ground assaults that forced them to capitulate.*
OPPOSITE PAGE INSET: *The Allies captured the Remagen Bridge before it could be destroyed by the Germans. The bold seizure of the bridge opened up the belly of Germany to attack and signaled to the German armed forces that the Allies had gathered unstoppable momentum.* **LEFT INSET:** *Infantrymen hitch a ride aboard a tank carrying an obstacle-eliminating dozer blade on its front, shown passing through one of the tank barriers of the vaunted Siegfried Line near Roetgen. Other cities in the area, Stalberg and Aachen, were also captured in September 1944. Dozer blades like the one shown had been especially effective earlier in breaking through the German hedgerow defenses in the French Bocage.*

BELOW: *Engineers cross the Seine River under heavy fire (note the spouts where the bullets are hitting the water). The ferry shown appears to have been improvised from motor-driven boats and a timber platform. One of the engineers present at the crossing said, "We had to get our truck across on a little old ferry, and the 'krauts zinged at us every foot of the way... Engineers are expected to do the impossible. We did it."* **RIGHT:** *Armor from General George Patton's Third Army drive over a pontoon bridge across the Rhine River south of Koblenz. The engineers who constructed these bridges often suffered heavy machine-gun and mortar barrages during construction. Many of these men were wounded or killed in the process, despite the smoke-screens that were frequently created to obscure the engi-neers while they performed these dangerous tasks.*

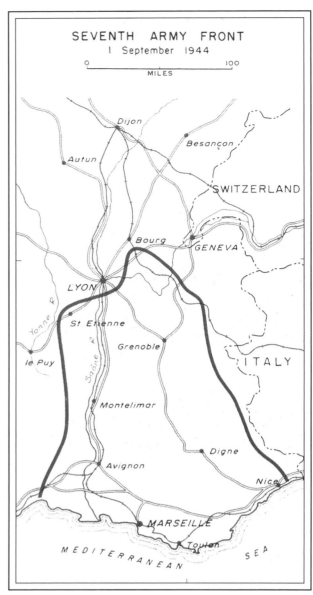

SEVENTH ARMY FRONT
1 September 1944

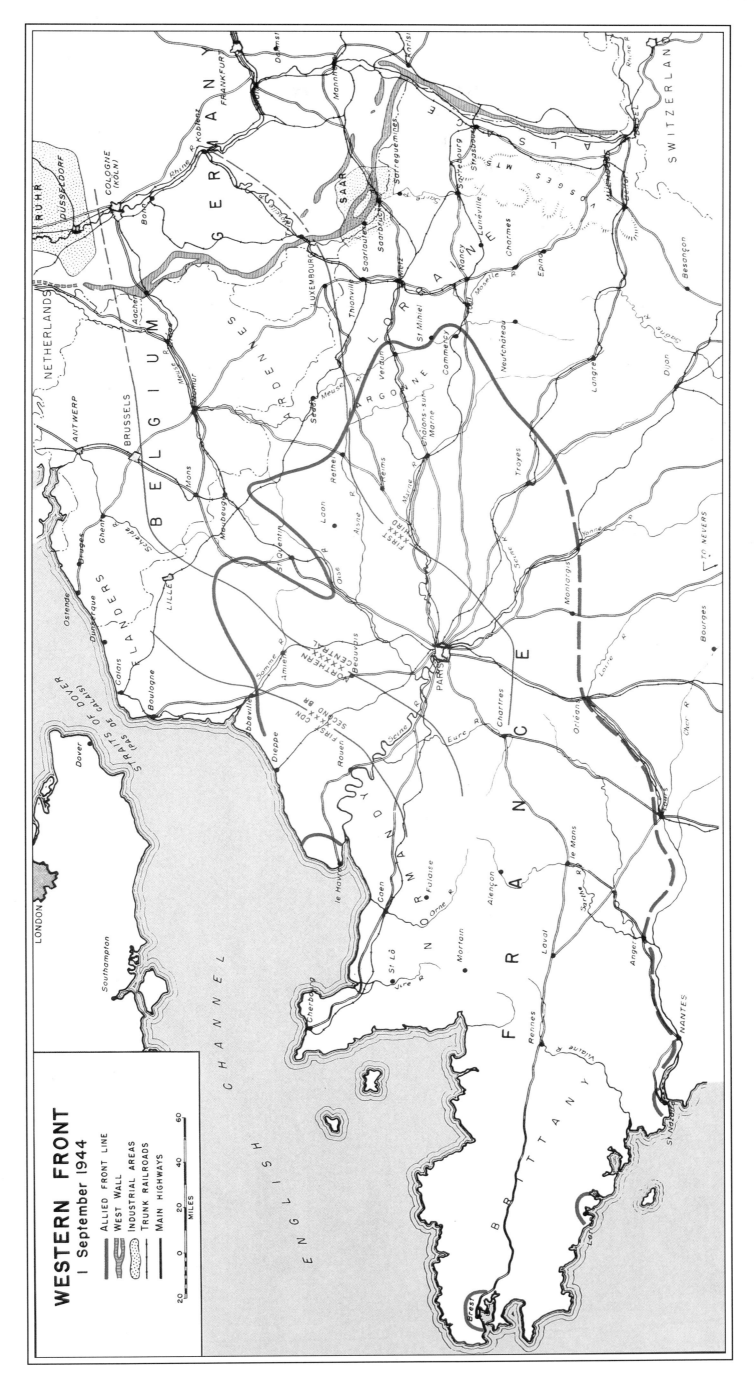

WESTERN FRONT
1 September 1944

ALLIED FRONT LINE
WEST WALL
INDUSTRIAL AREAS
TRUNK RAILROADS
MAIN HIGHWAYS

MILES
20 0 20 40 60

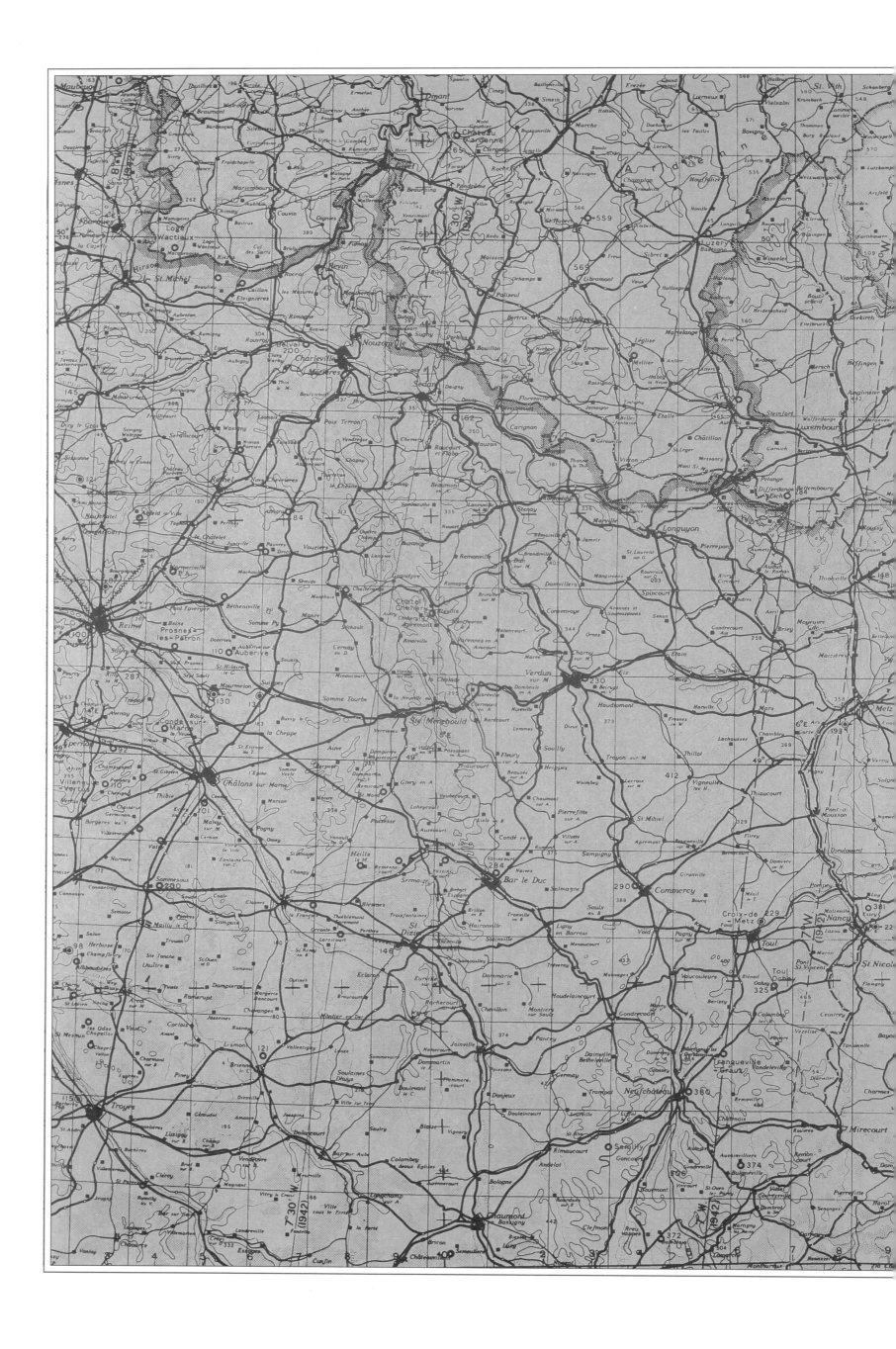

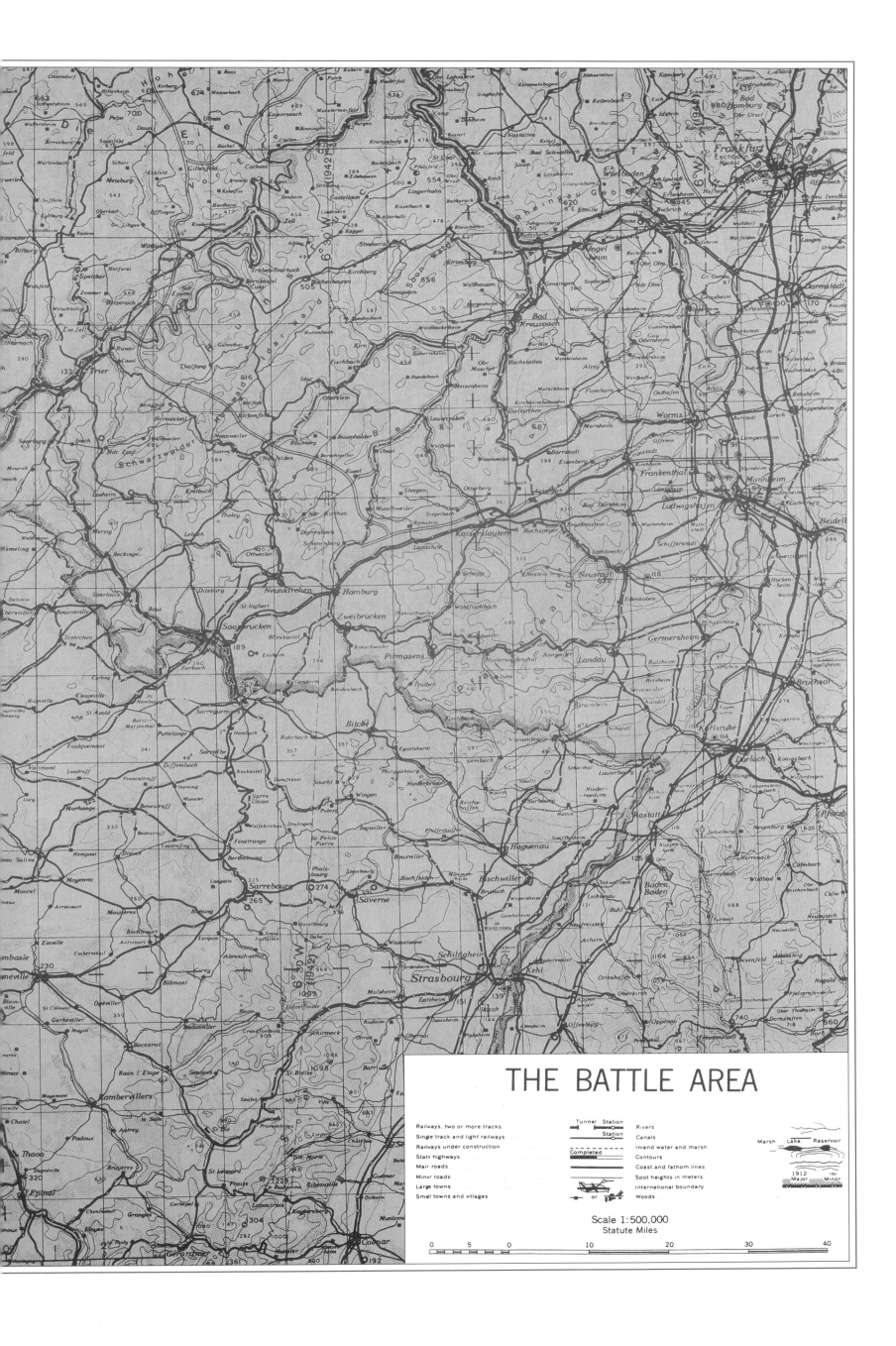

THE BATTLE AREA

Railways, two or more tracks	Rivers
Single track and light railways	Canals
Railways under construction	Inland water and marsh
State highways	Contours
Main roads	Coast and fathom lines
Minor roads	Spot heights in meters
Large towns	International boundary
Small towns and villages	Woods

Tunnel Station
Station
Completed

Marsh Lake Reservoir
1912   1791
Major Minor

Scale 1:500,000
Statute Miles

0   5   0   10   20   30   40

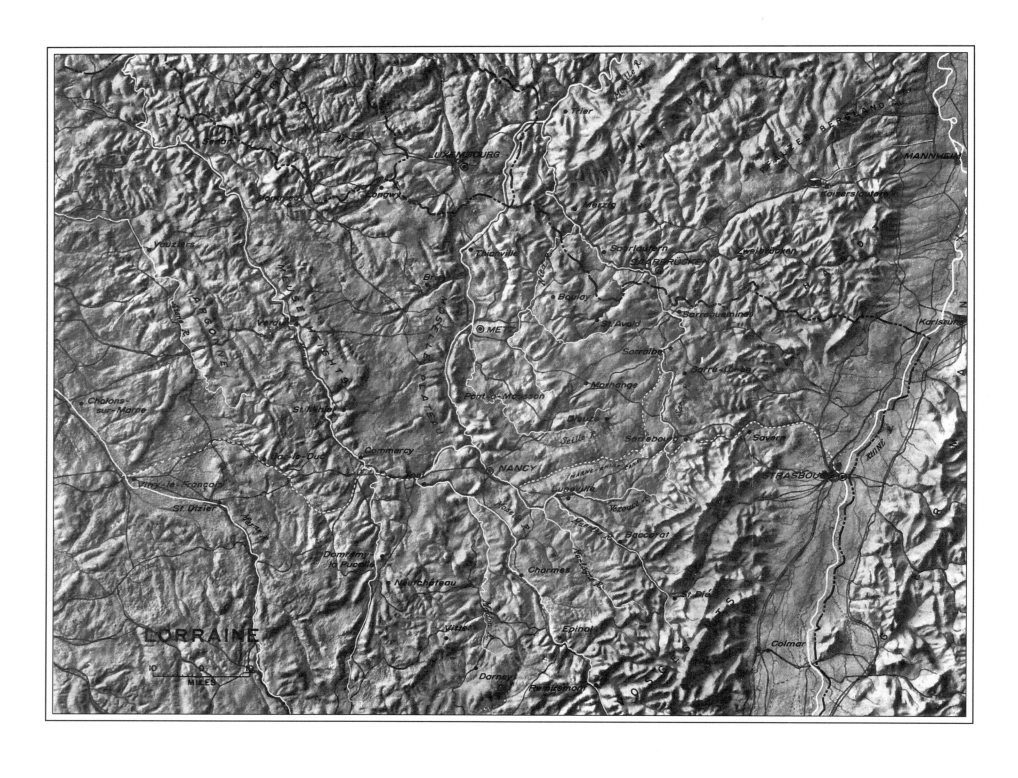

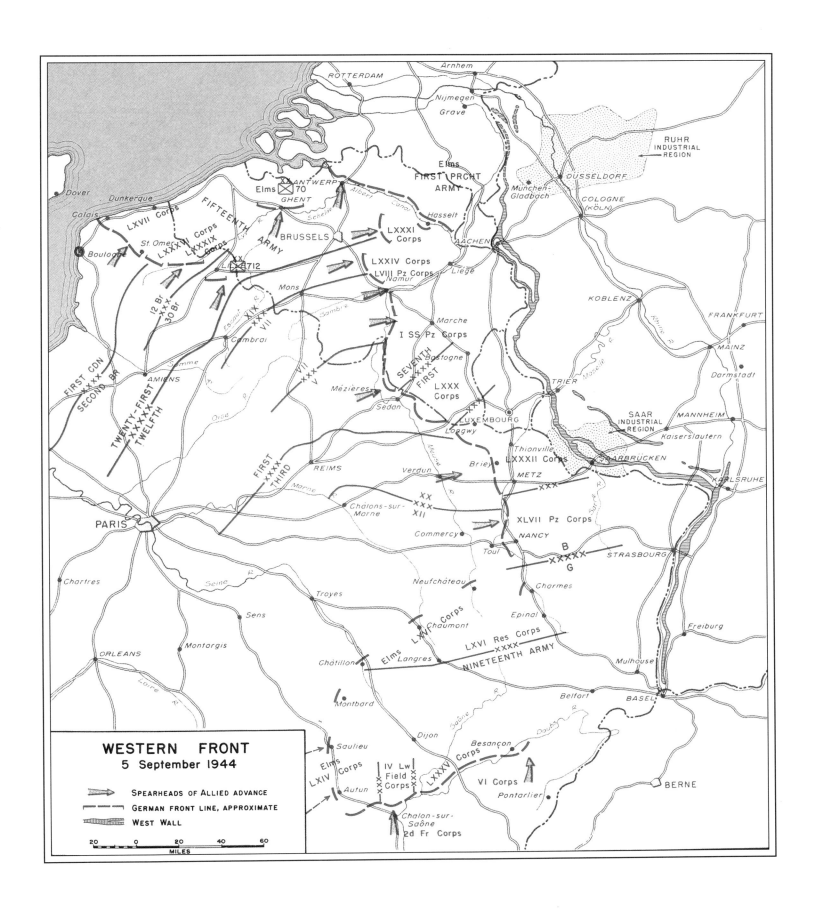

ROTTERDAM
Arnhem
Nijmegen
Grave

RUHR
INDUSTRIAL
REGION

Dover
Dunkerque
Calais
Boulogne
St Omer

Elms
Elms
ANTWERP
GHENT
Albert Canal
Scheldt

FIRST PRCHT
ARMY

München-Gladbach
DÜSSELDORF
COLOGNE
(KÖLN)

LXVII Corps
FIFTEENTH
ARMY
LXXXII Corps
LXXXIX Corps

Hasselt
BRUSSELS
LXXXI Corps
AACHEN

12 Br
XXX
30 Br
LXIX B712

Mons
Scheldt
XIX
XXX
VII
Sambre
Namur
LXXIV Corps
LVIII Pz Corps
Liège

FIRST CDN
XXXX Br
SECOND Br
AMIENS
Cambrai
Somme
V
Mézières
Sedan
I SS Pz Corps
Bastogne
Marche

KOBLENZ
FRANKFURT
MAINZ
Darmstadt

TWENTY-FIRST
XXXXX
TWELFTH

SEVENTH
FIRST
LXXX
Corps
TRIER
Luxembourg
Longwy

SAAR
INDUSTRIAL
REGION
MANNHEIM
Kaiserslautern

FIRST
THIRD
REIMS
Marne
Verdun
Brie
Thionville
LXXXII Corps
METZ
SAARBRÜCKEN

PARIS
Châlons-sur-Marne
XX
XXX
XII
Commercy
XLVII Pz Corps
NANCY
Toul
B
XXXXX
G
STRASBOURG
KARLSRUHE

Chartres
Seine R
Troyes
Neufchâteau
Charmes

Sens
Epinal
Freiburg

ORLEANS
Montargis
Loire R
Châtillon
LXIV Corps
Chaumont
Elms
Langres
LXVI Res Corps
XXXX
NINETEENTH ARMY
Mulhouse

Montbard
Belfort
BASEL

Saulieu
Dijon
Saône R
Besançon
Doubs R
LXXXV Corps
VI Corps
BERNE

Elms
LXIV Corps
Autun
IV Lw
Field
Corps
Pontarlier

Chalon-sur-Saône
2d Fr Corps

WESTERN FRONT
5 September 1944

SPEARHEADS OF ALLIED ADVANCE
GERMAN FRONT LINE, APPROXIMATE
WEST WALL

20 0 20 40 60
MILES

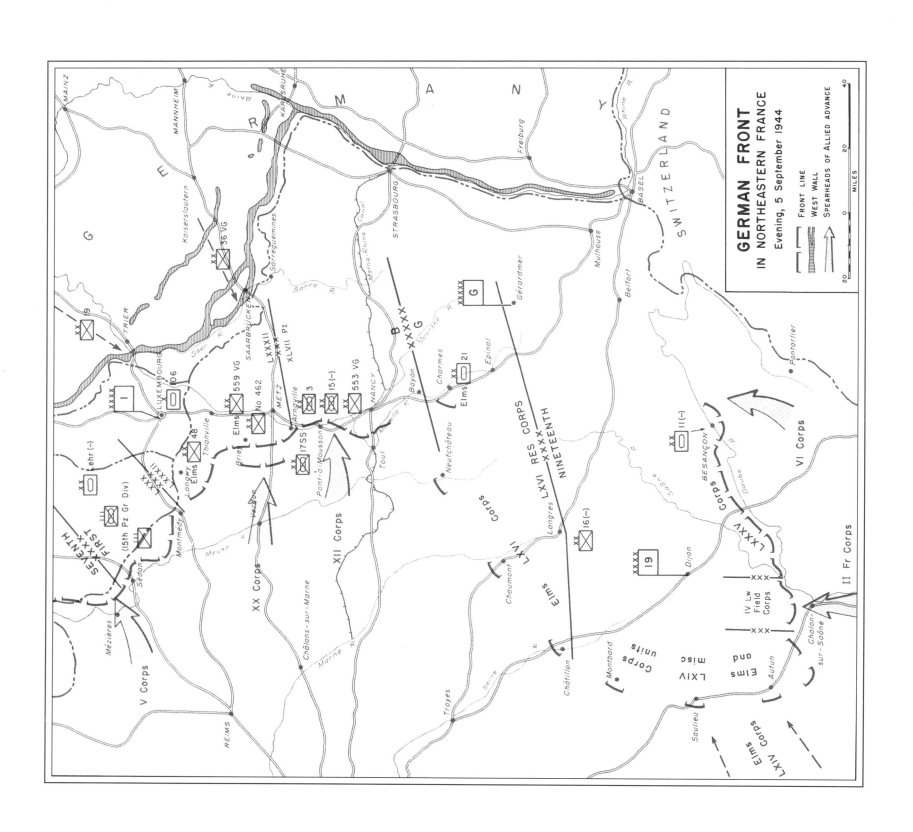

GERMAN FRONT
IN NORTHEASTERN FRANCE
Evening, 5 September 1944

Front Line
West Wall
Spearheads of Allied Advance

MILES

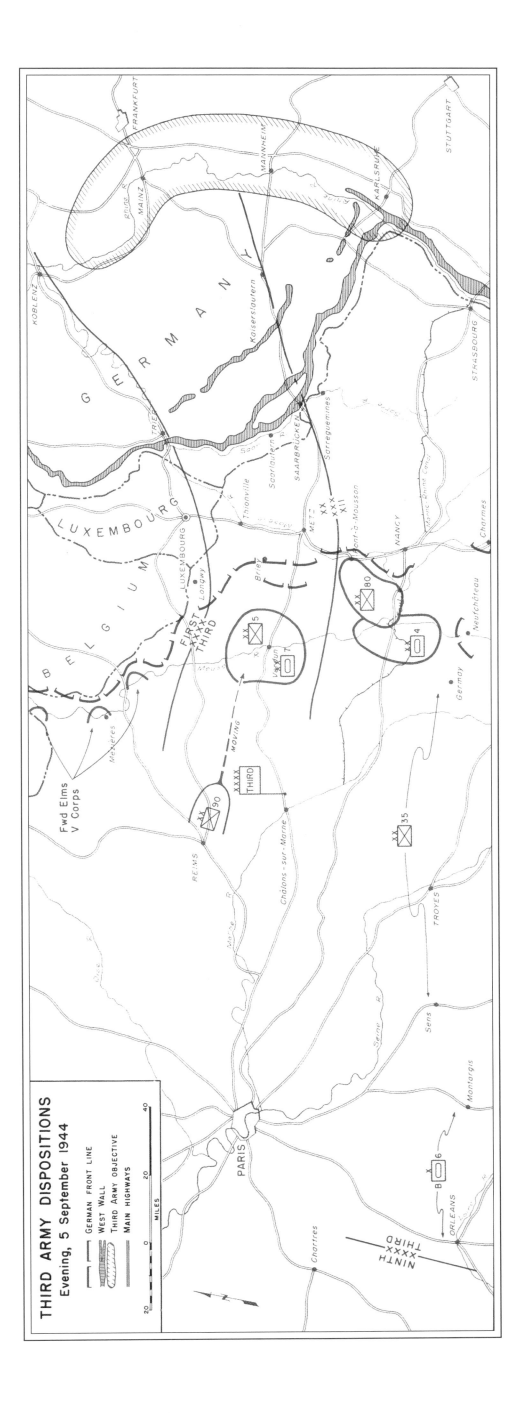

THIRD ARMY DISPOSITIONS
Evening, 5 September 1944

GERMAN FRONT LINE
WEST WALL
THIRD ARMY OBJECTIVE
MAIN HIGHWAYS

MILES
20   0   20   40

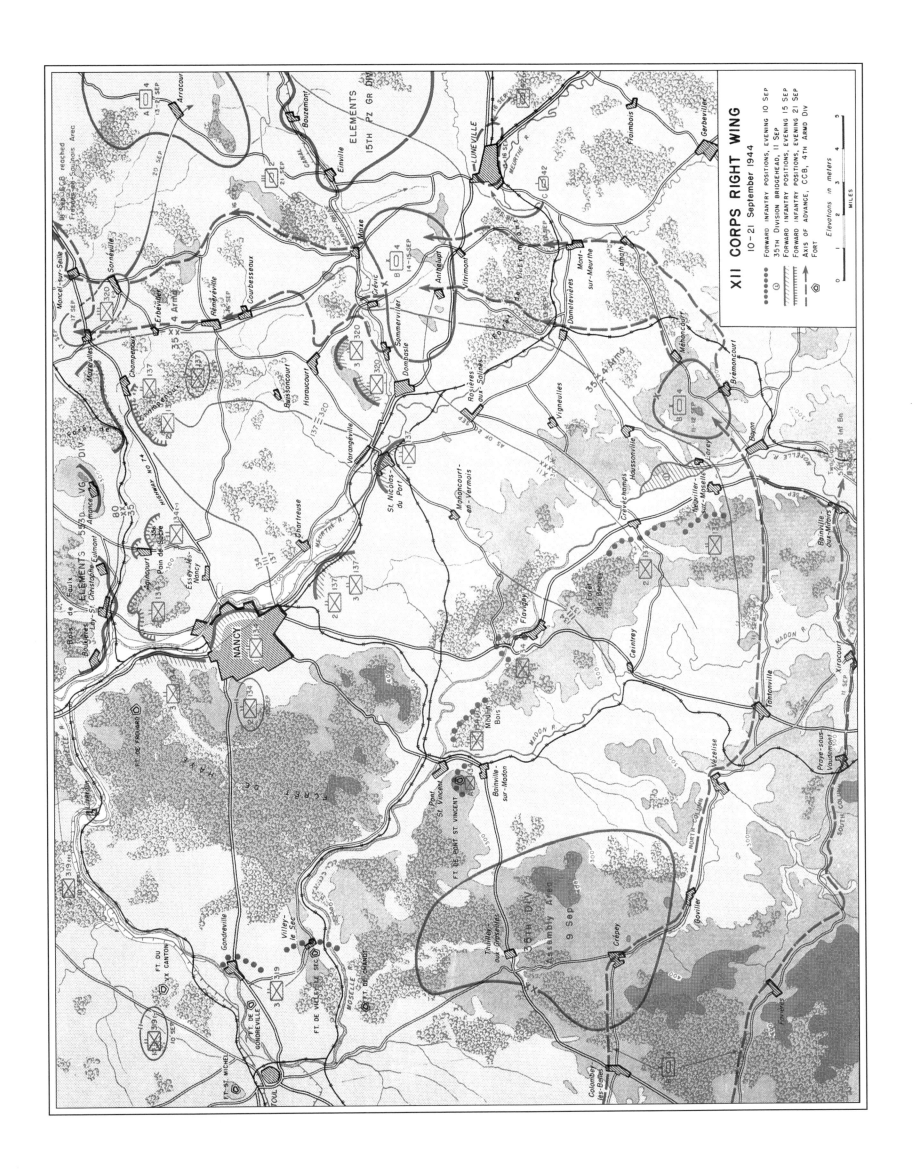

XII CORPS RIGHT WING
10–21 September 1944

●●●● FORWARD INFANTRY POSITIONS, EVENING 10 SEP
Ⓒ 35TH DIVISION BRIDGEHEAD, 11 SEP
//// FORWARD INFANTRY POSITIONS, EVENING 15 SEP
——— FORWARD INFANTRY POSITIONS, EVENING 21 SEP
⟶ AXIS OF ADVANCE, CCB, 4TH ARMD DIV
◉ FORT

Elevations in meters

0 1 2 3 4 5
MILES

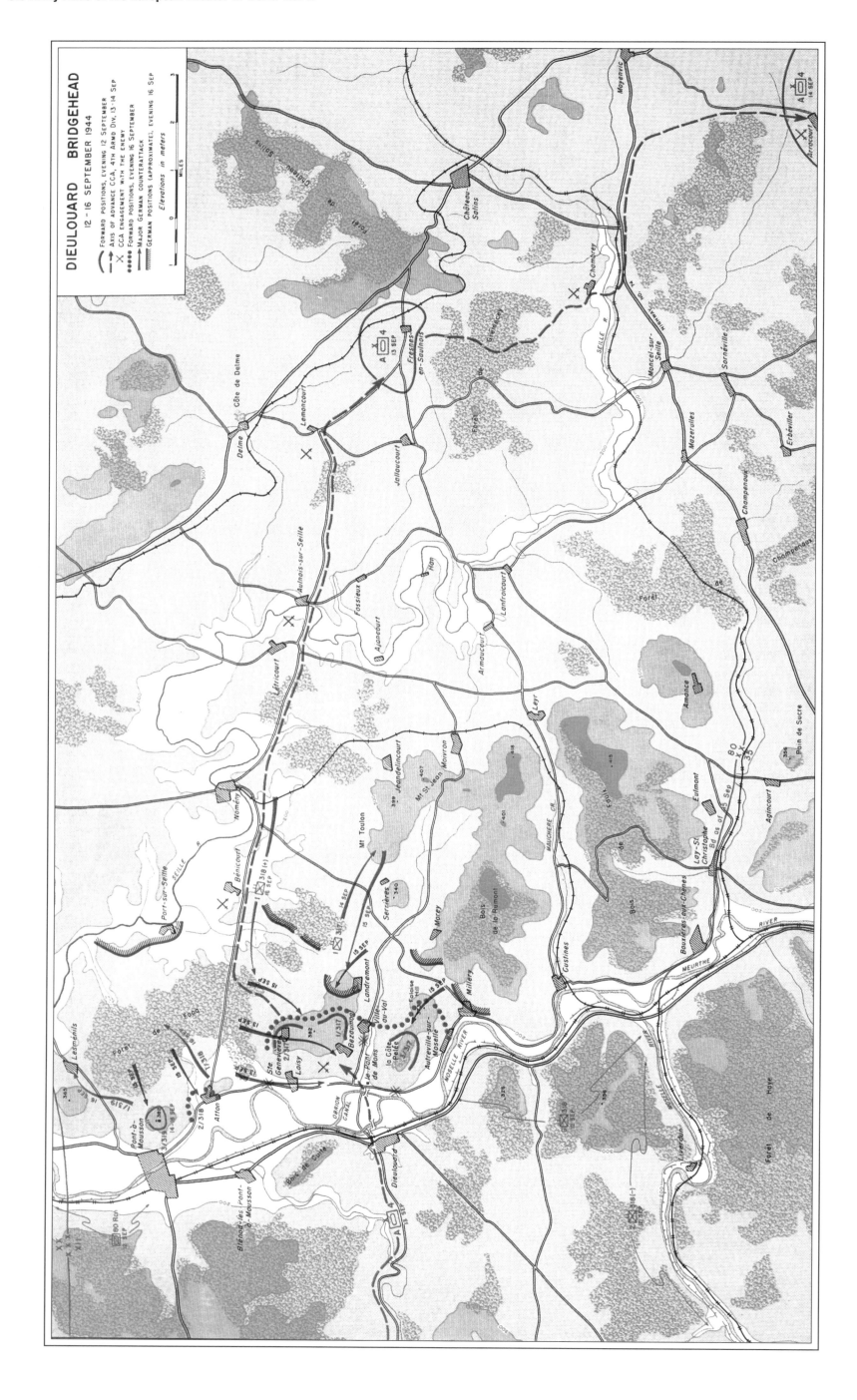

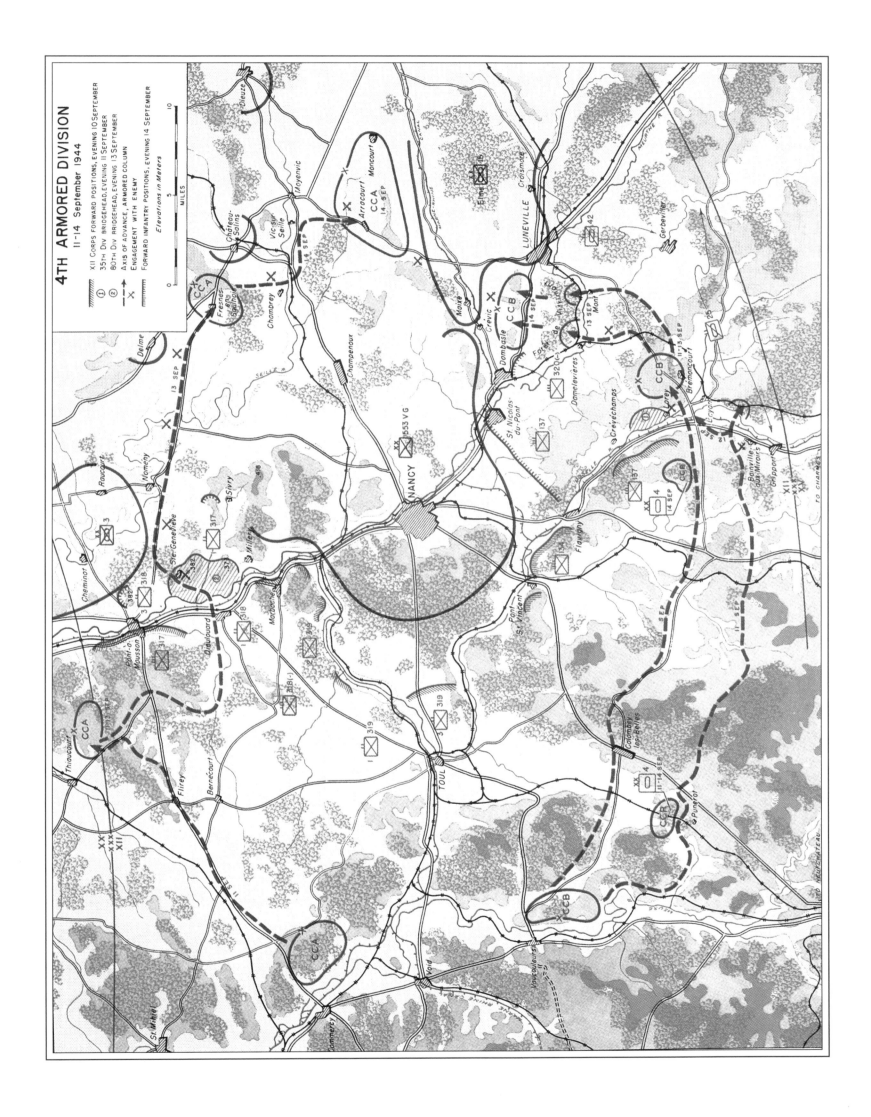

4TH ARMORED DIVISION

11–14 September 1944

XII CORPS FORWARD POSITIONS, EVENING 10 SEPTEMBER
35TH DIV BRIDGEHEAD, EVENING 11 SEPTEMBER
80TH DIV BRIDGEHEAD, EVENING 13 SEPTEMBER
AXIS OF ADVANCE, ARMORED COLUMN
ENGAGEMENT WITH ENEMY
FORWARD INFANTRY POSITIONS, EVENING 14 SEPTEMBER

Elevations in Meters

MILES

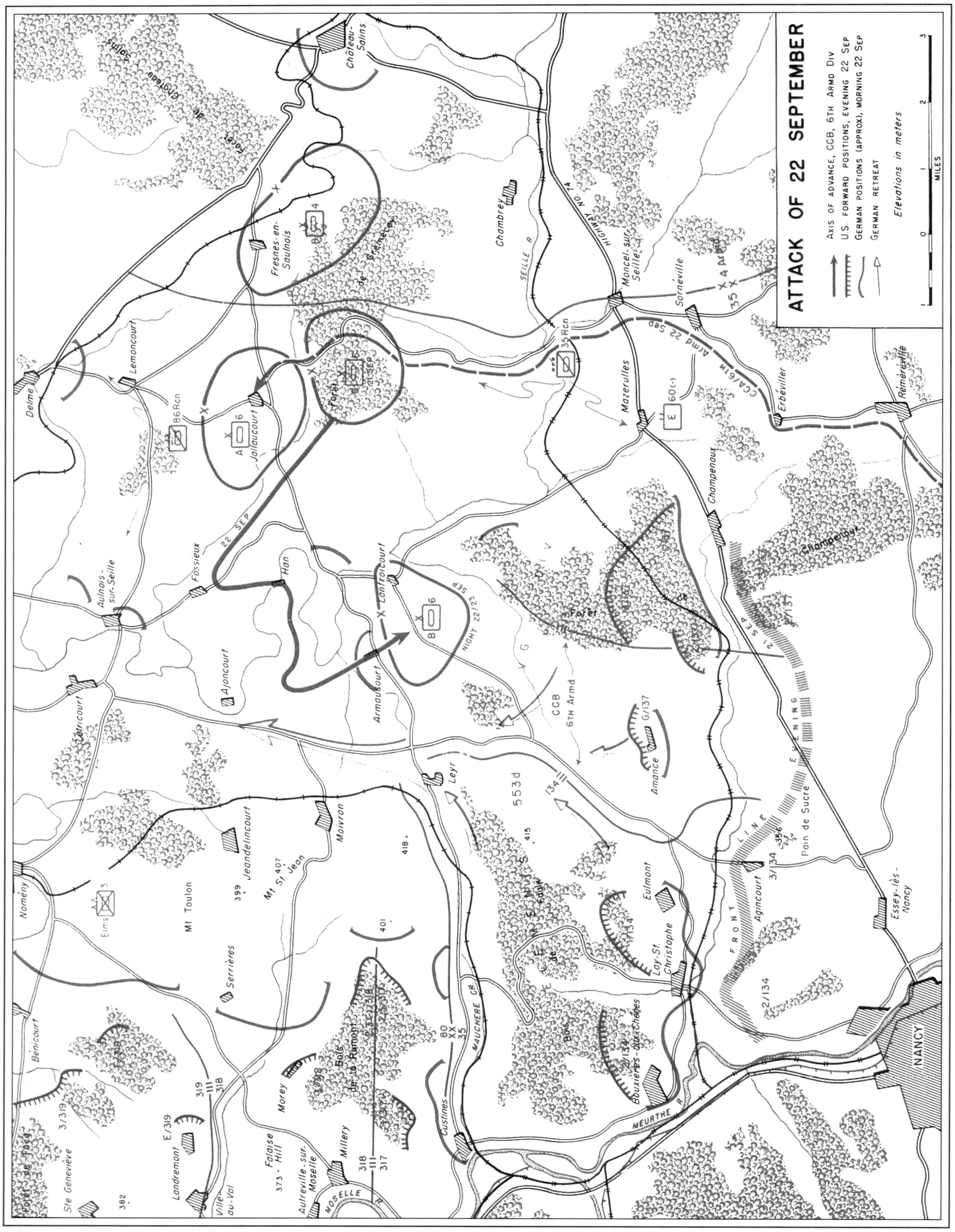
ATTACK OF 22 SEPTEMBER
Axis of advance, CCB, 6th Armd Div
U.S. forward positions, evening 22 Sep
German positions (approx), morning 22 Sep
German retreat
Elevations in meters
0 1 2 3
MILES
Château-Salins
Chambrey
Fresnes-en-Saulnois
Moncel-sur-Seille
Sornéville
Mazerulles
Erbéviller
Réméréville
Champenoux
Delme
Lemoncourt
Jallaucourt
Aulnois-sur-Seille
Fossieux
Han
Lanfroicourt
Ajoncourt
Armaucourt
Leyr
Amance
Eulmont
Agincourt
Pain de Sucre
Essey-lès-Nancy
Lay-St. Christophe
Bouxières-aux-Chênes
Nomeny
Mt Toulon
Serrières
Jeandelaincourt
Mt St. Jean
Moivron
Bénicourt
Morey
Millery
Custines
Landremont
Ste Geneviève
Autreville-sur-Moselle
Ville-au-Val
Falaise Hill
NANCY
MEURTHE R.
MOSELLE R.
MAUCHERE CR.
SEILLE R.
HIGHWAY NO. 74
553d
CCB 6th Armd
FRONT LINE EVENING 21 SEP
NIGHT 22/23 SEP
22 SEP
CCA/6th Armd 22 Sep
35 Rcn
86 Rcn
80 XX 35
Bois de la Rumont
Forêt de Champenoux
Forêt de Gremecey
Forêt de Château Salins

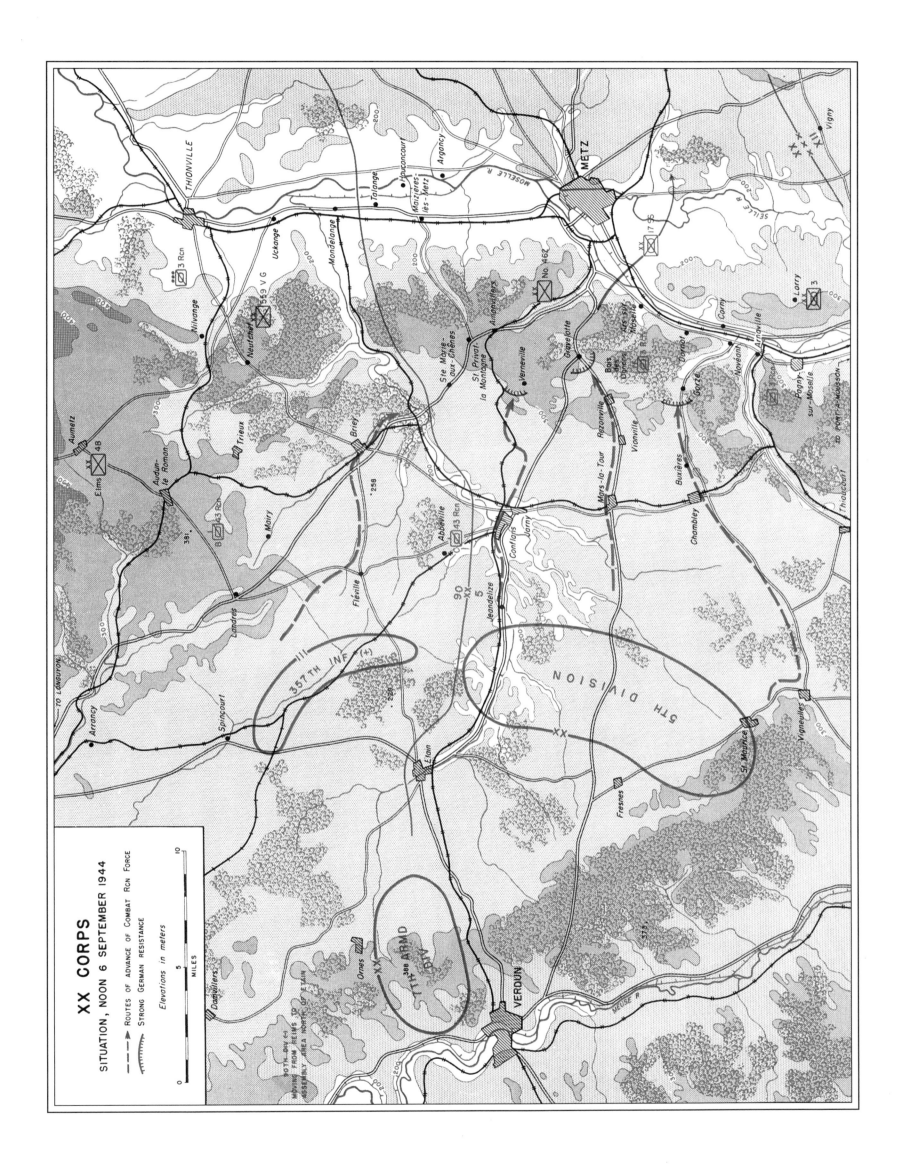

XX CORPS

SITUATION, NOON 6 SEPTEMBER 1944

➤➤➤ ROUTES OF ADVANCE OF COMBAT RCN FORCE

▬▬▬ STRONG GERMAN RESISTANCE

Elevations in meters

MILES

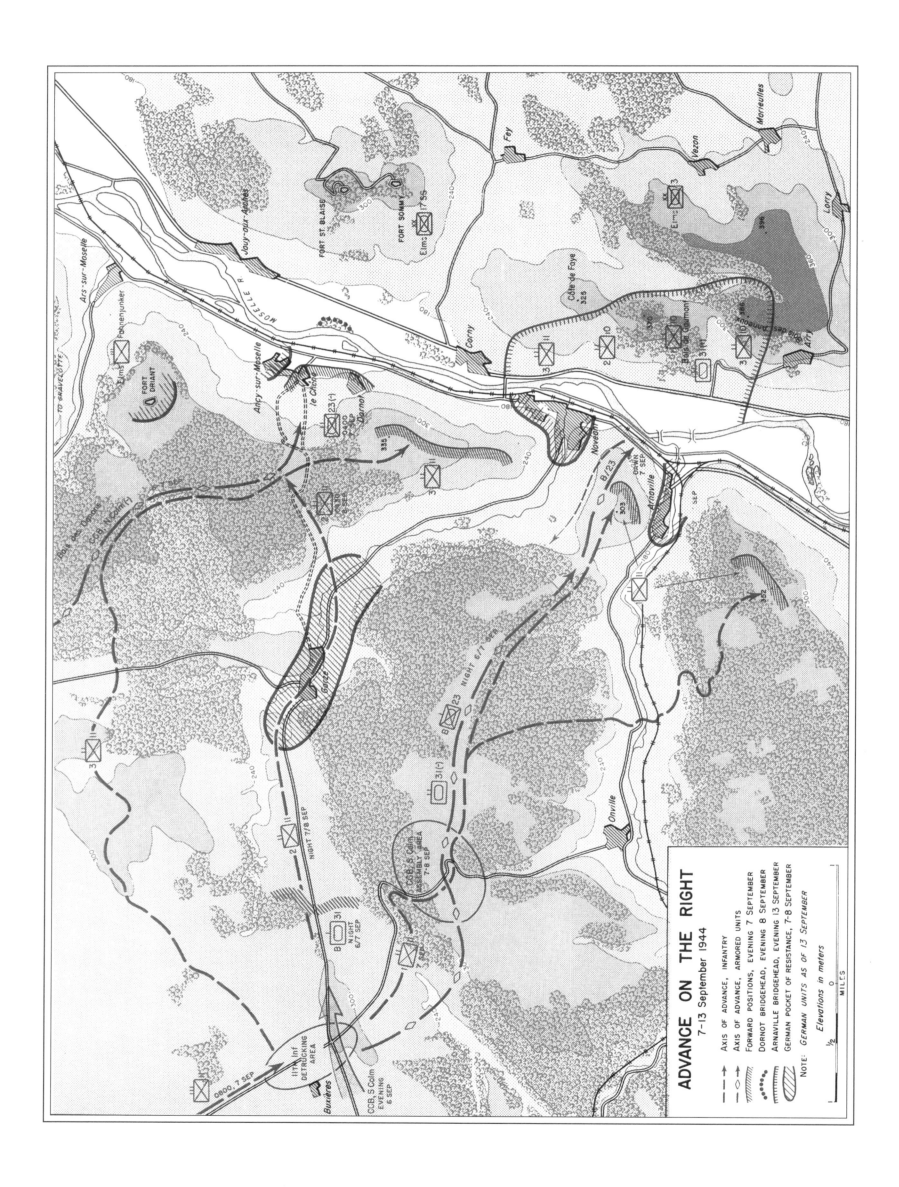

ADVANCE ON THE RIGHT

7–13 September 1944

AXIS OF ADVANCE, INFANTRY

AXIS OF ADVANCE, ARMORED UNITS

FORWARD POSITIONS, EVENING 7 SEPTEMBER

DORNOT BRIDGEHEAD, EVENING 8 SEPTEMBER

ARNAVILLE BRIDGEHEAD, EVENING 13 SEPTEMBER

GERMAN POCKET OF RESISTANCE, 7–8 SEPTEMBER

NOTE: GERMAN UNITS AS OF 13 SEPTEMBER

Elevations in meters

MILES

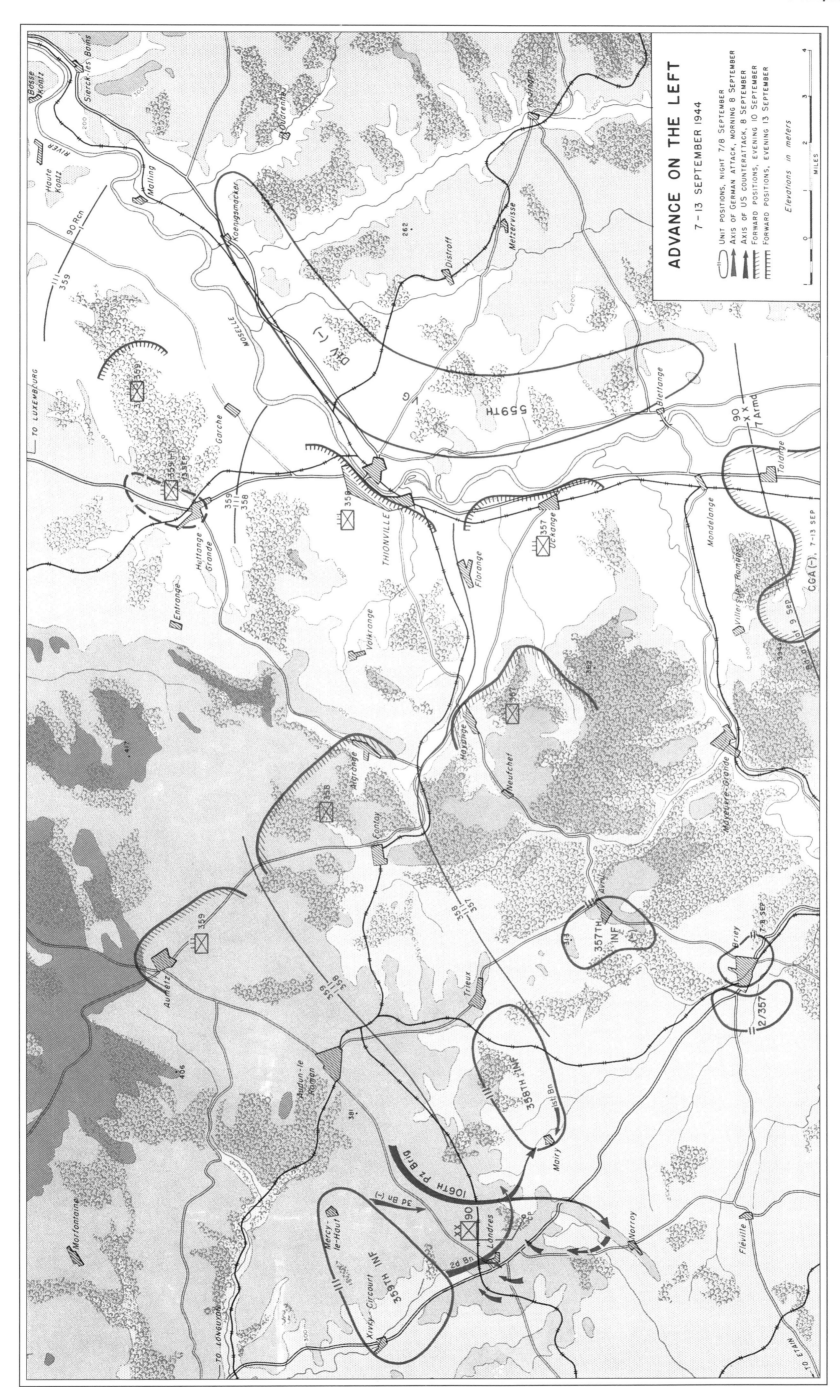

ADVANCE ON THE LEFT

7 – 13 SEPTEMBER 1944

Unit positions, night 7/8 September
Axis of German attack, morning 8 September
Axis of US counterattack, 8 September
Forward positions, evening 10 September
Forward positions, evening 13 September

Elevations in meters

0   1   2   3   4

MILES

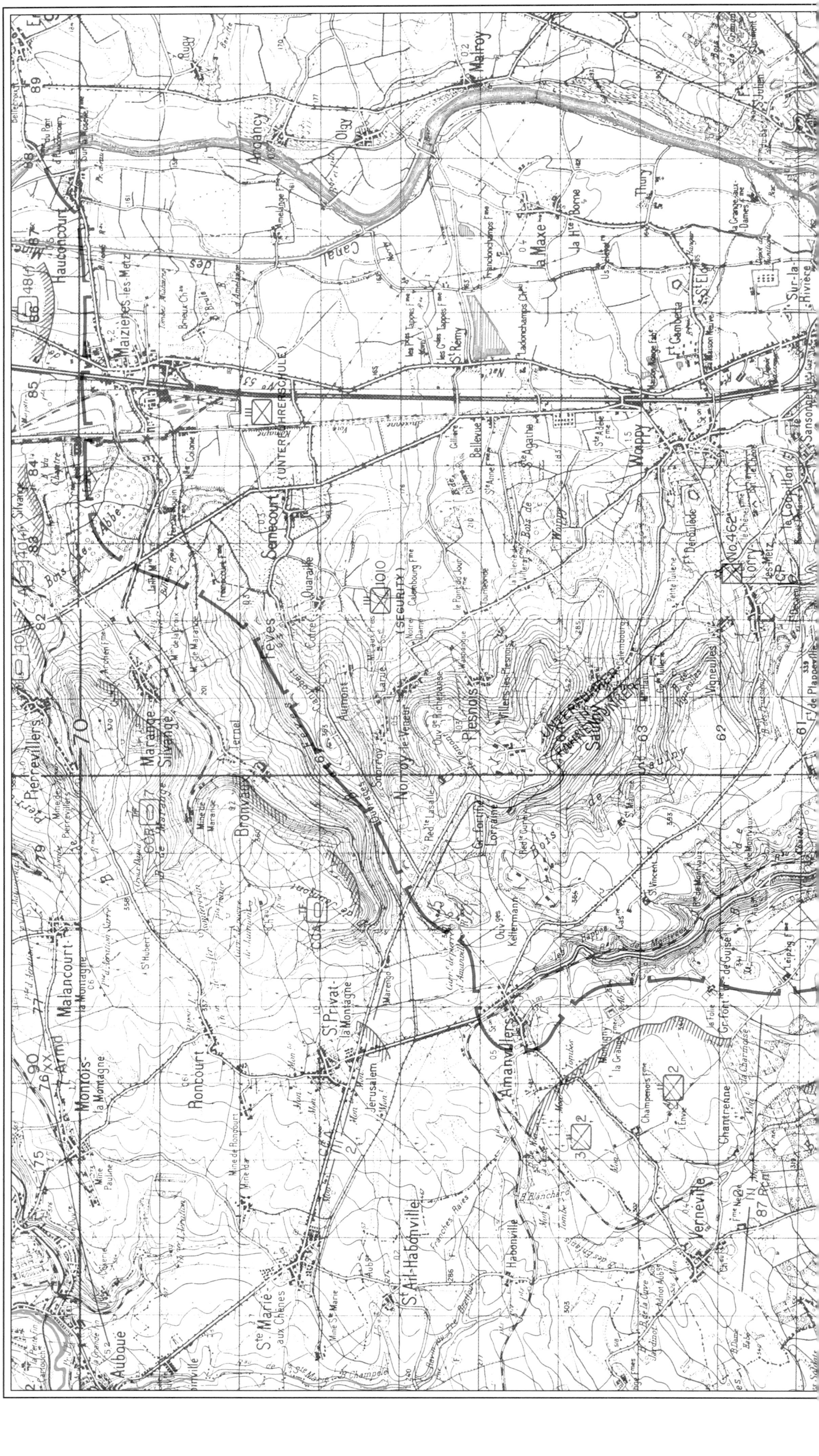
Malroy
Argancy
Olgy
Rugy
Hauconcourt
Maizières-les-Metz
La Maxe
Thury
St Rémy
(UNTERFÜHRERSCHULE)
Semécourt
Fèves
(SECURITY)
Woippy
Bellevue
Plesnois
Norroy-le-Veneur
Marange-Silvange
Pierrevillers
Bronvaux
Saulny
Vigneulles
Lorry
Amanvillers
St Privat-la Montagne
Roncourt
Montois-la Montagne
Malancourt
Jerusalem
Chantrenne
Habonville
St Ail-Habonville
Ste Marie-aux Chênes
Auboué
Verneville

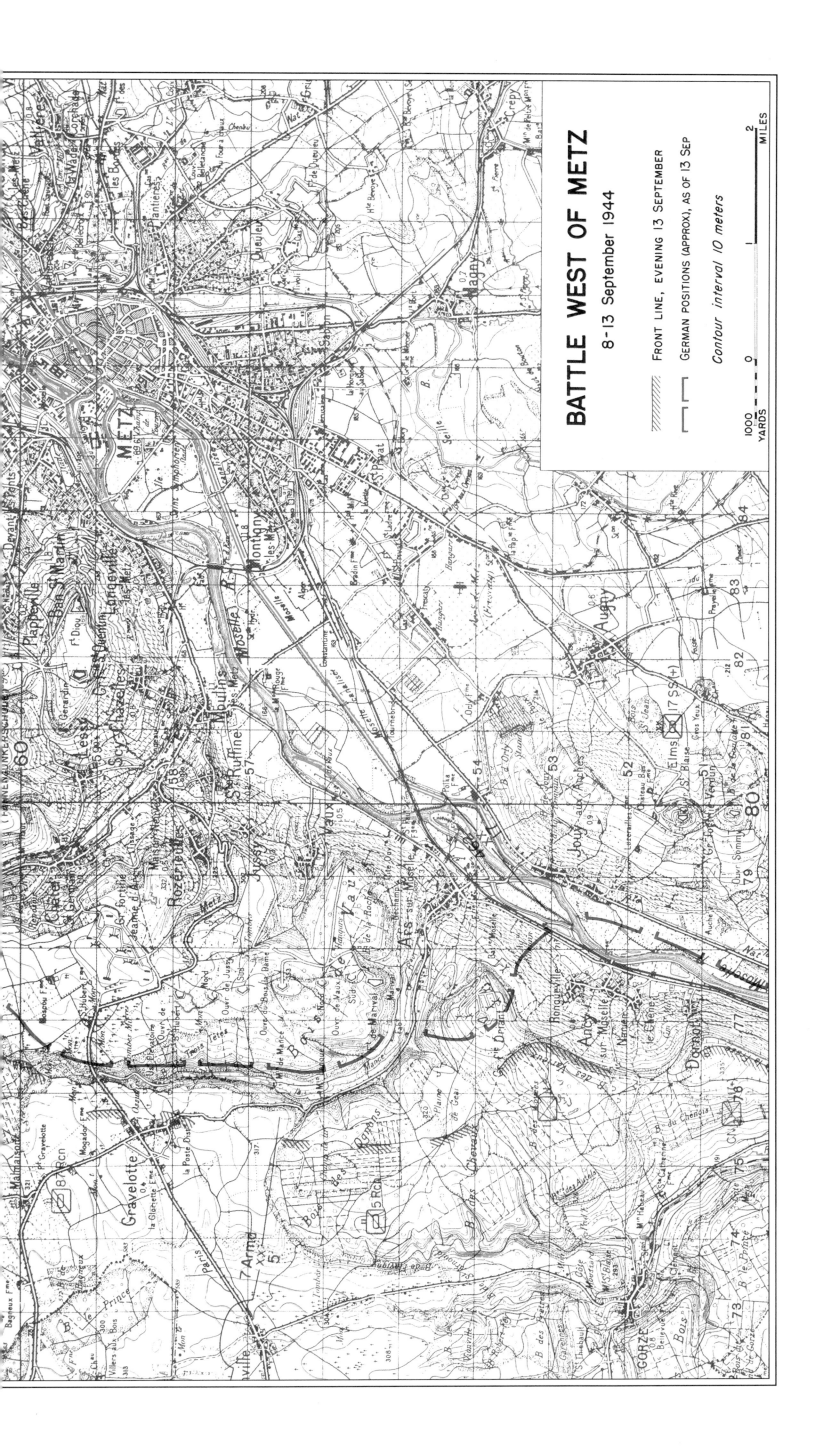

BATTLE WEST OF METZ

8–13 September 1944

FRONT LINE, EVENING 13 SEPTEMBER

GERMAN POSITIONS (APPROX), AS OF 13 SEP

Contour interval 10 meters

1000 0 1 2
YARDS MILES

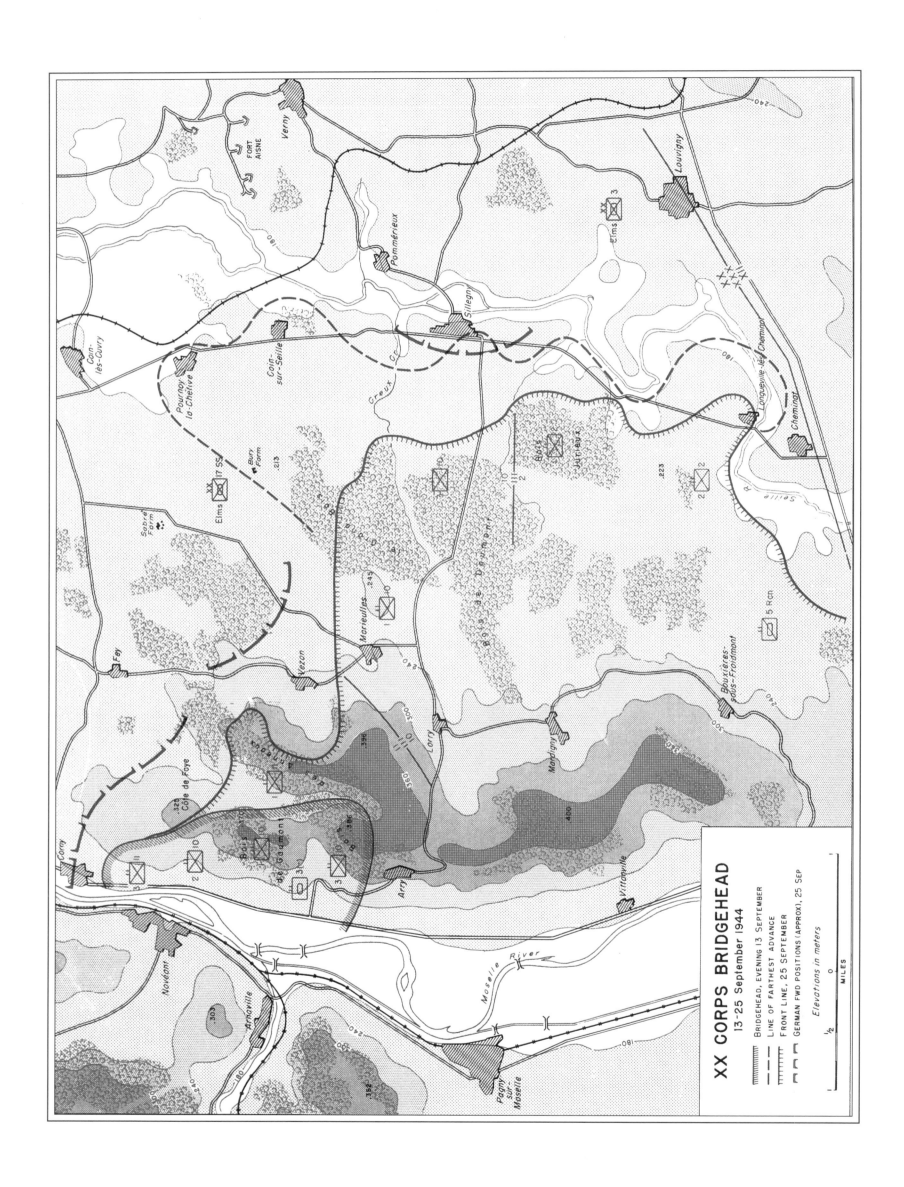

XX CORPS BRIDGEHEAD
13-25 September 1944

BRIDGEHEAD, EVENING 13 SEPTEMBER
LINE OF FARTHEST ADVANCE
FRONT LINE, 25 SEPTEMBER
GERMAN FWD POSITIONS (APPROX), 25 Sep

Elevations in meters

½   0

MILES

GERMAN PLAN OF COUNTERATTACK
3–15 September 1944

DISPOSITION OF THIRD ARMY UNITS, 3 SEPTEMBER
FIFTH PANZER ARMY CONCENTRATION AREA AS PLANNED
DIRECTION OF PROJECTED ATTACK
SPEARHEADS OF THIRD ARMY UNITS, 11 SEPTEMBER
GERMAN FRONT LINE (APPROX.), 11 SEPTEMBER
GERMAN UNITS AS OF 11 SEPTEMBER

ELEVATIONS IN FEET
1000   2000   3000 AND ABOVE

MILES
0   10   20   30

XV CORPS DRIVE TO THE VEZOUSE RIVER
11-24 September 1944

XII CORPS FORWARD POSITIONS, 10 SEPTEMBER
AXIS OF ADVANCE, 79TH INFANTRY DIVISION
AXIS OF ADVANCE, 2D FRENCH ARMD DIVISION
D, L, R, V   COMBAT COMMANDS, 2D FRENCH ARMD DIVISION
GERMAN FORWARD POSITIONS (APPROX), 11 SEPTEMBER
AXIS OF GERMAN COUNTERATTACK
FORWARD ELEMENTS SEVENTH ARMY, 20 SEPTEMBER
U. S. FORWARD POSITIONS, EVENING 24 SEPTEMBER (ALL COLORS)

Note: *Figure near an arrowhead indicates the date on which this point was reached.*

ELEVATIONS IN METERS

| 0 | 300 | 400 | 600 AND ABOVE |

10   0   10
MILES

Ligny-en-
Barrois

Void

Gondrecourt

Vaucouleurs

79TH DIV
10 SEP

Joinville

Prez-sous-Lafauche

Bar-sur-Aube

L 11 SEP

R

11 SEP

12 SEP
[MORAINE]

Bourmont

AUBE R.

GP OTTENBACHER

2D FR
ARMD DIV
10 SEP

D

13 SEP
CHAUMONT

Elms
2d Fr Armd Div

Clefmont

TO LANGRES

TO
LANGRES

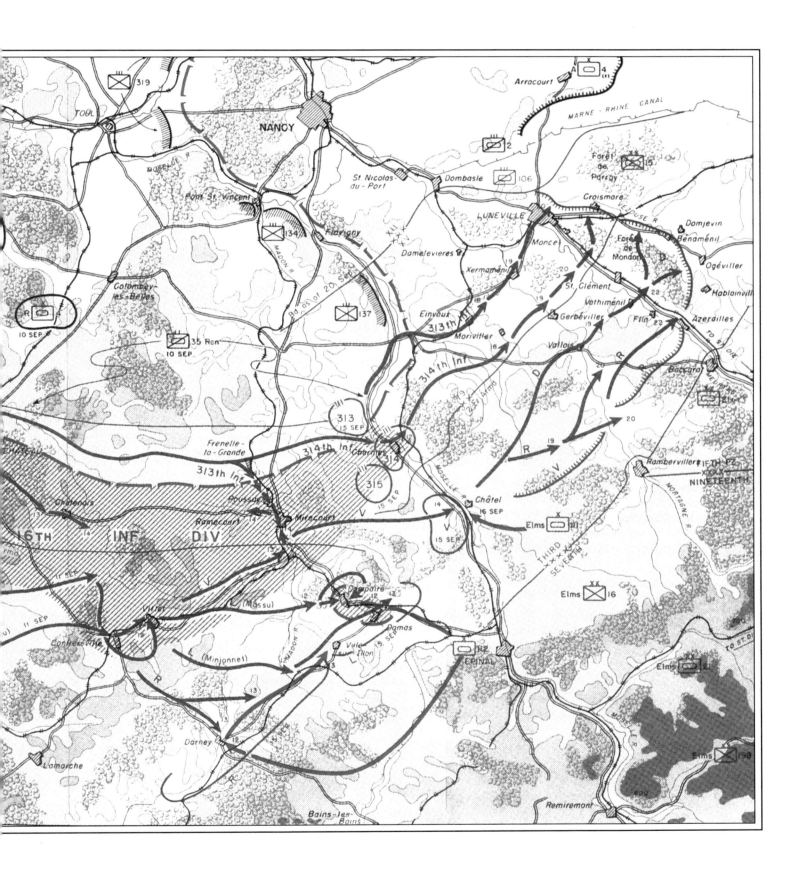

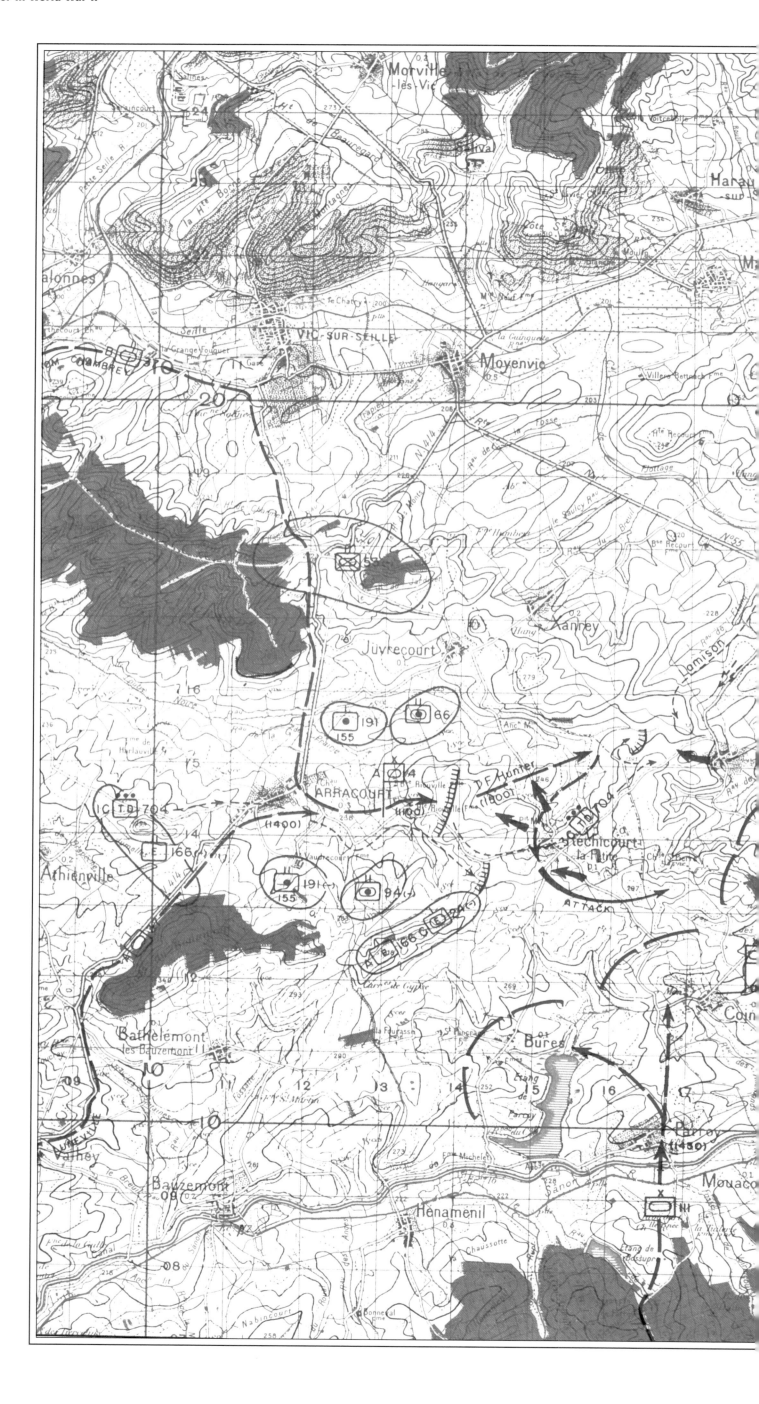

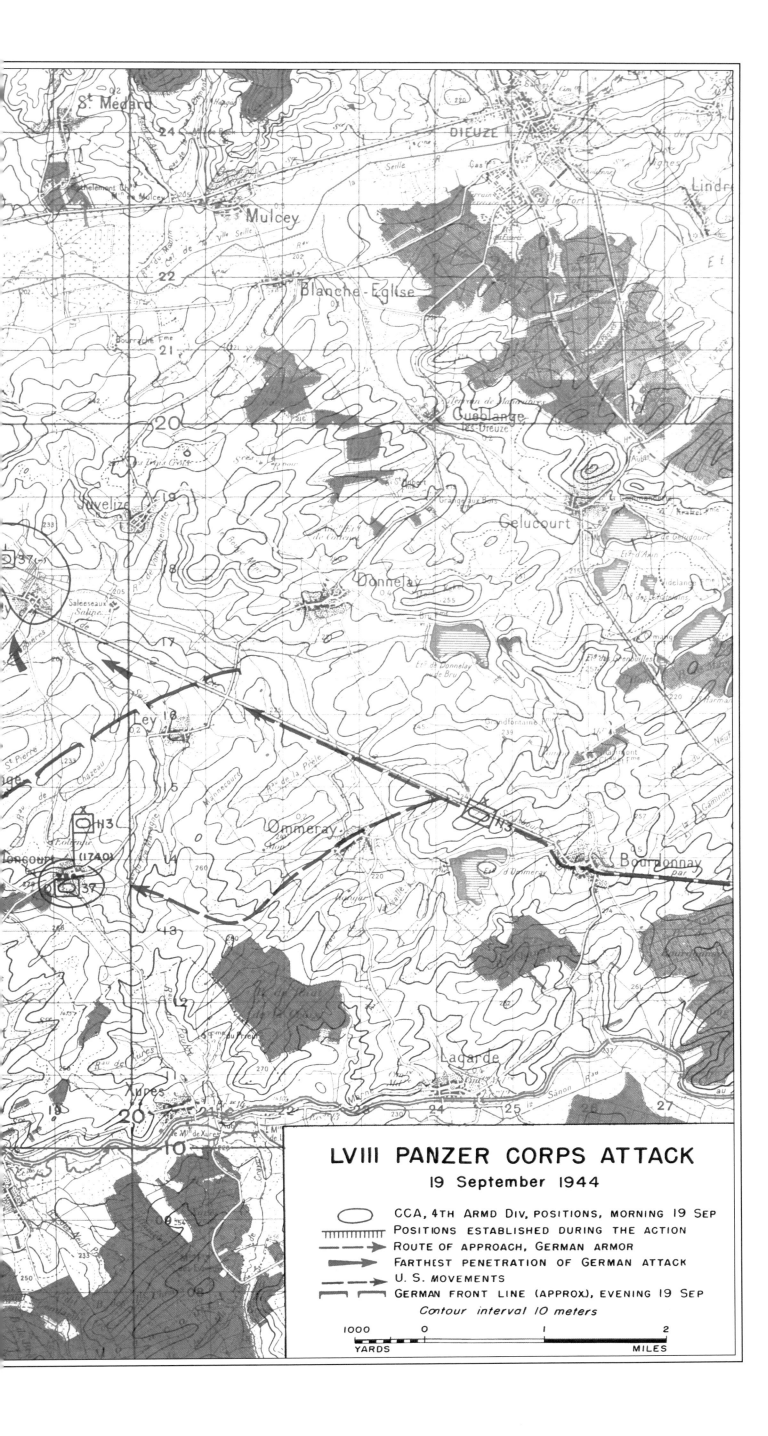

LVIII PANZER CORPS ATTACK
19 September 1944

⬭ CCA, 4TH ARMD DIV, POSITIONS, MORNING 19 SEP
▭ POSITIONS ESTABLISHED DURING THE ACTION
⟶ ROUTE OF APPROACH, GERMAN ARMOR
⟶ FARTHEST PENETRATION OF GERMAN ATTACK
⤍ U. S. MOVEMENTS
⊐ ⊏ GERMAN FRONT LINE (APPROX), EVENING 19 SEP
Contour interval 10 meters

1000   0   1   2

YARDS   MILES

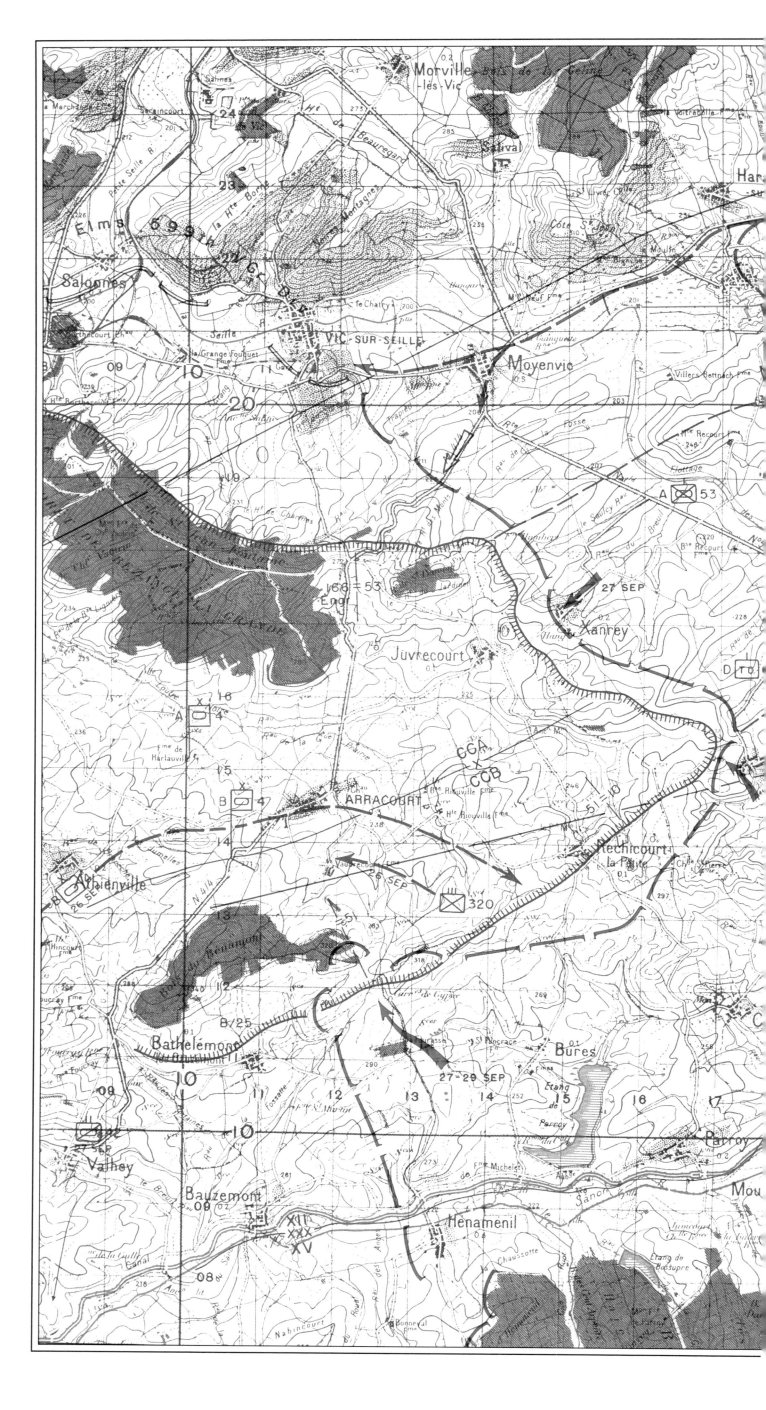

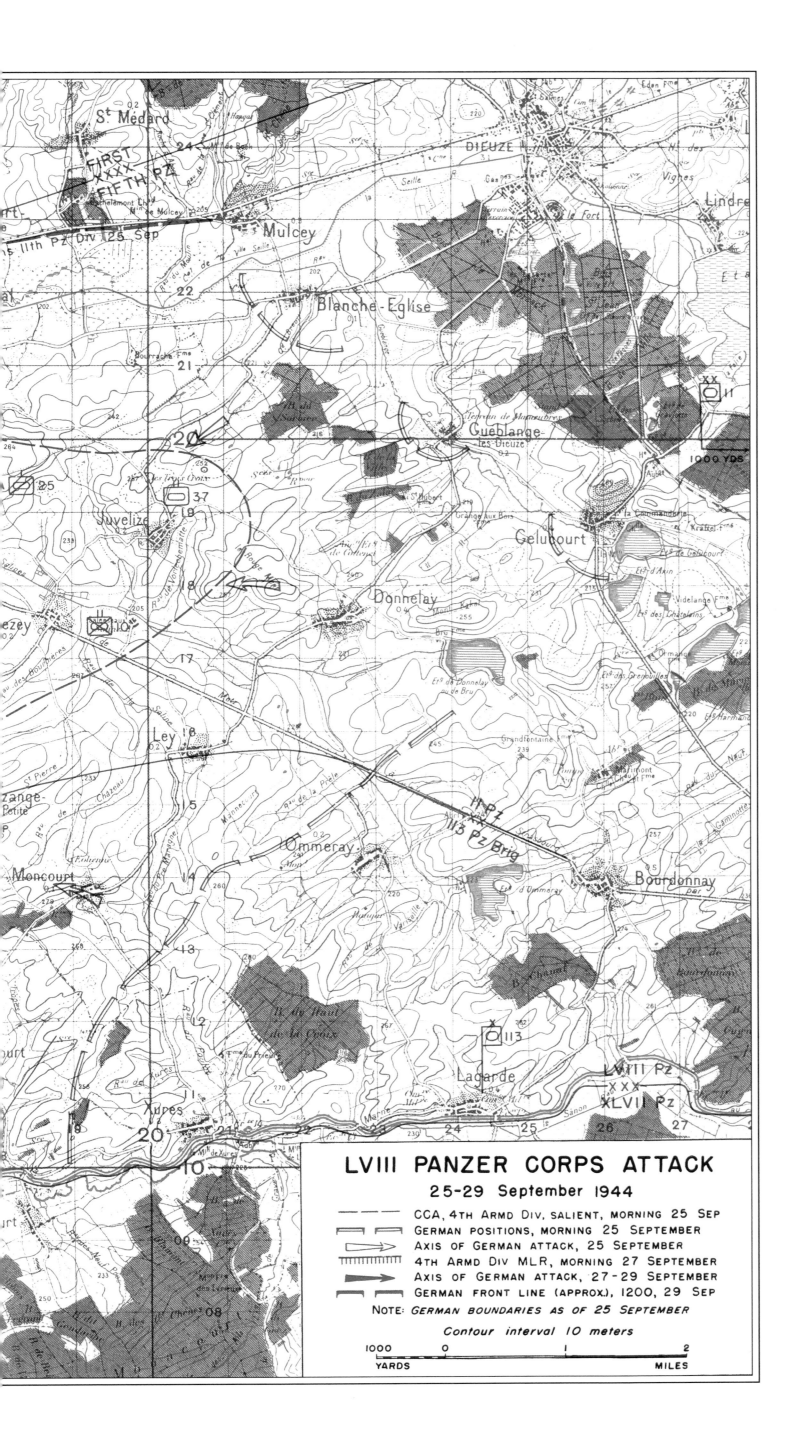

LVIII PANZER CORPS ATTACK

25-29 September 1944

— — —	CCA, 4TH ARMD DIV, SALIENT, MORNING 25 SEP
⊏ ⊐	GERMAN POSITIONS, MORNING 25 SEPTEMBER
⇨	AXIS OF GERMAN ATTACK, 25 SEPTEMBER
⊤⊤⊤⊤⊤⊤	4TH ARMD DIV MLR, MORNING 27 SEPTEMBER
→	AXIS OF GERMAN ATTACK, 27-29 SEPTEMBER
▬ ▬	GERMAN FRONT LINE (APPROX.), 1200, 29 SEP

NOTE: *GERMAN BOUNDARIES AS OF 25 SEPTEMBER*

Contour interval 10 meters

1000   0   1   2

YARDS   MILES

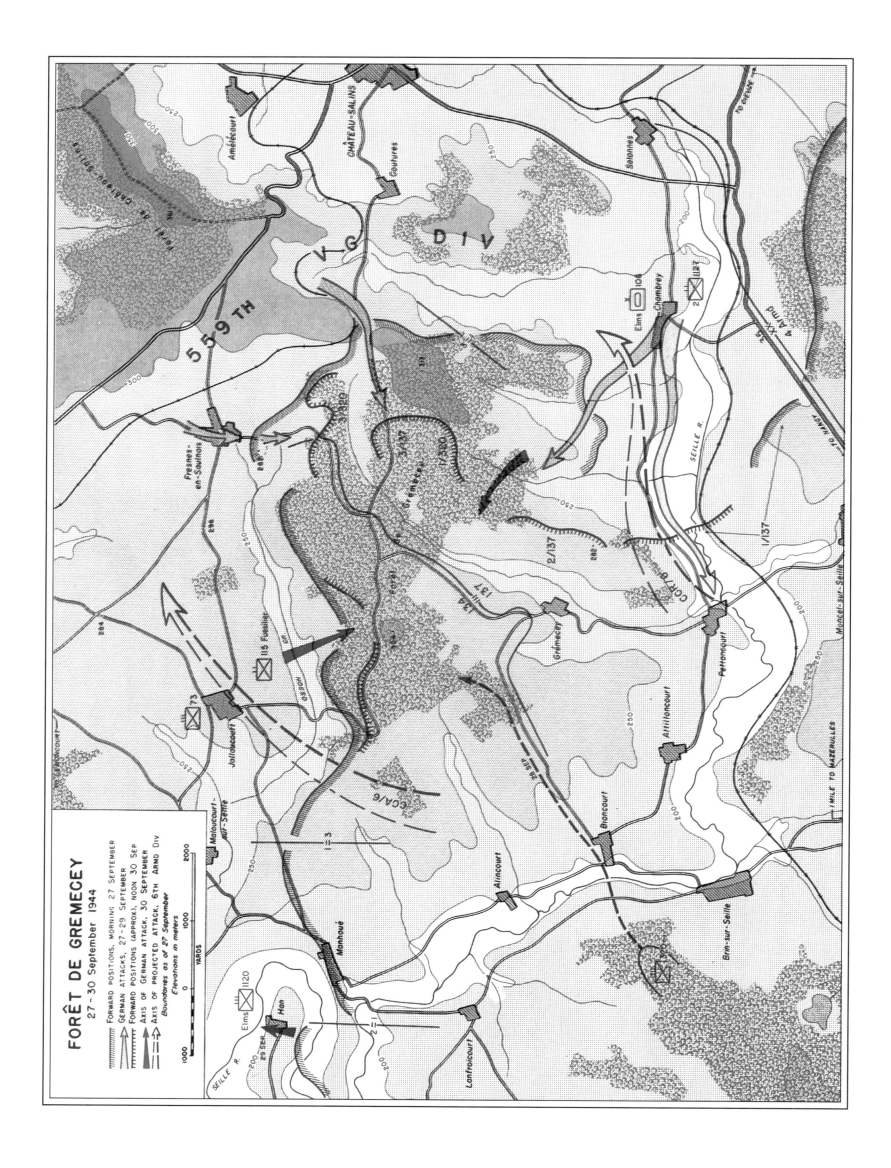

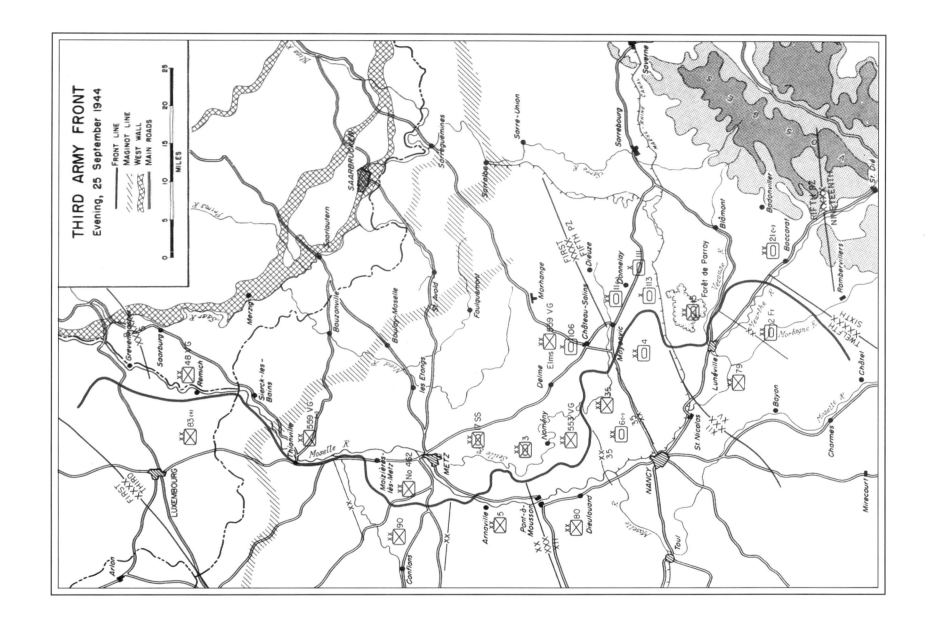

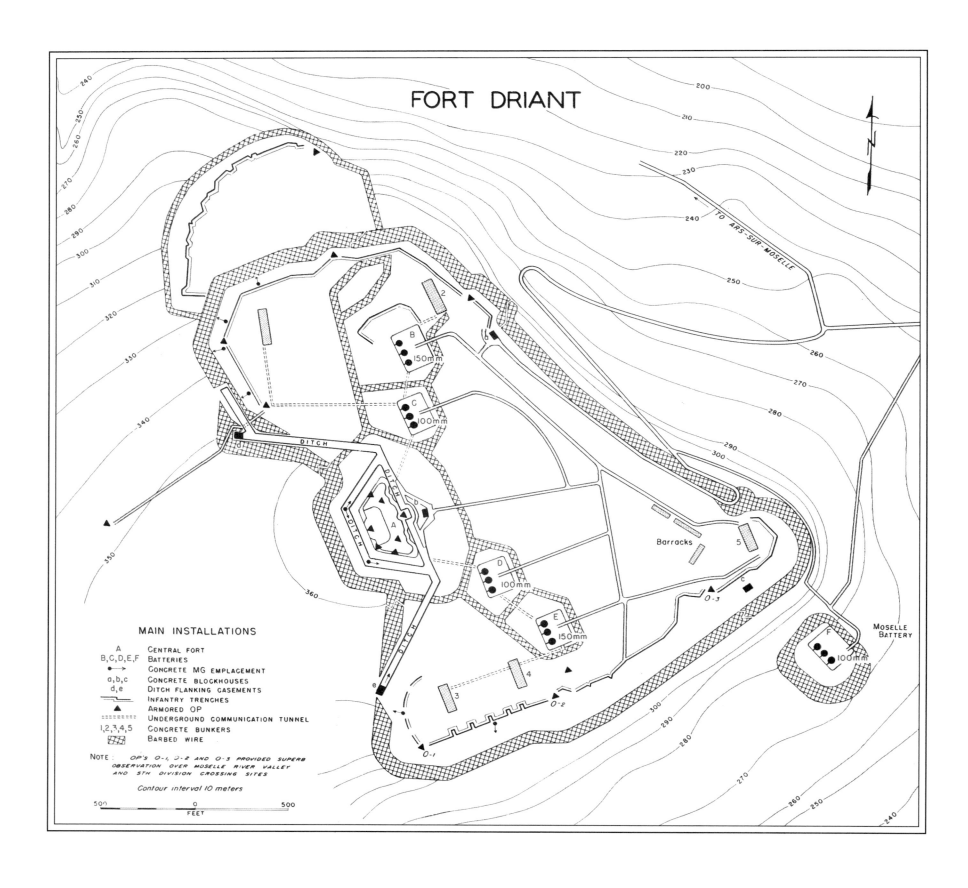

FORT DRIANT

MAIN INSTALLATIONS

A	CENTRAL FORT
B,C,D,E,F	BATTERIES
●—→	CONCRETE MG EMPLACEMENT
a,b,c	CONCRETE BLOCKHOUSES
d,e	DITCH FLANKING CASEMENTS
	INFANTRY TRENCHES
▲	ARMORED OP
┄┄┄	UNDERGROUND COMMUNICATION TUNNEL
1,2,3,4,5	CONCRETE BUNKERS
▨	BARBED WIRE

NOTE: *OP'S O-1, O-2 AND O-3 PROVIDED SUPERB OBSERVATION OVER MOSELLE RIVER VALLEY AND 5TH DIVISION CROSSING SITES*

Contour interval 10 meters

500   0   500
FEET

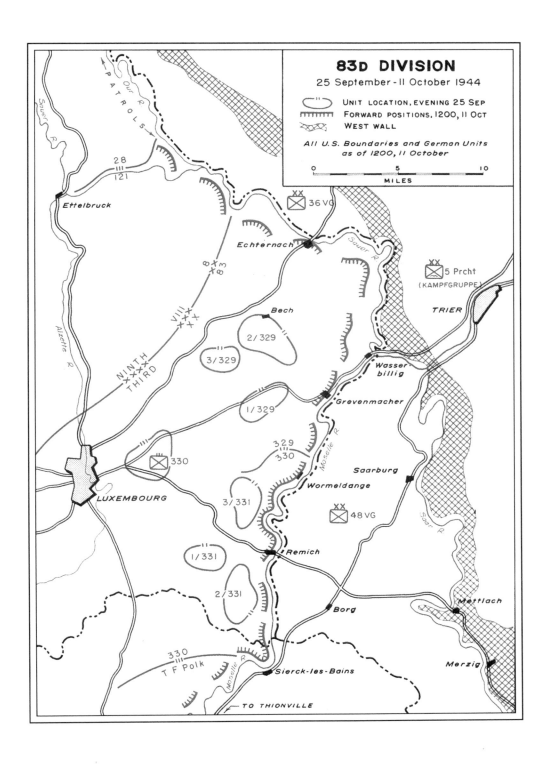

83D DIVISION

25 September – 11 October 1944

Unit location, evening 25 Sep
Forward positions, 1200, 11 Oct
West Wall

*All U.S. Boundaries and German Units
as of 1200, 11 October*

0   5   10
MILES

FIGHT FOR MAIZIERES–LES–METZ
3–30 October 1944

FRONT LINE (APPROX), DATE INDICATED
AXIS OF ATTACK, DATE INDICATED
EMPLACEMENT OF 155MM SP GUN
AREA OF LAST GERMAN RESISTANCE,
EVENING 29 OCTOBER

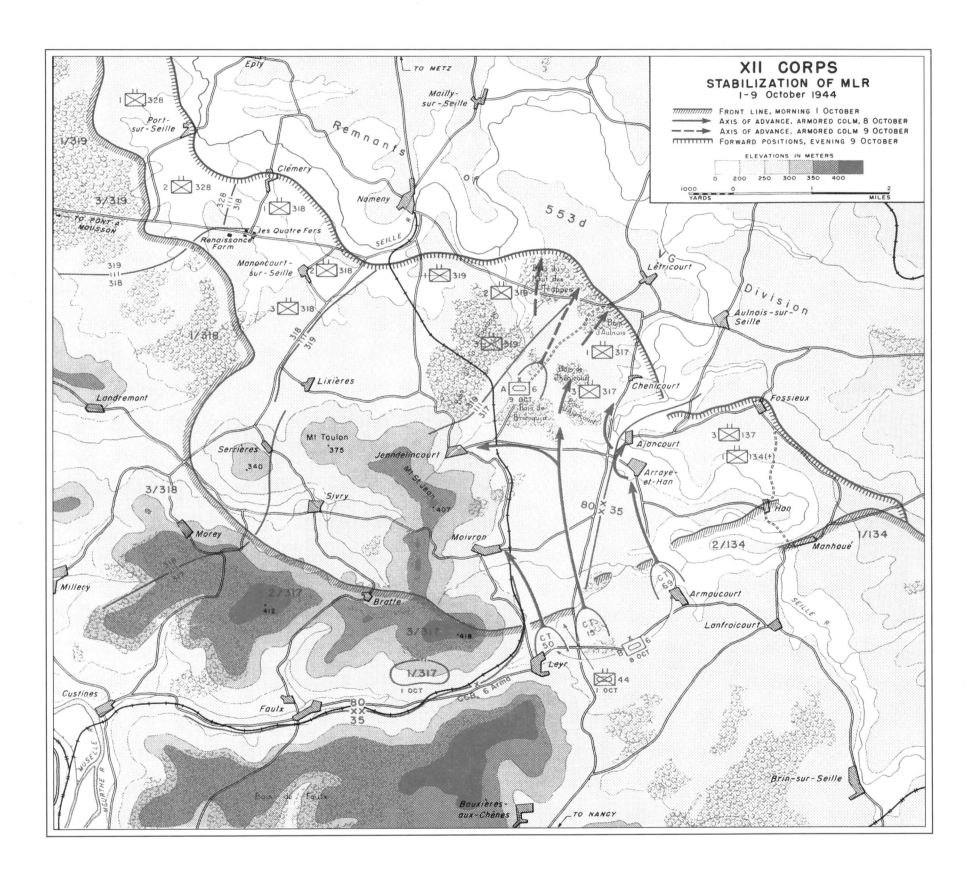

XII CORPS
STABILIZATION OF MLR
1-9 October 1944

FRONT LINE, MORNING 1 OCTOBER
AXIS OF ADVANCE, ARMORED COLM, 8 OCTOBER
AXIS OF ADVANCE, ARMORED COLM 9 OCTOBER
FORWARD POSITIONS, EVENING 9 OCTOBER

ELEVATIONS IN METERS
0   200   250   300   350   400
1000
0   2
YARDS   MILES

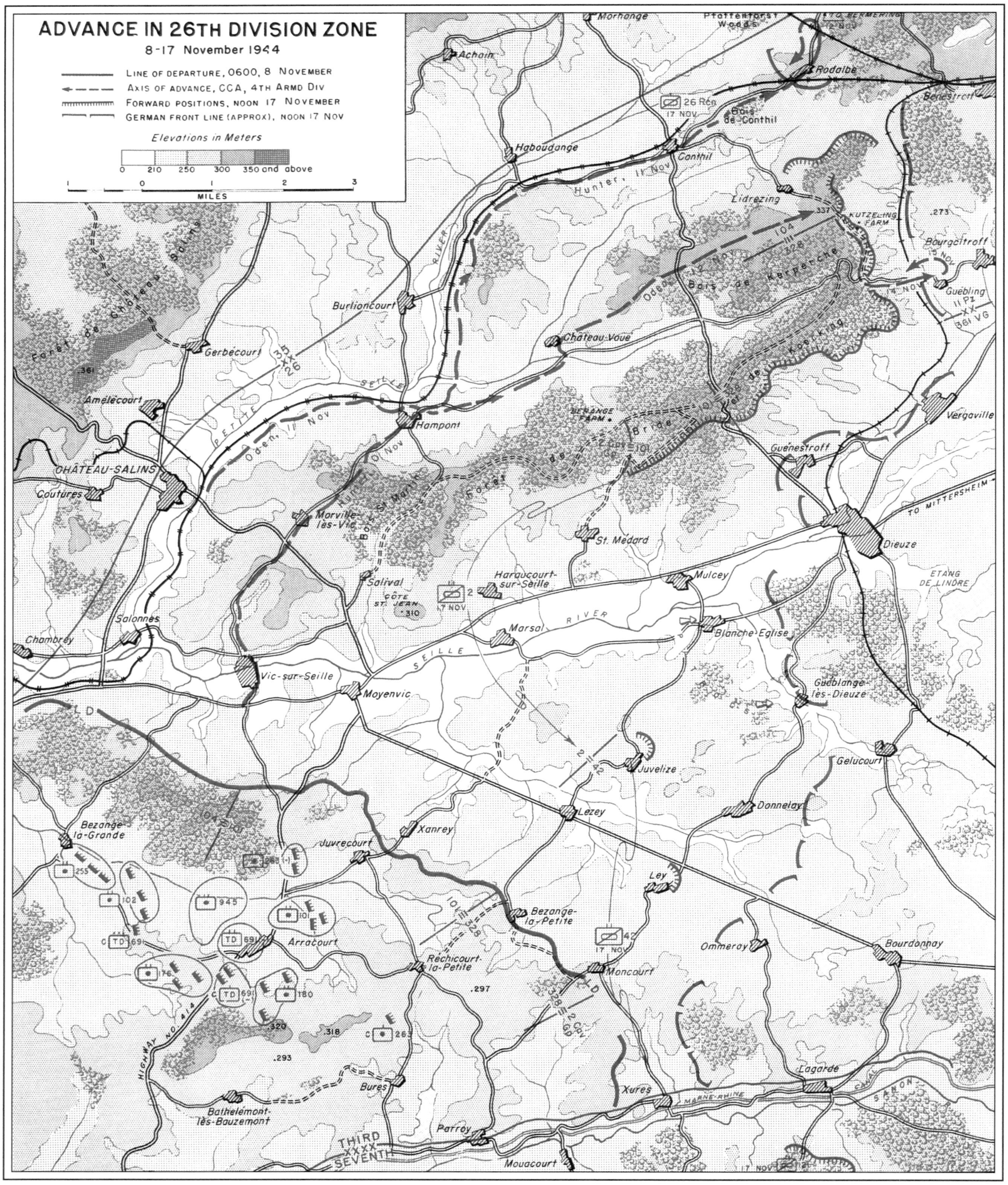

ADVANCE IN 26TH DIVISION ZONE
8-17 November 1944

LINE OF DEPARTURE, 0600, 8 NOVEMBER	
AXIS OF ADVANCE, CCA, 4TH ARMD DIV	
FORWARD POSITIONS, NOON 17 NOVEMBER	
GERMAN FRONT LINE (APPROX), NOON 17 NOV	

Elevations in Meters

0   210   250   300   350 and above

MILES
0   1   2   3

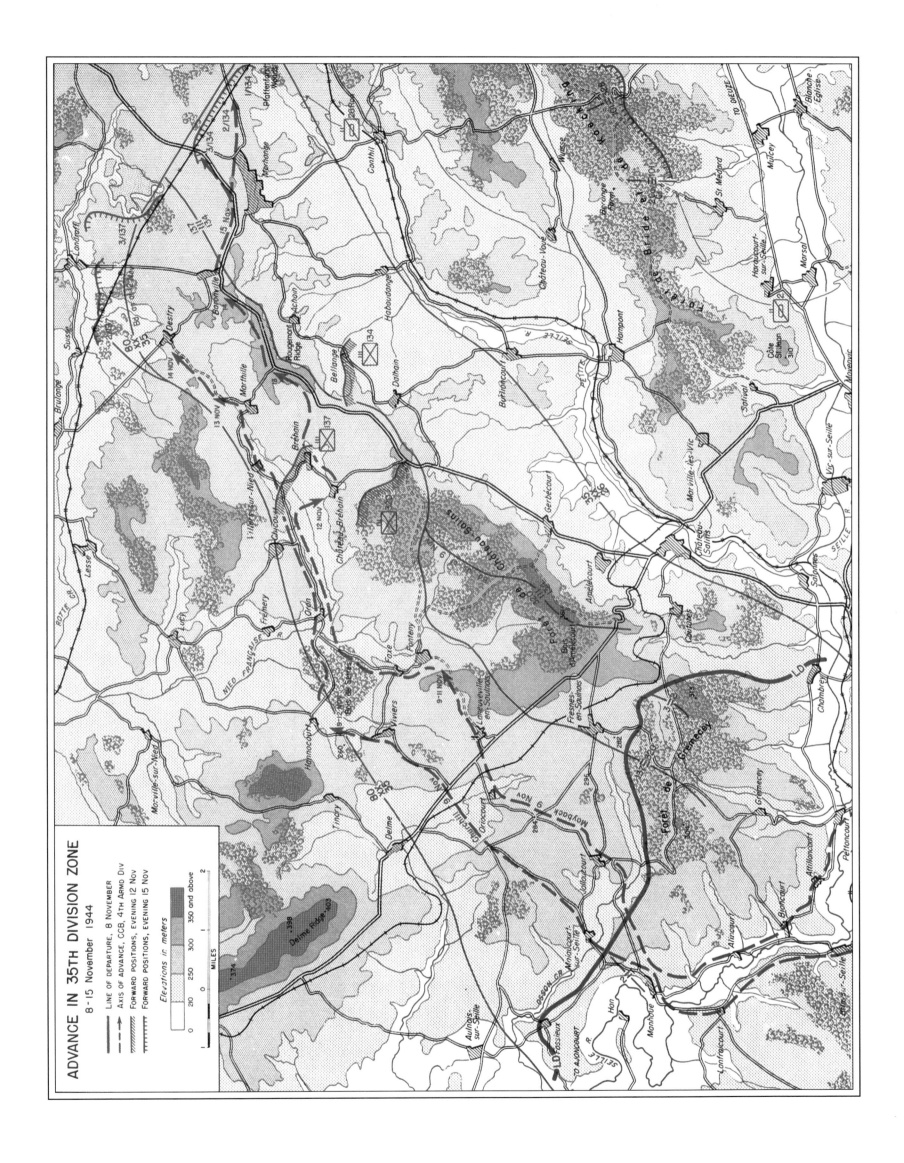

ADVANCE IN 35TH DIVISION ZONE
8–15 November 1944

LINE OF DEPARTURE, 8 NOVEMBER
AXIS OF ADVANCE, CCB, 4TH ARMD DIV
FORWARD POSITIONS, EVENING 12 Nov
FORWARD POSITIONS, EVENING 15 Nov

Elevations in meters

0 250 300 350 and above

MILES
0   1   2

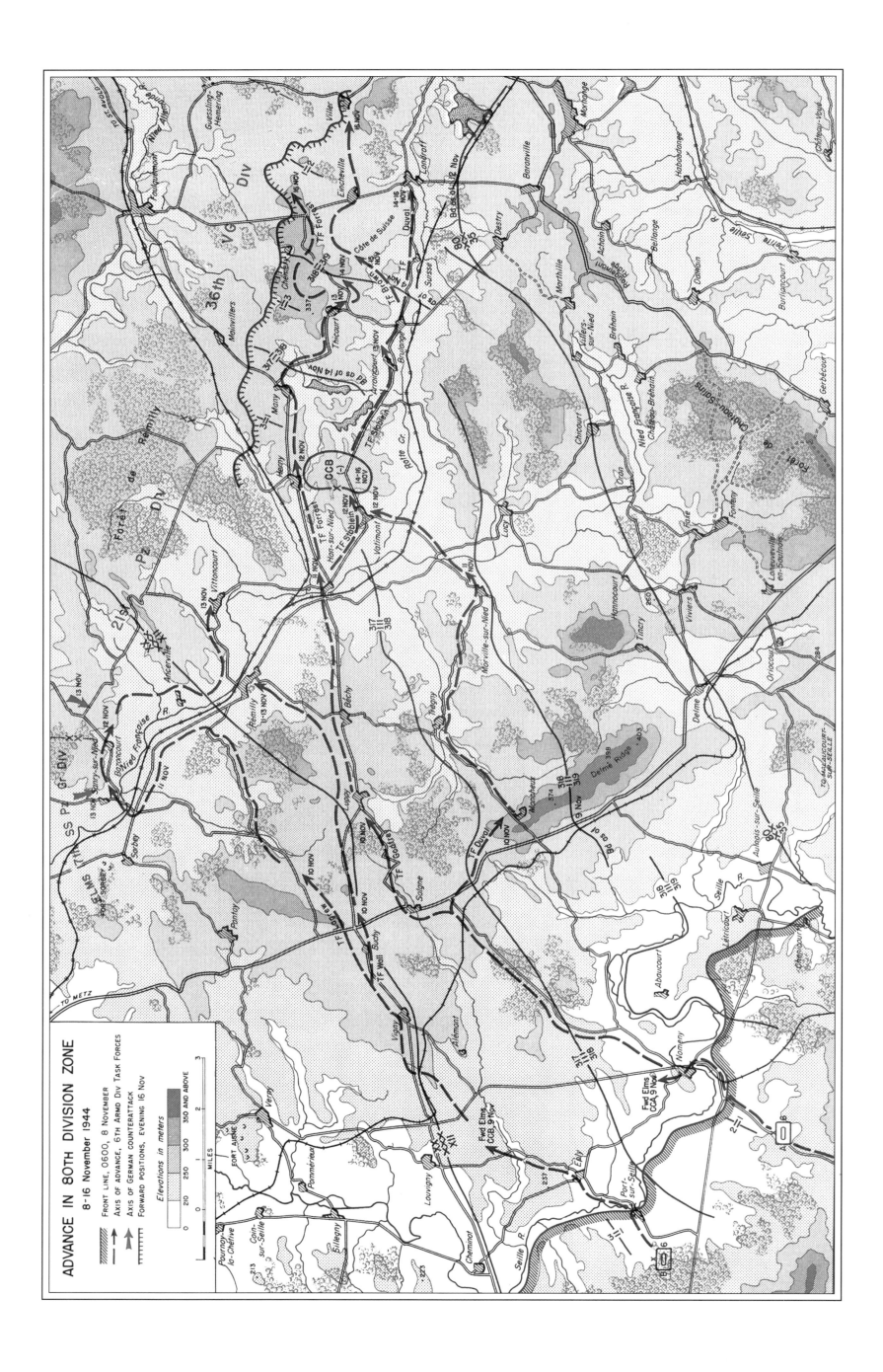

ADVANCE IN 80TH DIVISION ZONE

8-16 November 1944

FRONT LINE, 0600, 8 November
AXIS OF ADVANCE, 6TH ARMD DIV TASK FORCES
AXIS OF GERMAN COUNTERATTACK
FORWARD POSITIONS, EVENING 16 Nov

Elevations in meters

0   210   250   300   350 AND ABOVE

MILES
0   1   2   3

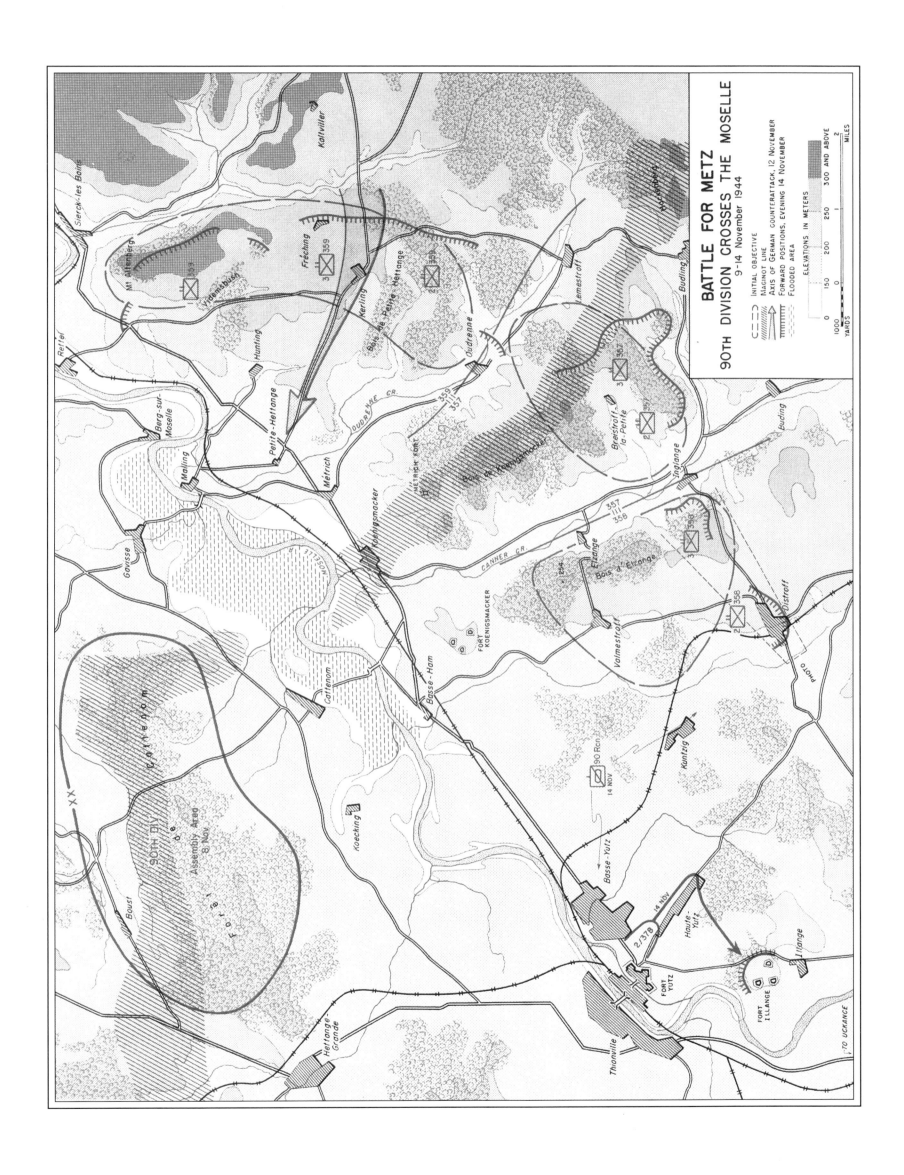

BATTLE FOR METZ
90TH DIVISION CROSSES THE MOSELLE
9–14 November 1944

INITIAL OBJECTIVE
MAGINOT LINE
AXIS OF GERMAN COUNTERATTACK, 12 November
FORWARD POSITIONS, EVENING 14 November
FLOODED AREA

ELEVATIONS IN METERS

0   150   200   250   300 AND ABOVE

0   1   2
MILES

1000   0   YARDS

BATTLE FOR METZ

ENVELOPMENT FROM THE SOUTH

8–19 November 1944

FRONT LINE, MORNING 8 NOVEMBER
5TH DIVISION OBJECTIVE
POSITIONS REACHED 12 NOVEMBER
AXIS OF ADVANCE, CCB, 6TH ARMD DIVISION
AXIS OF GERMAN COUNTERATTACK, 13 NOVEMBER
FORWARD POSITIONS, 1100N 19 NOVEMBER
GERMAN POCKET, NOON 19 NOVEMBER

ELEVATIONS IN METERS

0   200   250   300   350 and above

MILES

0   1   2   3

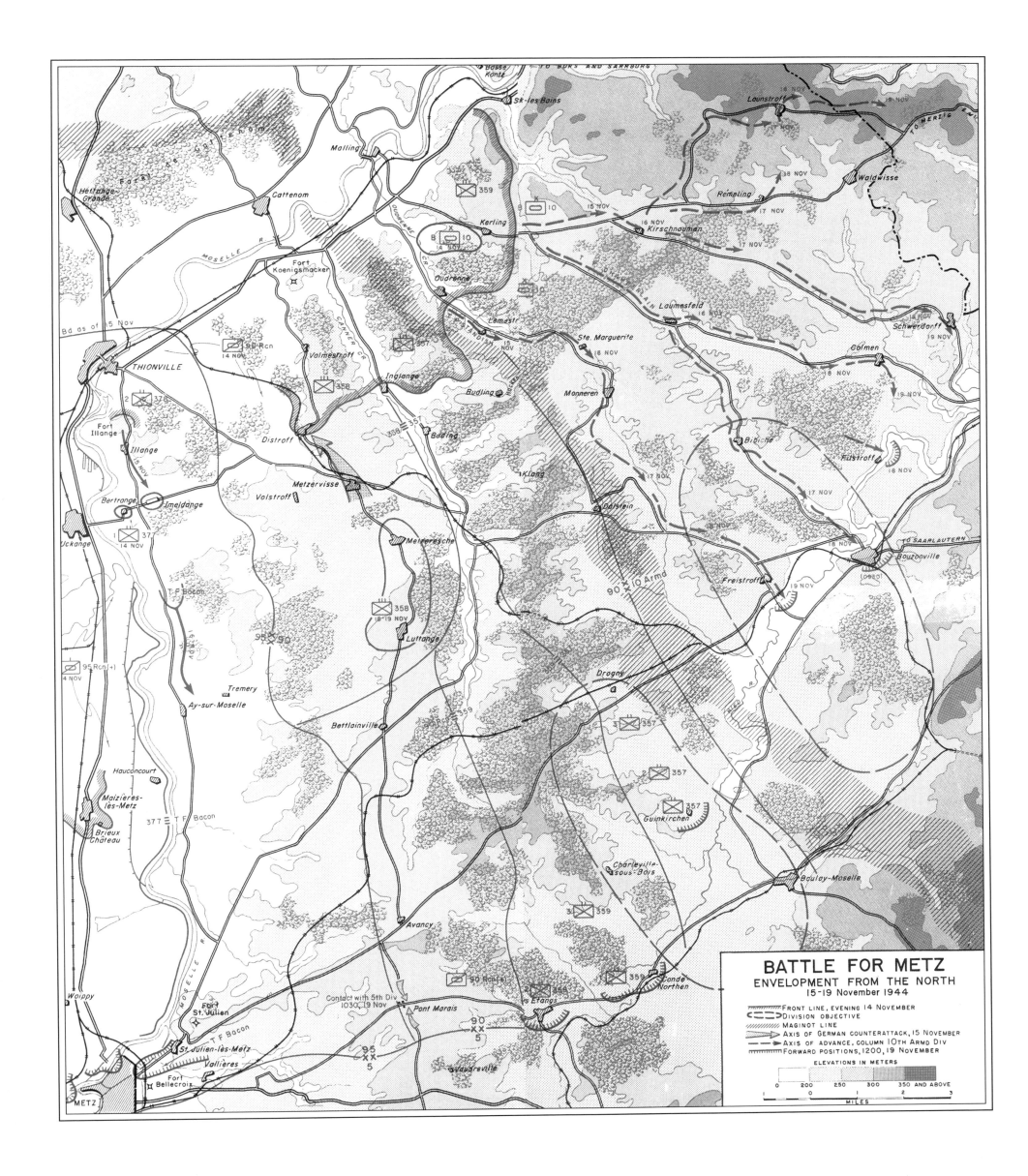

BATTLE FOR METZ
ENVELOPMENT FROM THE NORTH
15-19 November 1944

Front line, evening 14 November
Division objective
Maginot line
Axis of German counterattack, 15 November
Axis of advance, column 10th Armd Div
Forward positions, 1200, 19 November

ELEVATIONS IN METERS

0   200   250   300   350 AND ABOVE

0   1   2   3
MILES

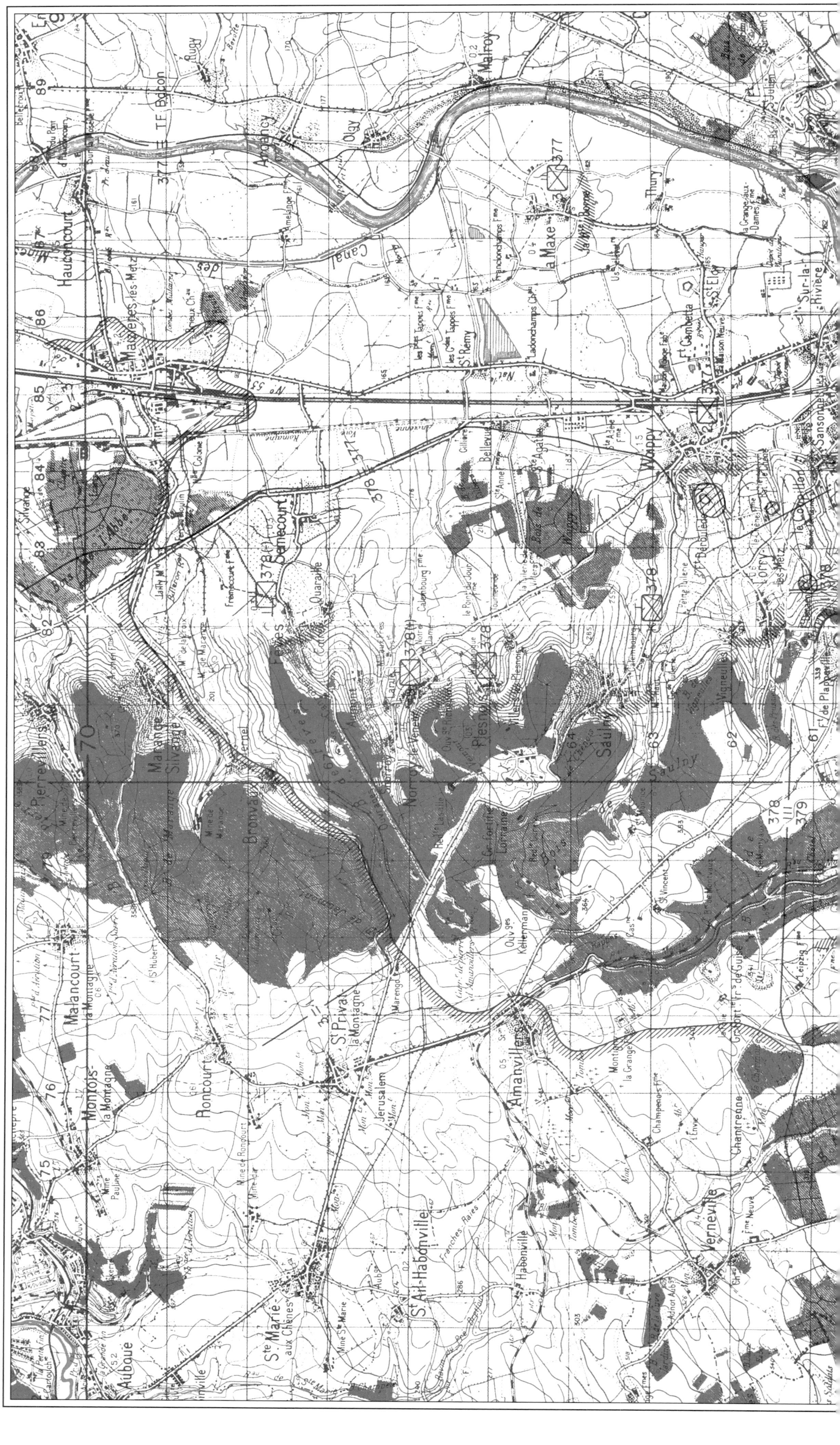
TF Bacon
377
378
Hauconcourt
Maizières-les-Metz
Malroy
Olgy
Argancy
Rugy
la Maxe
Thury
St Rémy
Woippy
Semécourt
Fèves
Norroy-le-Veneur
Plesnois
Saulny
Lorry
Amanvillers
St Privat la Montagne
Roncourt
Montois la Montagne
Malancourt la Montagne
Marange Silvange
Bronvaux
Pierrevillers
Ste Marie-aux-Chênes
St Ail-Habonville
Habonville
Verneville
Chantrenne
Jerusalem
Auboué

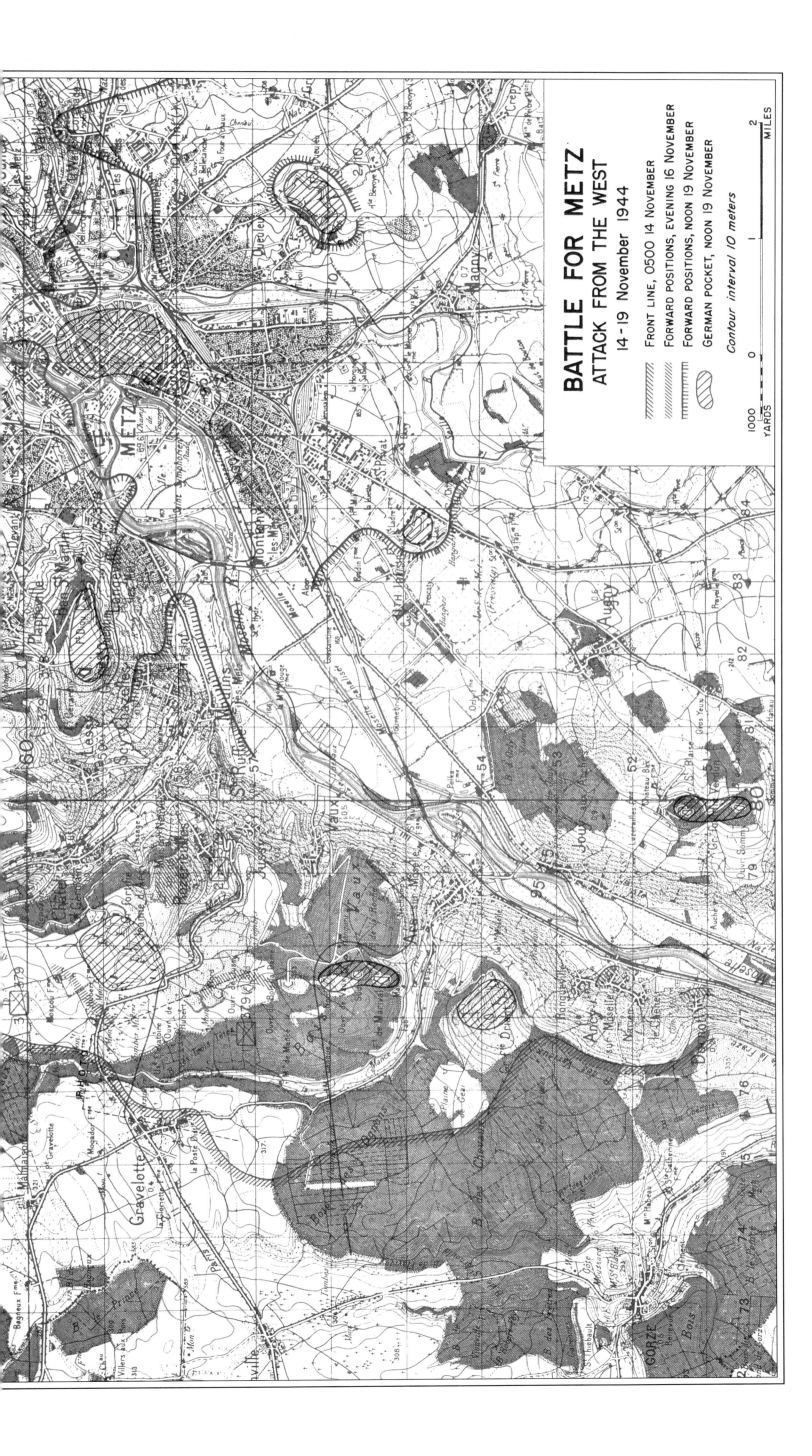

BATTLE FOR METZ
ATTACK FROM THE WEST
14–19 November 1944

///	FRONT LINE, 0500 14 November
///	FORWARD POSITIONS, EVENING 16 November
|||||||	FORWARD POSITIONS, NOON 19 November
▨	GERMAN POCKET, NOON 19 November

Contour interval 10 meters

1000 0   1   2
YARDS   MILES

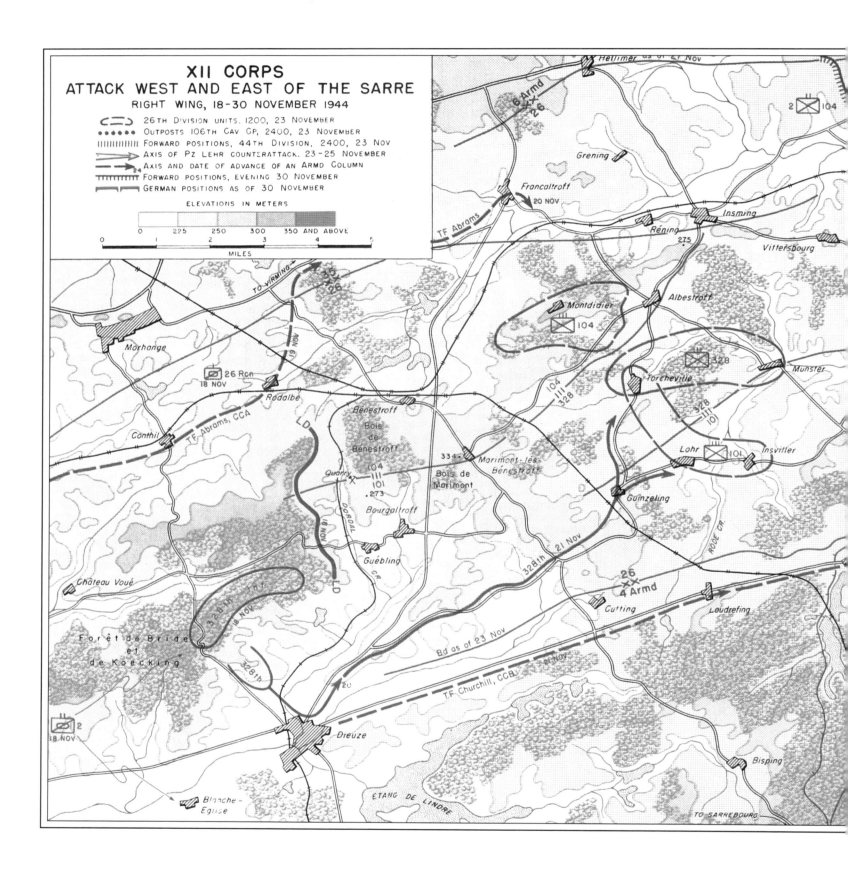

XII CORPS
ATTACK WEST AND EAST OF THE SARRE
RIGHT WING, 18-30 NOVEMBER 1944

⊂⊃ 26TH DIVISION UNITS, 1200, 23 NOVEMBER
•••••• OUTPOSTS 106TH CAV GP, 2400, 23 NOVEMBER
‖‖‖‖‖ FORWARD POSITIONS, 44TH DIVISION, 2400, 23 NOV
↦ AXIS OF PZ LEHR COUNTERATTACK, 23-25 NOVEMBER
➤ AXIS AND DATE OF ADVANCE OF AN ARMD COLUMN
⊤⊤⊤⊤ FORWARD POSITIONS, EVENING 30 NOVEMBER
⊔⊔⊔⊔ GERMAN POSITIONS AS OF 30 NOVEMBER

ELEVATIONS IN METERS

| 0 | 225 | 250 | 300 | 350 AND ABOVE |

0   1   2   3   4   5
MILES

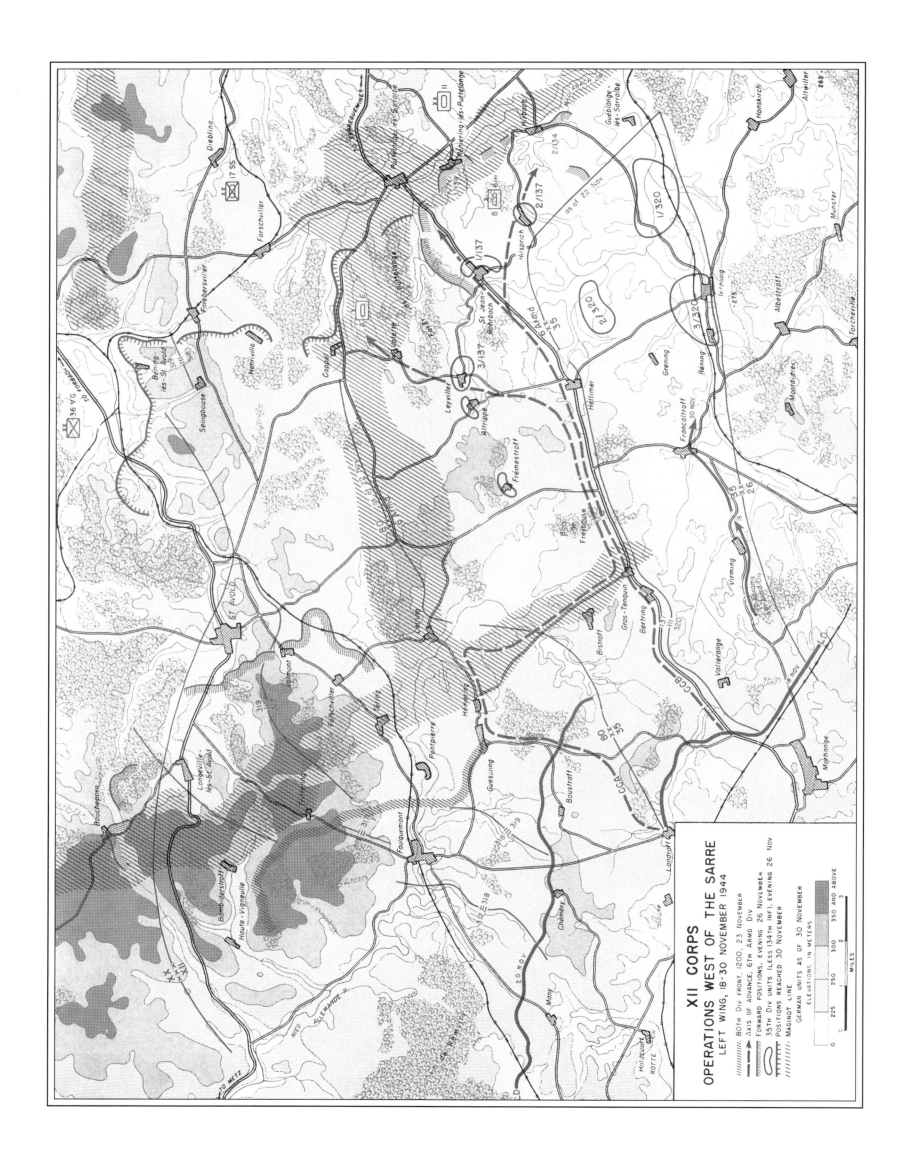

XII CORPS

OPERATIONS WEST OF THE SARRE

LEFT WING, 18-30 NOVEMBER 1944

⫼⫼⫼⫼⫼ 80TH DIV FRONT, 1200, 23 NOVEMBER
━━━━━ AXIS OF ADVANCE, 6TH ARMD DIV
━ ━ ━ ━ FORWARD POSITIONS, EVENING 26 NOVEMBER
⟓ 35TH DIV UNITS (LESS 134TH INF), EVENING 26 NOV
⟓ POSITIONS REACHED 30 NOVEMBER
⫽⫽⫽⫽⫽ MAGINOT LINE
GERMAN UNITS AS OF 30 NOVEMBER
ELEVATIONS IN METERS

225	250	300
350 AND ABOVE

0   1   2   3
MILES

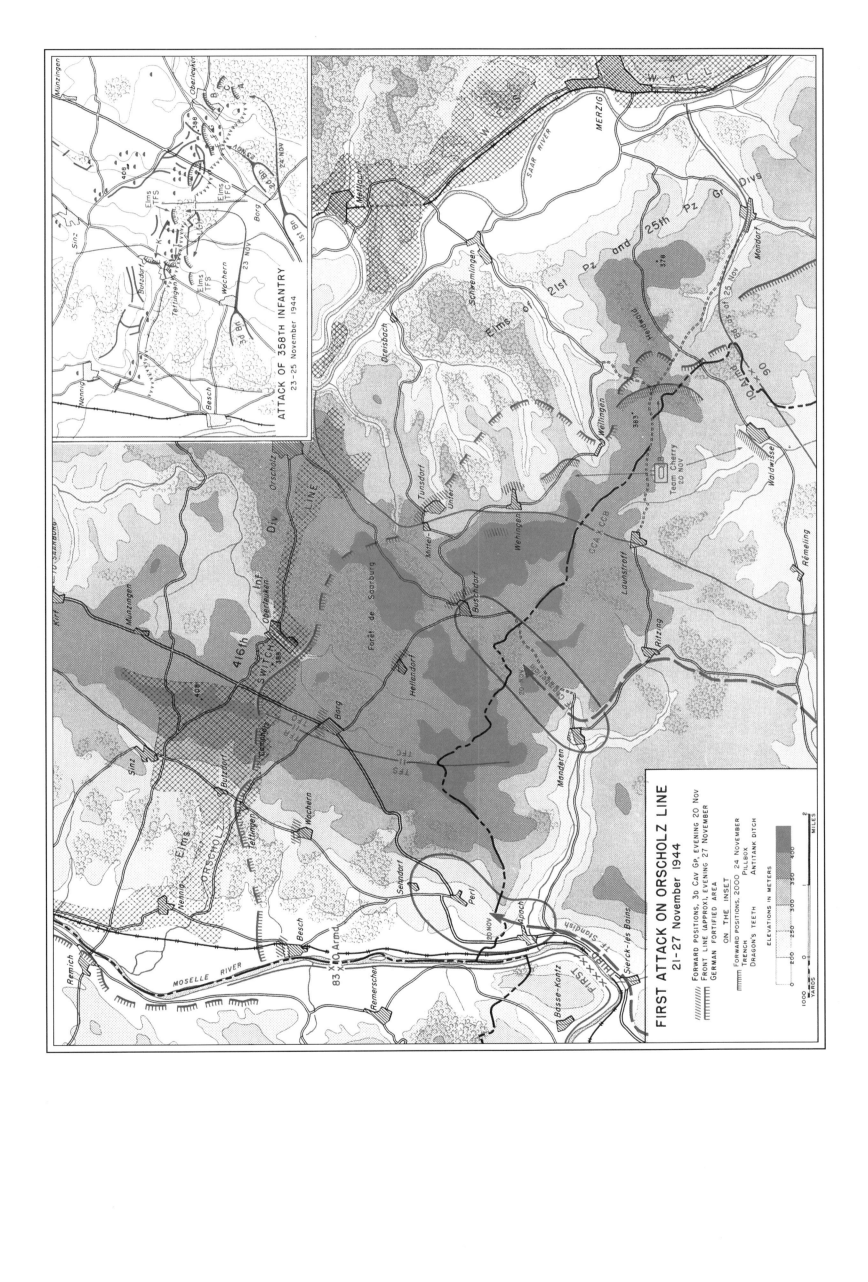

ATTACK OF 358TH INFANTRY
23-25 November 1944

FIRST ATTACK ON ORSCHOLZ LINE
21-27 November 1944

Forward positions, 3d Cav Gp, evening 20 Nov
Front line (approx), evening 27 November
German fortified area
ON THE INSET
Forward positions, 2000 24 November
Trench   Pillbox
Dragon's teeth Antitank ditch
ELEVATIONS IN METERS

MILES
YARDS

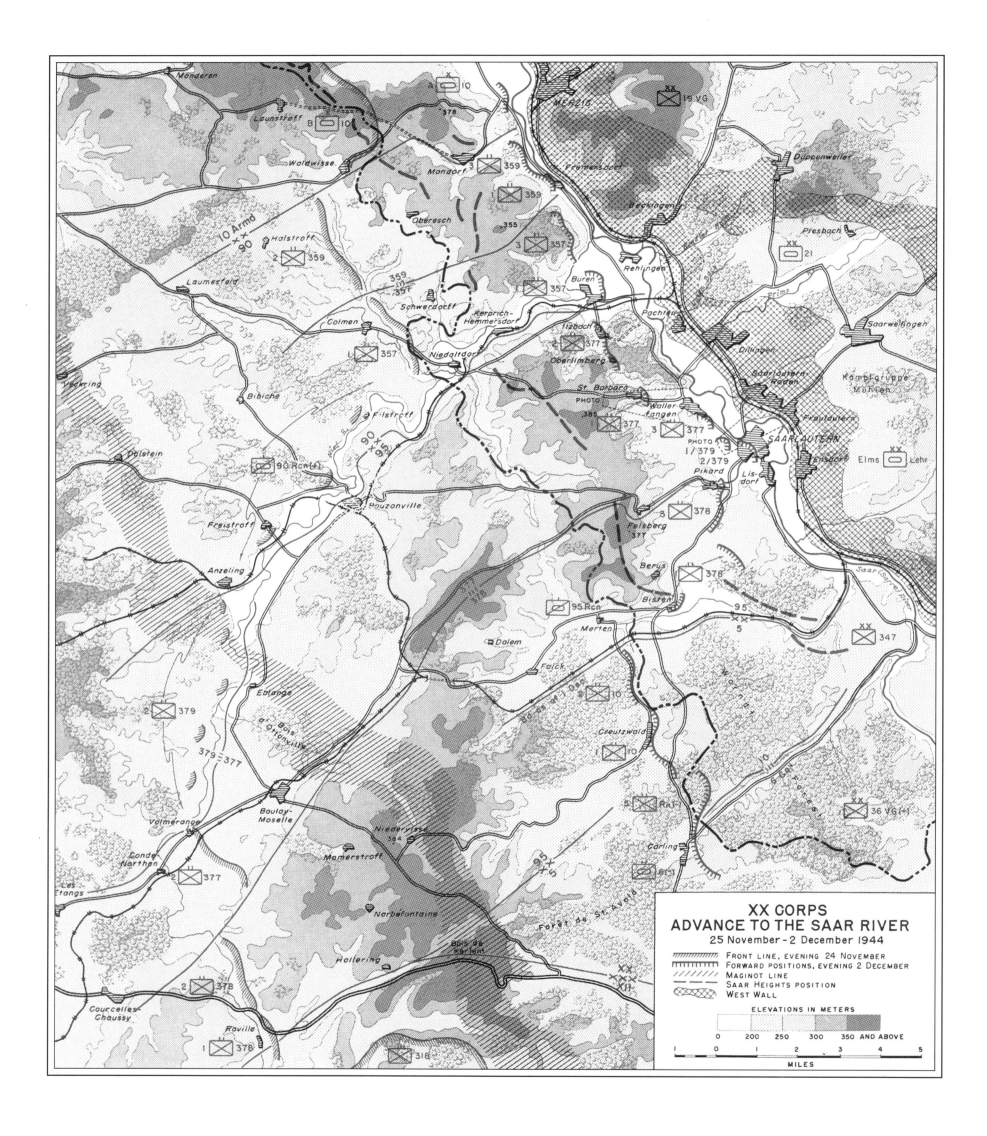

XX CORPS
ADVANCE TO THE SAAR RIVER
25 November - 2 December 1944

FRONT LINE, EVENING 24 NOVEMBER
FORWARD POSITIONS, EVENING 2 DECEMBER
MAGINOT LINE
SAAR HEIGHTS POSITION
WEST WALL

ELEVATIONS IN METERS

0   200   250   300   350 AND ABOVE

1   0   1   2   3   4   5
MILES

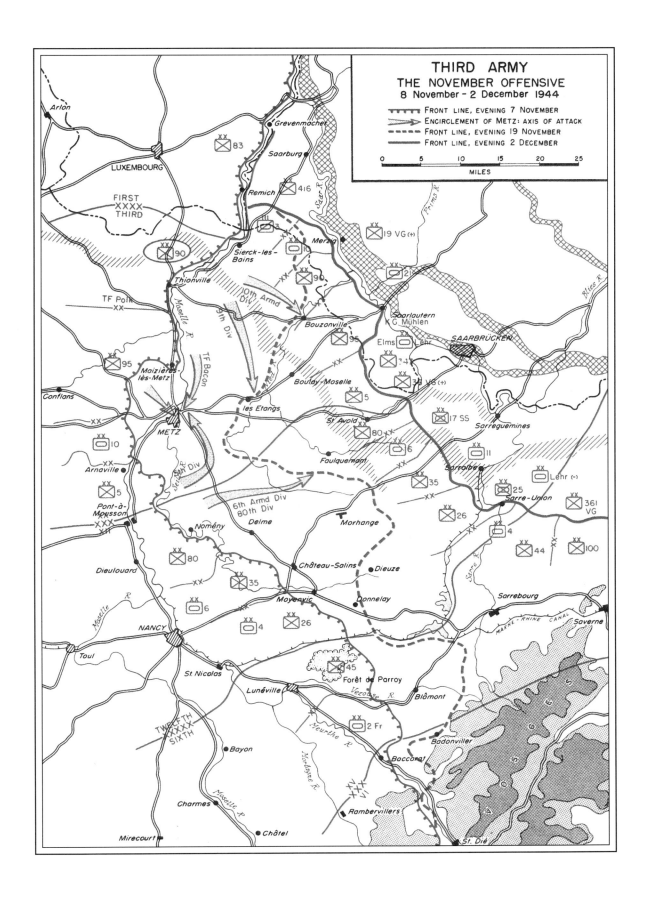

THIRD ARMY
THE NOVEMBER OFFENSIVE
8 November – 2 December 1944

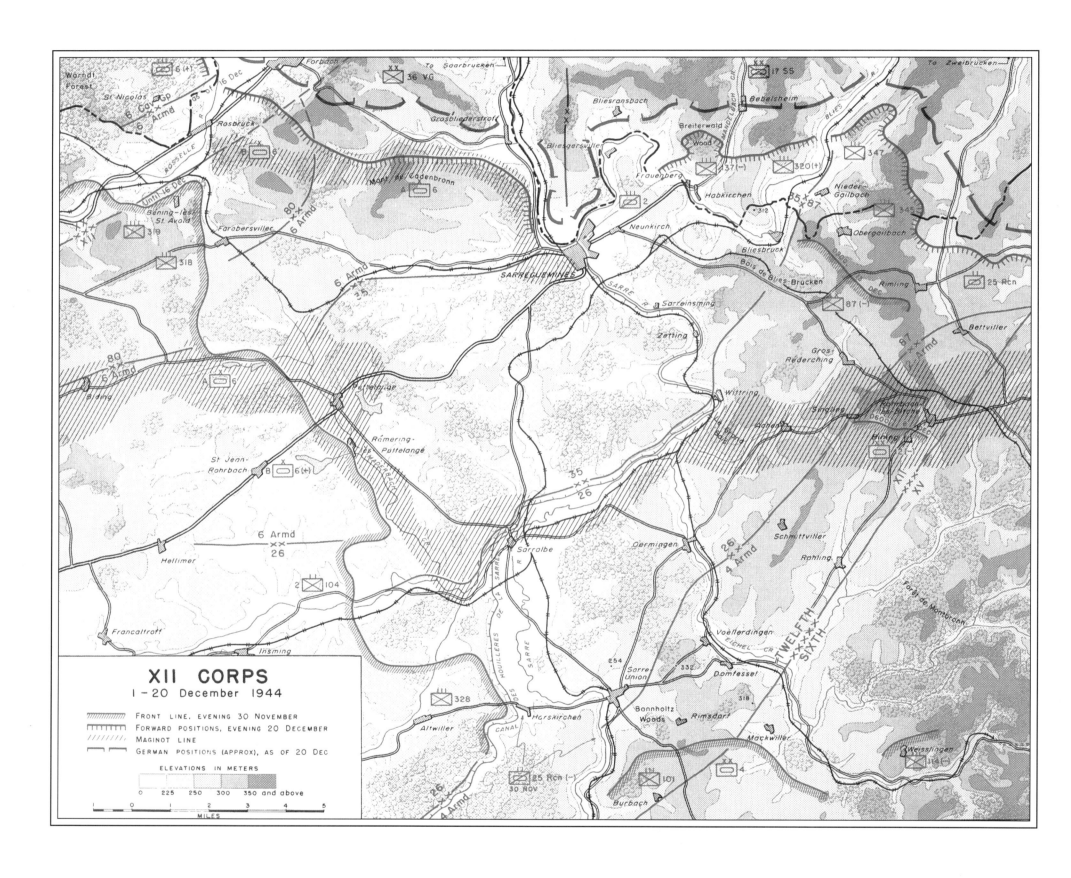

XII CORPS
1–20 December 1944

////////	FRONT LINE, EVENING 30 NOVEMBER
┴┴┴┴┴	FORWARD POSITIONS, EVENING 20 DECEMBER
/////////	MAGINOT LINE
	GERMAN POSITIONS (APPROX), AS OF 20 DEC

ELEVATIONS IN METERS

0   225   250   300   350 and above

0   1   2   3   4   5
MILES

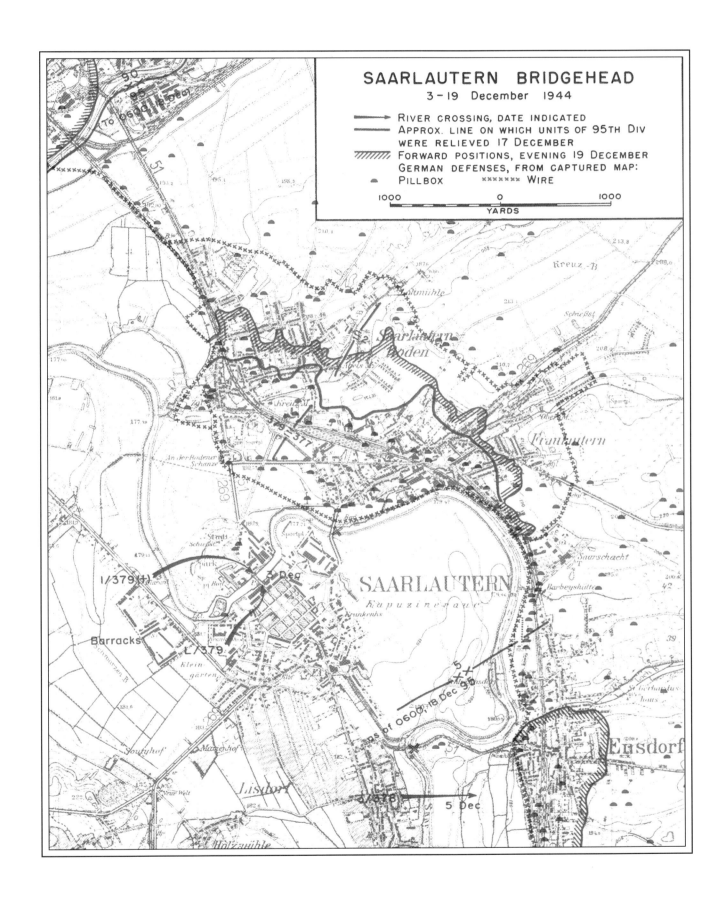

SAARLAUTERN BRIDGEHEAD
3–19 December 1944

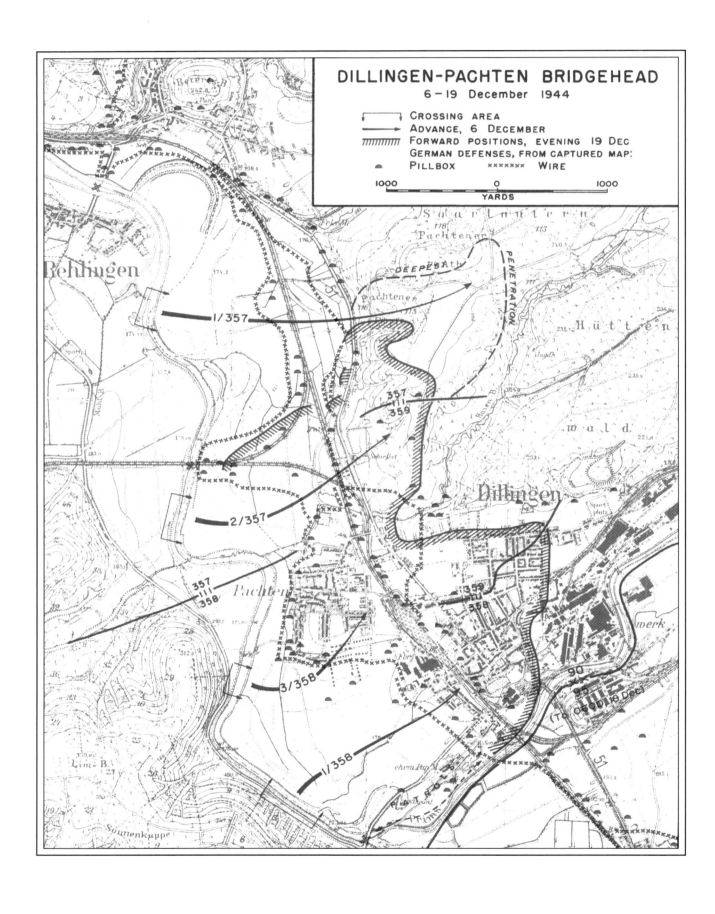

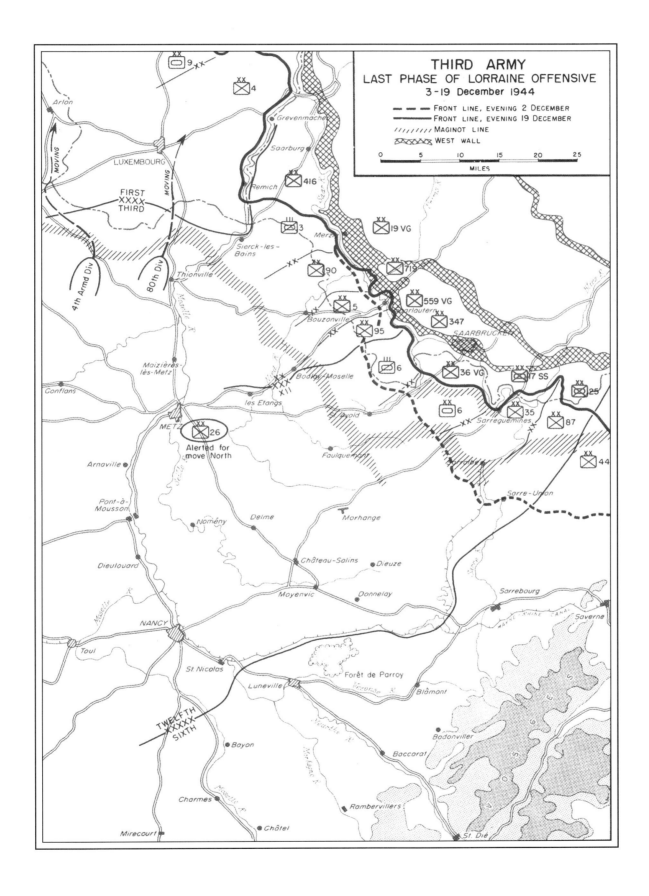

THIRD ARMY
LAST PHASE OF LORRAINE OFFENSIVE
3-19 December 1944

FRONT LINE, EVENING 2 DECEMBER
FRONT LINE, EVENING 19 DECEMBER
MAGINOT LINE
WEST WALL

0   5   10   15   20   25
MILES

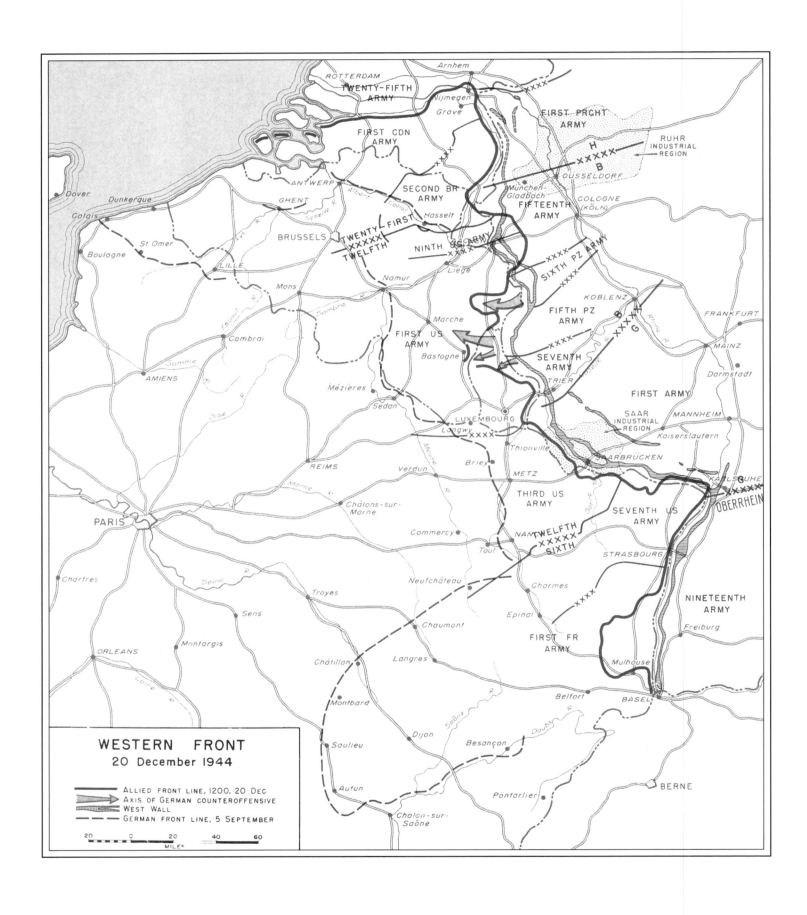

WESTERN FRONT
20 December 1944

ALLIED FRONT LINE, 1200, 20 DEC
AXIS OF GERMAN COUNTEROFFENSIVE
WEST WALL
GERMAN FRONT LINE, 5 SEPTEMBER

20   0   20   40   60
MILES

ABOVE: *Columns of U.S. First Army infantrymen reach to the horizon as they march in double file on the road to the fortress city of Aachen, Germany. On October 20, after a bitter, protracted frontal assault, Aachen was finally taken. Meanwhile, from the North Sea to Switzerland, Allied forces continued to press the Germans relentlessly.*

LEFT: *In September 1944, American infantrymen of the 60th Infantry Regiment proceed into a Belgian town shielded by a tank. The relationship was reciprocal: not only did the tank afford protection for infantrymen in such cases, the infantrymen protected the tank from small, devastating antitank weapons wielded by German foot soldiers. Tanks stripped of their ordinary complement of infantry were highly vulnerable.*

The Siegfried Line Campaign

August 26–December 15, 1944

AFTER A RAPID AND EXHAUSTING ADVANCE ACROSS France, by early September, Allied forces ran into stiffening resistance along the Siegfried Line, also called the West Wall, a three-mile-deep belt of defenses. The need to establish a port closer to the front line to bring in supplies for the invasion of Germany had become urgent. Eisenhower thought the capture of Antwerp would resolve the problem, and British General Bernard Montgomery, commander of 21st Army Group, was given the task of taking it.

The headstrong Montgomery, however, had other ideas. He argued for a powerful thrust across the Rhine onto the North German plain and the Ruhr industrial district. Finally, Montgomery and Eisenhower compromised and attempted to do both. Eisenhower insisted, though, that Antwerp be Montgomery's first priority. Afterward, the American general could lead his great drive, called Operation MARKET-GARDEN, through Arnhem and Nijmegen, across the Rhine River.

Montgomery failed to live up to his promise concerning the port, however, sending only a weak Canadian force to capture Antwerp and stabilize the area around the Scheldt Estuary (which allowed access to the North Sea). While the Canadians captured Antwerp, they were unable to obtain control of both banks of the Scheldt, and German forces remained to threaten the entire sector.

Operation MARKET-GARDEN nonetheless went forward, and on September 17, a fleet of some 4,700 planes dropped 35,000 troops behind the German lines. Because of poor planning and execution, however, the mission was a total disaster, and a number of units were surrounded, killed, and captured.

In October, a bitter and protracted frontal assault to take Aachen finally succeeded on October 20. But it was not until December that Patton's army was able to take Metz, and still the Rhine had yet to be crossed. Meanwhile, from October 6 to December 9, some of the worst fighting of the war took place in the Hürtgen Forest. The forest was considered a key to the capture of critical dams along the Roer River, so American troops were poured into the well-defended tangle of woods. More than 10,000 of them were ground up by German defenders.

LEFT: *American tanks, trucks, and other vehicles advance into Germany along a superhighway, known as the autobahn, a revolutionary road concept developed under Hitler's auspices for wartime use by the German military. A long column of German POWs, sandwiched between U.S. columns, marches down the median on its way to a detention camp well behind the front as Allied forces whiz past in the opposite direction in both lanes of the autobahn, headed toward the heart of Germany.* OPPOSITE PAGE INSET: *British Field Marshal Bernard Montgomery and American Generals Dwight Eisenhower and Omar Bradley (left to right) pore over a terrain map while discussing operations. While Eisenhower and Montgomery did not always agree on the strategy for the war in Europe, they were able to overcome their differences in the common cause of defeating the enemy.* LEFT INSET: *American soldiers observe a passage through the formidable defenses of the Siegfried Line. The pointed objects shown in the middle of the picture were known as "dragon's teeth," polyhedron-shaped concrete tank obstacles that were sometimes booby-trapped in the spaces between the "teeth." Behind such obstacles were artillery positions, usually sited on the heights, concrete pillboxes, and elaborate trench systems and wire entanglements. When a section of these defenses was challenged, the Germans immediately reinforced that sector of their line.*

RIGHT, TOP AND BOTTOM:
In mid-October 1944, U.S. First Army soldiers, supported by a tank, hunt for snipers and other resisters in the outskirts of Aachen, Germany. While half of the bombarded city was being wrested from German control by U.S. forces, other units were in the process of smashing German troop and armor concentrations northeast of the city. In the top photo, GIs round the corner in the middle of house-to-house fighting; in the bottom photo, taken not long after, American soldiers carry a wounded man, apparently a GI, to the relative safety of the building protected by the tank.

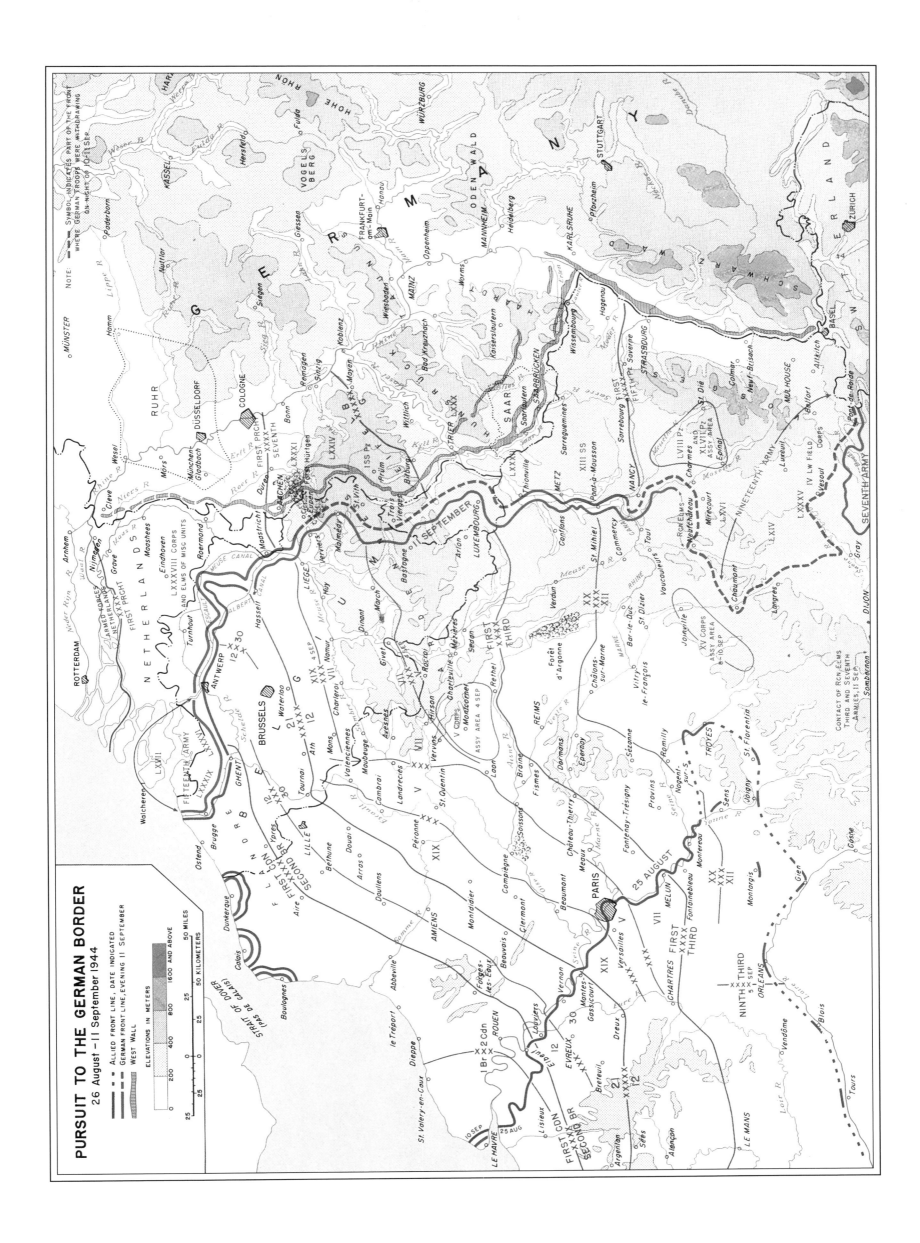

PURSUIT TO THE GERMAN BORDER
26 August–11 September 1944

Allied front line, date indicated
German front line, evening 11 September
WEST WALL

ELEVATIONS IN METERS

200   400   800   1600 AND ABOVE

MILES

KILOMETERS

NOTE — SYMBOL INDICATES PART OF THE FRONT WHERE GERMAN TROOPS WERE WITHDRAWING ON NIGHT OF 10–11 SEP.

V CORPS HITS THE WEST WALL
11-19 September 1944

⬭   ASSEMBLY AREAS, NIGHT 11 SEP

– – –   EXTENT OF U.S. PENETRATION, NIGHT 17 SEP

▨   WEST WALL

⬅   AXIS OF GERMAN COUNTERATTACK

Elevations in meters

1   0   1   2   3   4 MILES

1   0   1   2   3   4 KILOMETERS

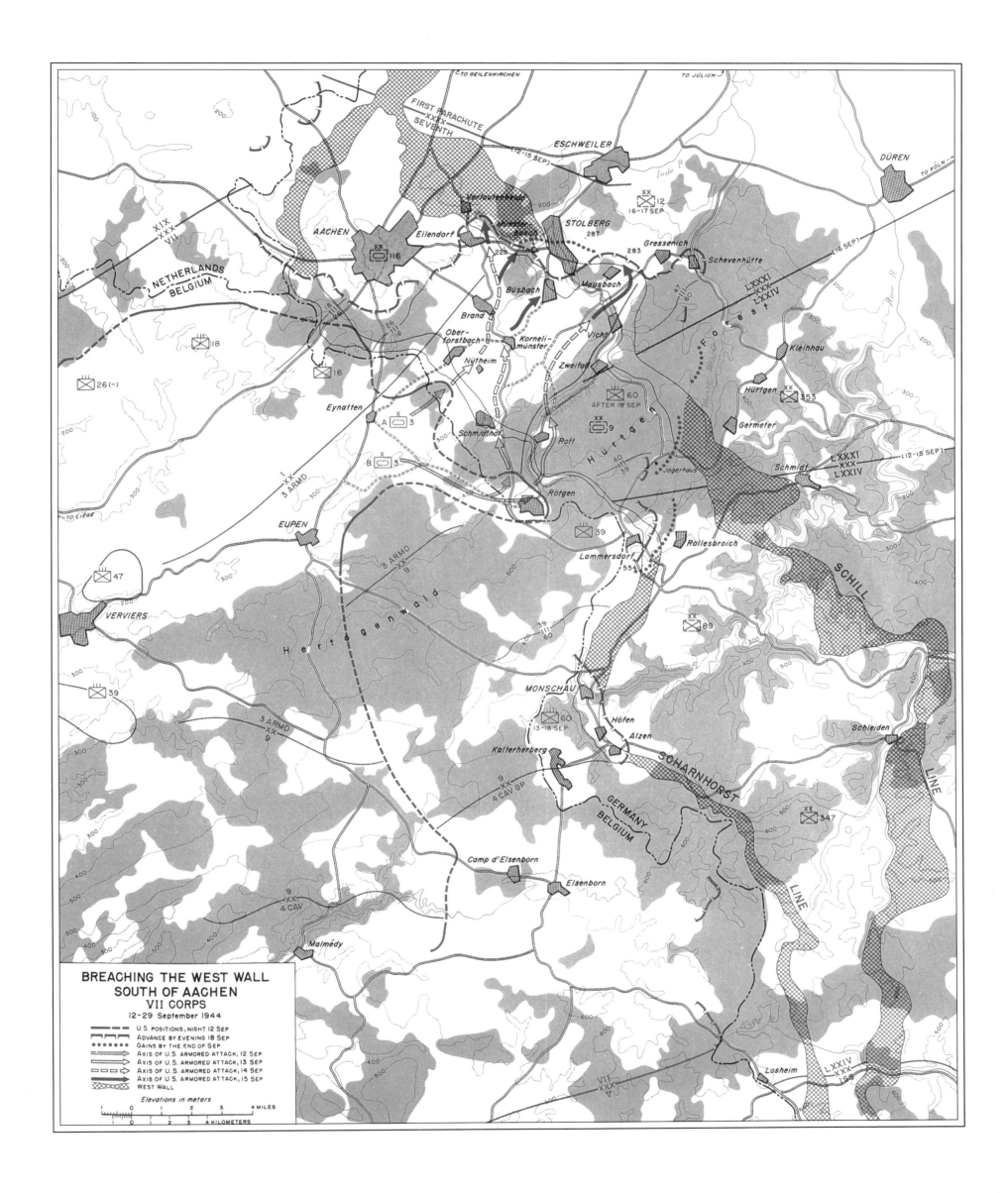

**BREACHING THE WEST WALL
SOUTH OF AACHEN
VII CORPS**
12-29 September 1944

U.S. POSITIONS, NIGHT 12 SEP
ADVANCE BY EVENING 18 SEP
GAINS BY THE END OF SEP
AXIS OF U.S. ARMORED ATTACK, 12 SEP
AXIS OF U.S. ARMORED ATTACK, 13 SEP
AXIS OF U.S. ARMORED ATTACK, 14 SEP
AXIS OF U.S. ARMORED ATTACK, 15 SEP
WEST WALL

Elevations in meters

4 MILES

4 KILOMETERS

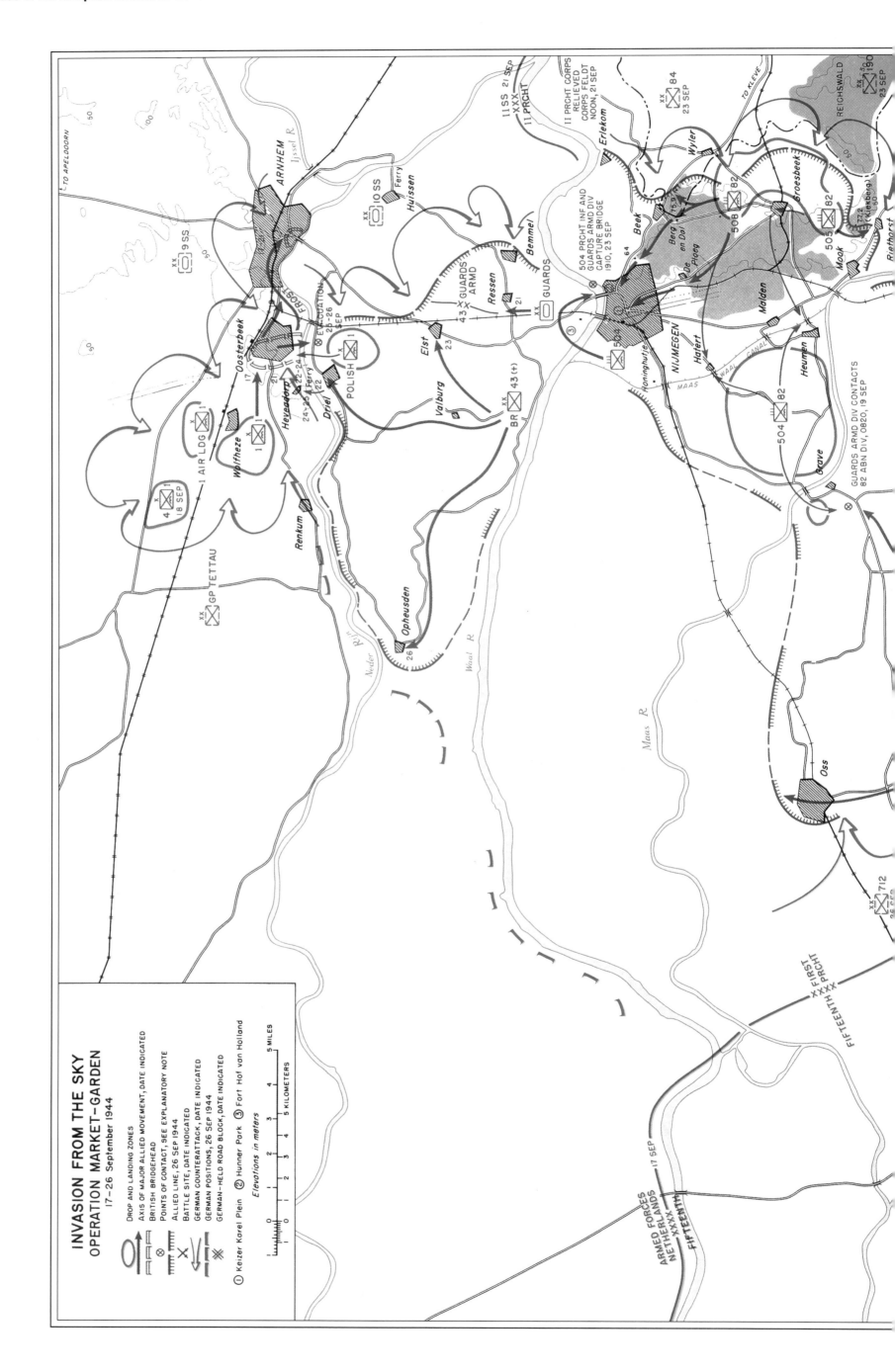

INVASION FROM THE SKY
OPERATION MARKET-GARDEN
17–26 September 1944

Drop and landing zones
Axis of major Allied movement, date indicated
British bridgehead
Points of contact, see explanatory note
Allied line, 26 SEP 1944
Battle site, date indicated
German counterattack, date indicated
German positions, 26 SEP 1944
German-held road block, date indicated

① Keizer Karel Plein ② Hunner Park ③ Fort Hof van Holland

Elevations in meters

SCALE
0   1   2   3   4   5 MILES
0   1   2   3   4   5 KILOMETERS

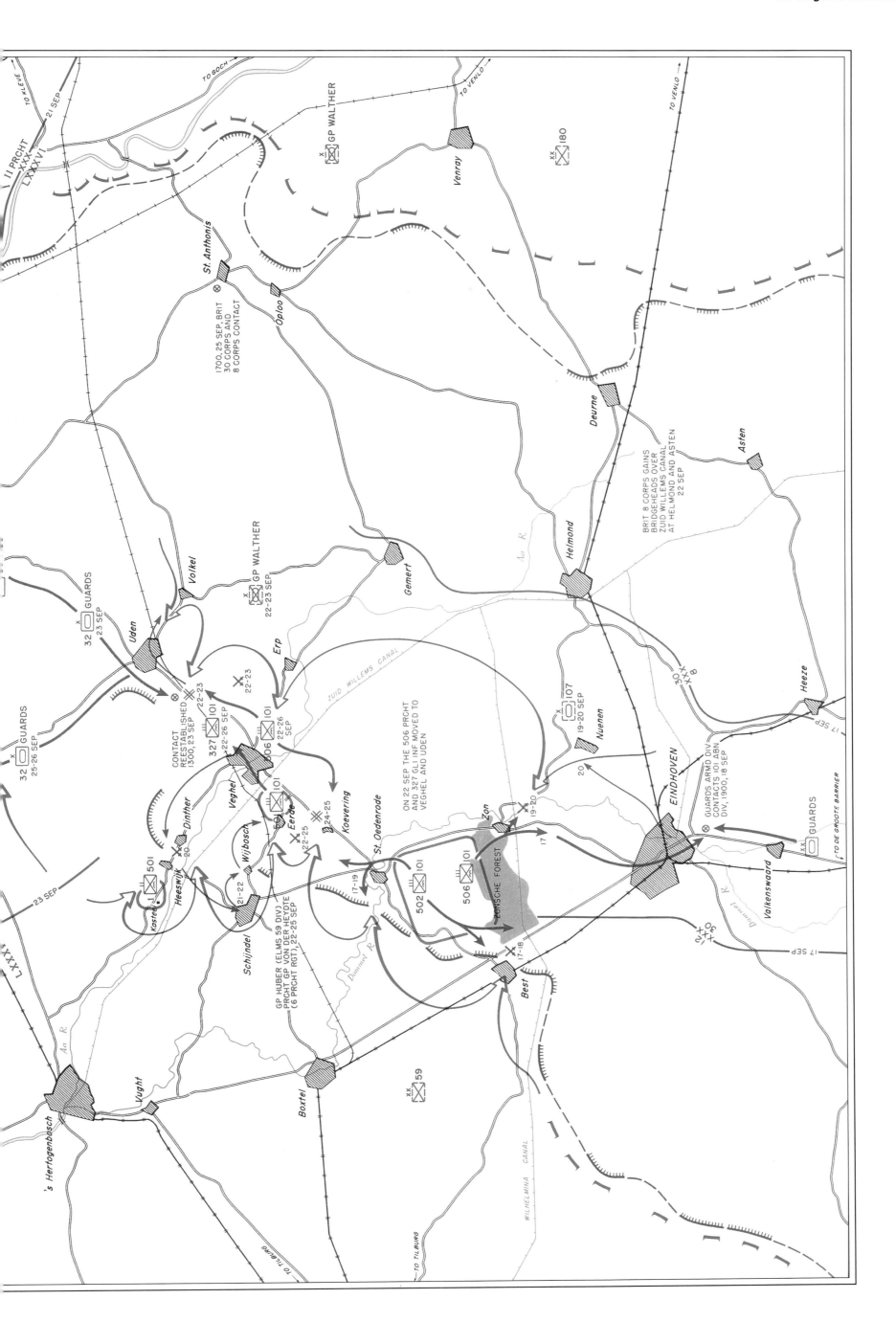

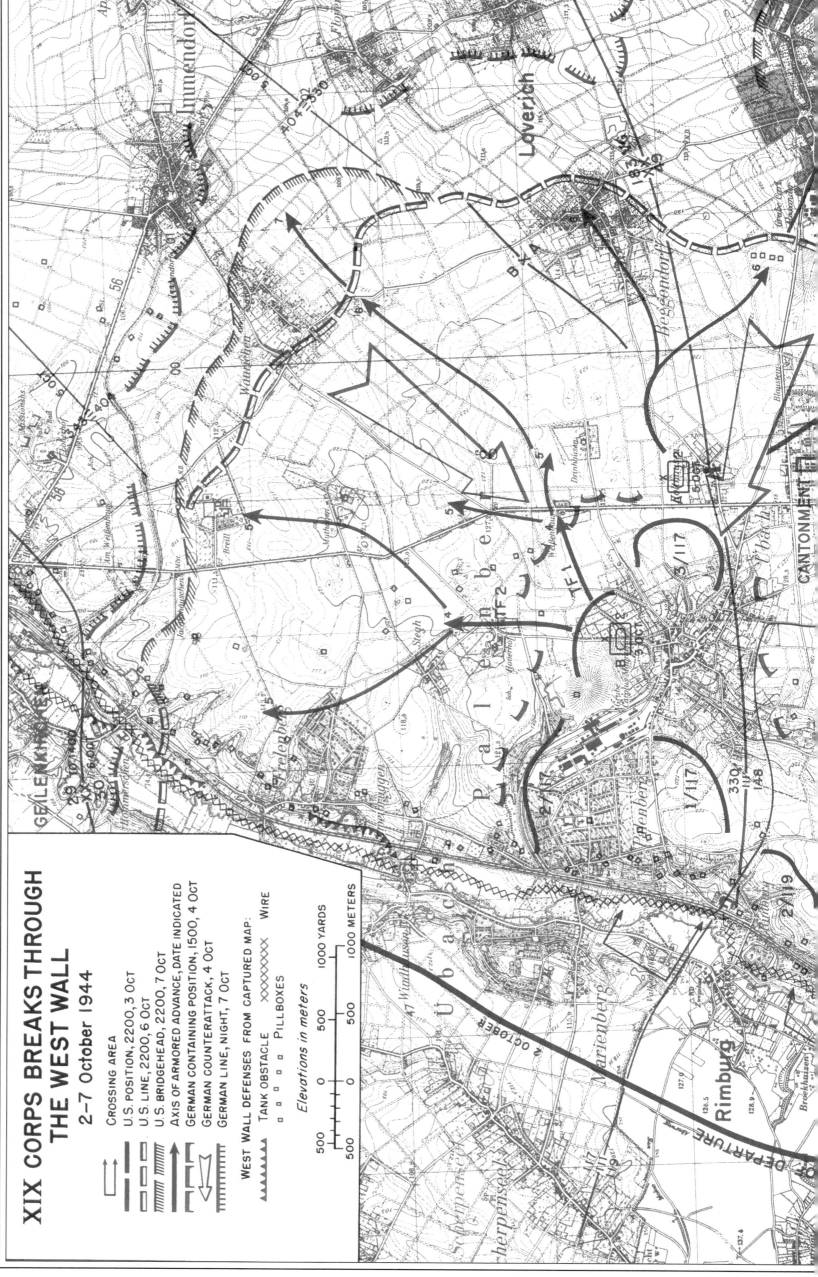

XIX CORPS BREAKS THROUGH THE WEST WALL
2-7 October 1944

CROSSING AREA

U.S. POSITION, 2200, 3 OCT

U.S. LINE, 2200, 6 OCT

U.S. BRIDGEHEAD, 2200, 7 OCT

AXIS OF ARMORED ADVANCE, DATE INDICATED

GERMAN CONTAINING POSITION, 1500, 4 OCT

GERMAN COUNTERATTACK, 4 OCT

GERMAN LINE, NIGHT, 7 OCT

WEST WALL DEFENSES FROM CAPTURED MAP:

TANK OBSTACLE   XXXXXXXXX WIRE

□ □ □ □ PILLBOXES

Elevations in meters

500   0   500   1000 YARDS

500   0   500   1000 METERS

THE HÜRTGEN FOREST
16 November – 9 December 1944

••••••••	AMERICAN FRONT LINE, MORNING 16 NOV
⊤⊤⊤⊤⊤⊤	FORWARD POSITIONS, NIGHT 19 NOV
⊤⊤⊤⊤⊤	FORWARD POSITIONS, NIGHT 22 NOV
⊤⊤⊤⊤⊤	FORWARD POSITIONS, NIGHT 29 NOV
	FINAL LINE REACHED: 8TH DIV ON 9 DEC, 4TH DIV ON 2 DEC, 1ST DIV ON 4 DEC, 104TH AND 30TH DIVS ON 6 DEC
➞	AXIS OF ARMORED DRIVE, DATE INDICATED
	GERMAN MAIN LINE OF RESISTANCE, MORNING 16 NOV
▭▭▭	GERMAN POSITIONS, MORNING 20 NOV
▭▭▭	GERMAN MAIN LINE OF RESISTANCE, 6 DEC WITH ADJUSTMENTS IN SECTOR OPPOSITE U.S. 8TH DIV
⬅	GERMAN COUNTERATTACK
▨▨	GERMAN-HELD PORTION OF WEST WALL, DATA FROM CAPTURED MAP

Elevations in meters

2 MILES

2 KILOMETERS

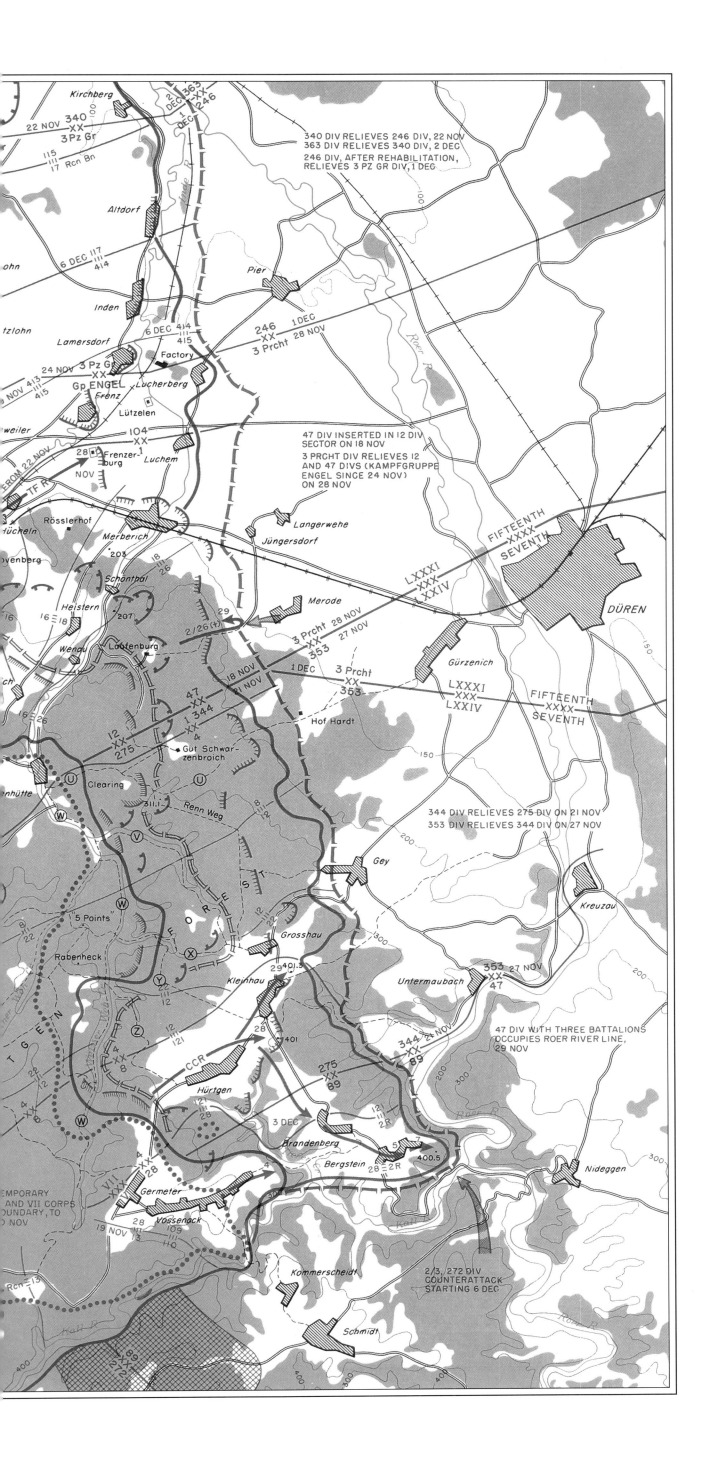

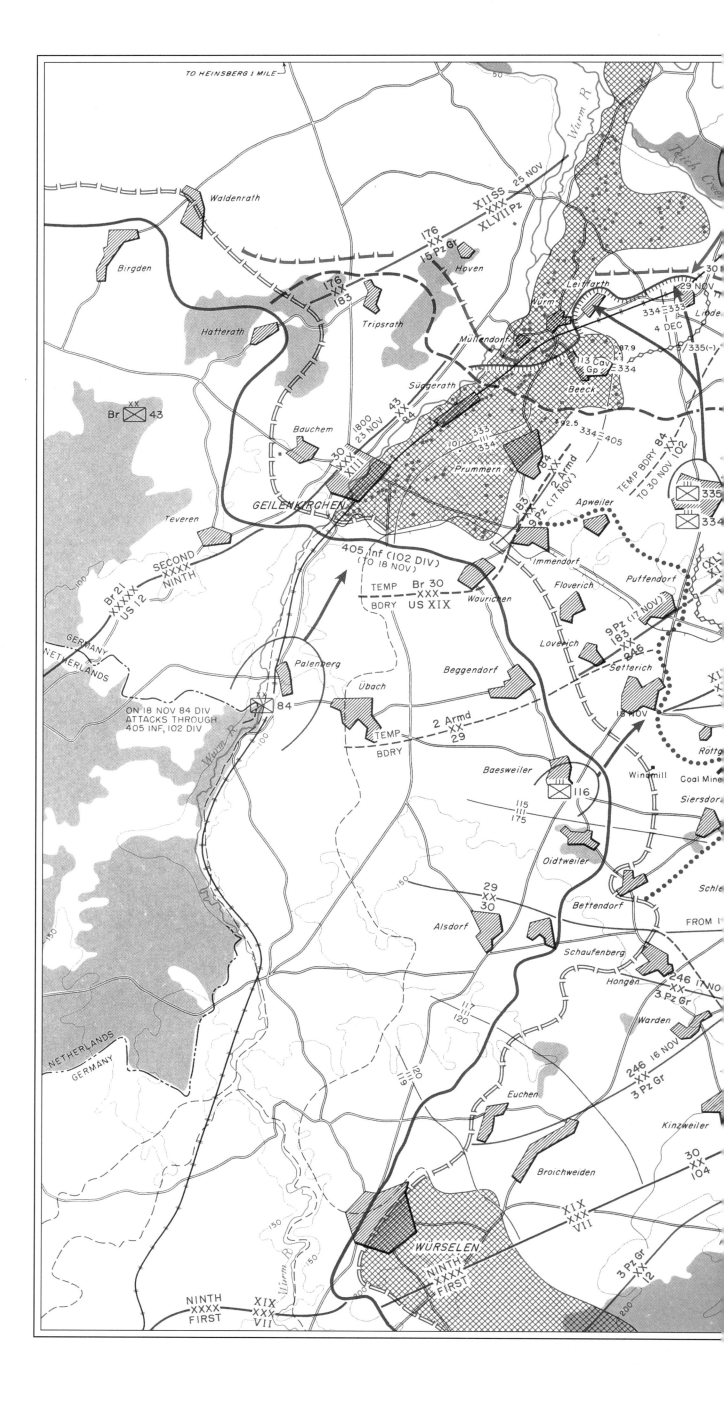

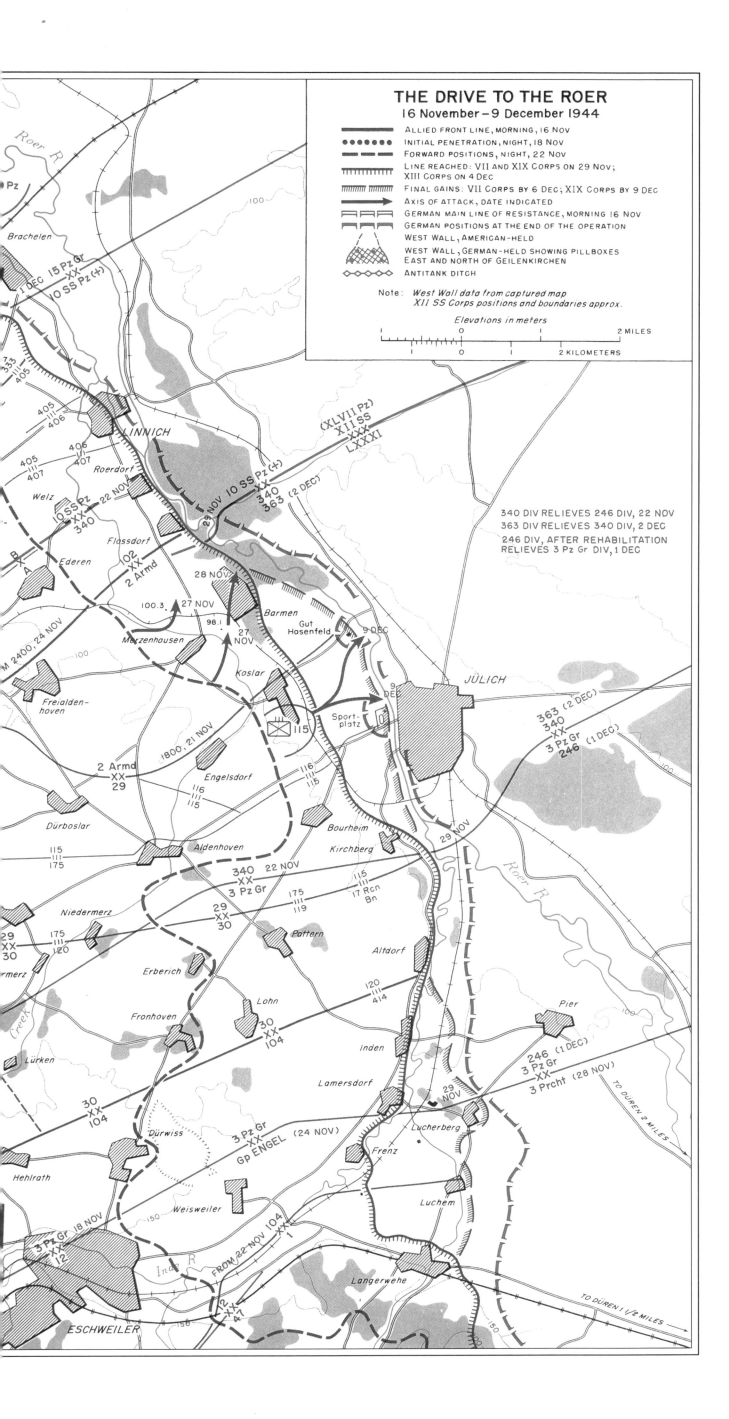

THE DRIVE TO THE ROER
16 November – 9 December 1944

ALLIED FRONT LINE, MORNING, 16 NOV
INITIAL PENETRATION, NIGHT, 18 NOV
FORWARD POSITIONS, NIGHT, 22 NOV
LINE REACHED: VII AND XIX CORPS ON 29 NOV; XIII CORPS ON 4 DEC
FINAL GAINS: VII CORPS BY 6 DEC; XIX CORPS BY 9 DEC
AXIS OF ATTACK, DATE INDICATED
GERMAN MAIN LINE OF RESISTANCE, MORNING 16 NOV
GERMAN POSITIONS AT THE END OF THE OPERATION
WEST WALL, AMERICAN-HELD
WEST WALL, GERMAN-HELD SHOWING PILLBOXES EAST AND NORTH OF GEILENKIRCHEN
ANTITANK DITCH

Note: *West Wall data from captured map*
XII SS Corps positions and boundaries approx.

Elevations in meters

2 MILES
2 KILOMETERS

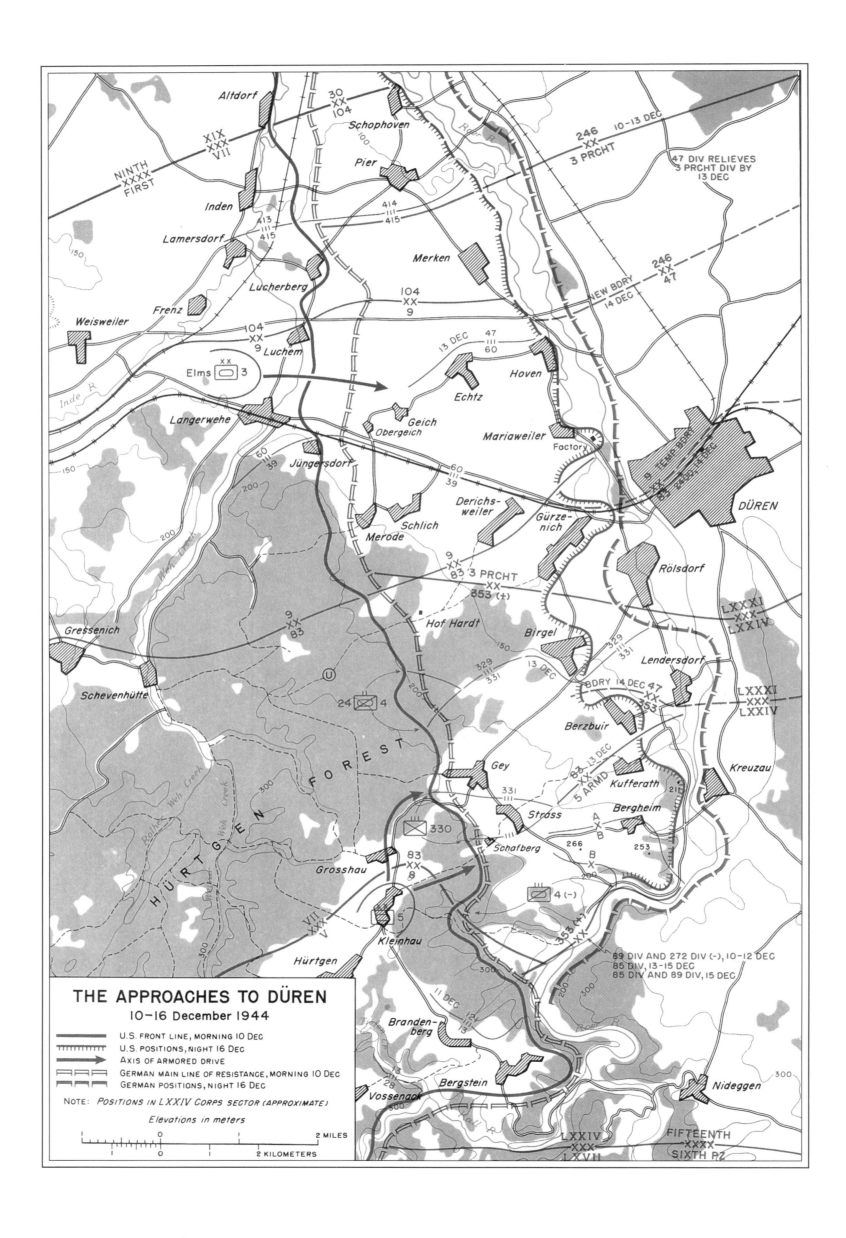

THE APPROACHES TO DÜREN
10–16 December 1944

▬▬▬▬▬	U.S. FRONT LINE, MORNING 10 DEC
▬▬▬▬▬	U.S. POSITIONS, NIGHT 16 DEC
➤➤➤	AXIS OF ARMORED DRIVE
◄◄◄	GERMAN MAIN LINE OF RESISTANCE, MORNING 10 DEC
◄◄◄	GERMAN POSITIONS, NIGHT 16 DEC

NOTE: POSITIONS IN LXXIV CORPS SECTOR (APPROXIMATE)

Elevations in meters

0   1   2 MILES

0   1   2 KILOMETERS

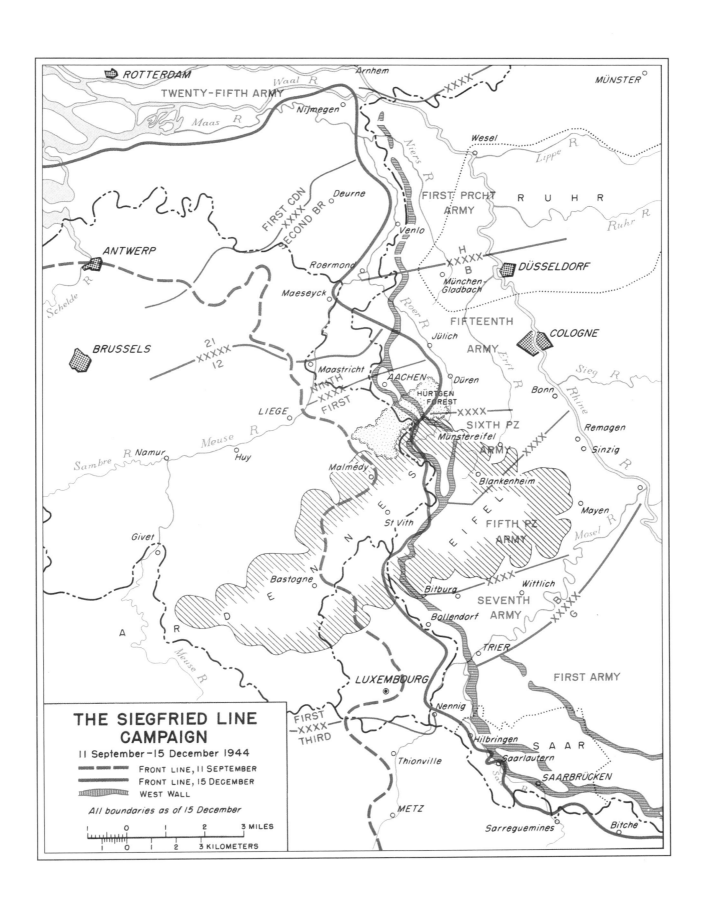

ROTTERDAM
TWENTY-FIFTH ARMY
Waal R Arnhem
XXXX
MÜNSTER
Maas R Nijmegen

FIRST CDN
XXXX
SECOND BR
Deurne
FIRST PRCHT
ARMY
Niers R
R U H R
Wesel
Lippe R
Ruhr R

ANTWERP
Venlo
Roermond
H
XXXXX
B
DÜSSELDORF
München-Gladbach
Schelde R

BRUSSELS
21
XXXXX
12
Maeseyck
FIRTEENTH
ARMY
COLOGNE
Roer R
Jülich
Sieg R
Erft R

NINTH
XXXX
FIRST
Maastricht
AACHEN
HÜRTGEN FOREST
Düren
Bonn
Rhine R

LIEGE
XXXX
SIXTH PZ
ARMY
Münstereifel
Remagen
Sinzig

Sambre R Namur
Meuse R
Huy
Malmédy
E
I
F
E
L
Blankenheim
Mayen
Mosel R

Givet
St Vith
FIFTH PZ
ARMY

A
R
D
E
N
N
E
S
Bastogne
Bitburg
XXXX
Wittlich
SEVENTH
ARMY
Mosel R
Bollendorf
TRIER
XXXX
G

Meuse R
LUXEMBOURG
FIRST ARMY
Nennig

FIRST
XXXX
THIRD
Hilbringen
S A A R
Saarlautern
Saar R
SAARBRÜCKEN
Thionville
METZ
Sarreguemines
Bitche

**THE SIEGFRIED LINE
CAMPAIGN**
11 September–15 December 1944

—————— FRONT LINE, 11 SEPTEMBER
—————— FRONT LINE, 15 DECEMBER
|||||||||||| WEST WALL

All boundaries as of 15 December

1 0 1 2 3 MILES
1 0 1 2 3 KILOMETERS

The Ardennes: Battle of the Bulge

December 1944–January 1945

THESE MAPS DEPICT THE GERMANS' ONLY MAJOR counterattack on the Western Front. By September 1944, the Germans had strengthened their border defenses. Hitler now sought a way to strike at the Allies with his remaining strength and resources. His focus settled on the Ardennes, the same place Germany had chosen to attack France and Britain at the start of the war. Because the Allies were weakly defending the area, it was an ideal attack site. Hitler's objective was Antwerp, the Allies' crucial—and lightly held—supply port.

By this time, U.S. intelligence was aware of the disappearance of Fifth and Sixth Panzer Armies and of the movement of trains and supplies toward the Ardennes. Patton suspected that the Germans had a plan afoot and had his staff create contingency plans to meet it. Other Allied commanders, though, were oblivious to what was happening, believing the Germans incapable of a major offensive.

Thinly scattered along the Allied front in the Ardennes were U.S. VII Corps and the 4th, 106th, and 28th Infantry Divisions. On the German side were General Sepp Dietrich's Sixth SS Panzer Army and General Hasso von Manteuffel's Fifth Panzer Army. The Germans had a three-to-one advantage in manpower and a two-to-one advantage in tanks.

On December 16, before dawn, the Germans bombarded U.S. positions in the Ardennes between Monschau and Echternach. Several hours later, armored and infantry columns assailed American positions along four axes of advance leading toward the Meuse River. Mist and rain prevented the Allied air forces from intervening. The U.S. 99th and 2d Infantry Divisions resisted the attack vigorously, the latter defending its positions on Eisenborn Ridge and refusing to retreat for three days. Some American units broke, but others continued to blow up bridges and rain down artillery fire on the advancing Germans until finally forced to retire.

Eisenhower rushed two armored divisions and the 101st and 82d Airborne Divisions to the front. By December 19, The 101st Airborne had relieved the surrounded Bastogne garrison, which had refused to retreat or surrender. By Christmas, the Germans had failed to reach the Meuse, and were forced to retreat under devastating air and ground fire. Patton's suggestion that the bulge be closed up from the southern shoulder and the German Army destroyed or captured failed to ignite support. The Americans suffered 81,000 casualties in the Ardennes, but the Germans lost 100,000 men and 800 tanks—losses they could ill afford.

LEFT: *A column of American troops wearing full field packs and wielding M1 Garand rifles marches down a snowy lane in the Ardennes Forest during the Battle of the Bulge. Many of the troops suffered from severe frostbite and others simply froze to death while valiantly resisting a concentrated German attack along their weakly manned front.* OPPOSITE PAGE INSET: *During the Battle of the Bulge, General Dwight D. Eisenhower assigned Field Marshal Bernard Montgomery, commander, 21st Army Group, to operational command of two U.S. armies. Montgomery is shown here with four of his commanders during the campaign (from left to right): Lieutenant General Miles Dempsey, British Second Army; Lieutenant General Courtney Hodges, U.S. First Army; Field Marshal Montgomery; Lieutenant General W.H. Simpson, U.S. Ninth Army; and Lieutenant General H.D.G. Crerar, Canadian First Army.* LEFT INSET: *German soldiers carry heavy ammunition boxes during the Battle of the Bulge. In December 1944, a powerful German offensive drove into the Ardennes Forest, its ultimate objective being the capture of the port city of Antwerp, Belgium. The offensive was ultimately repulsed, denying Germany some of its last precious resources. Sadly, the campaign exacted a devastating toll in human life, with nearly 190,000 soldiers dying on both sides.*

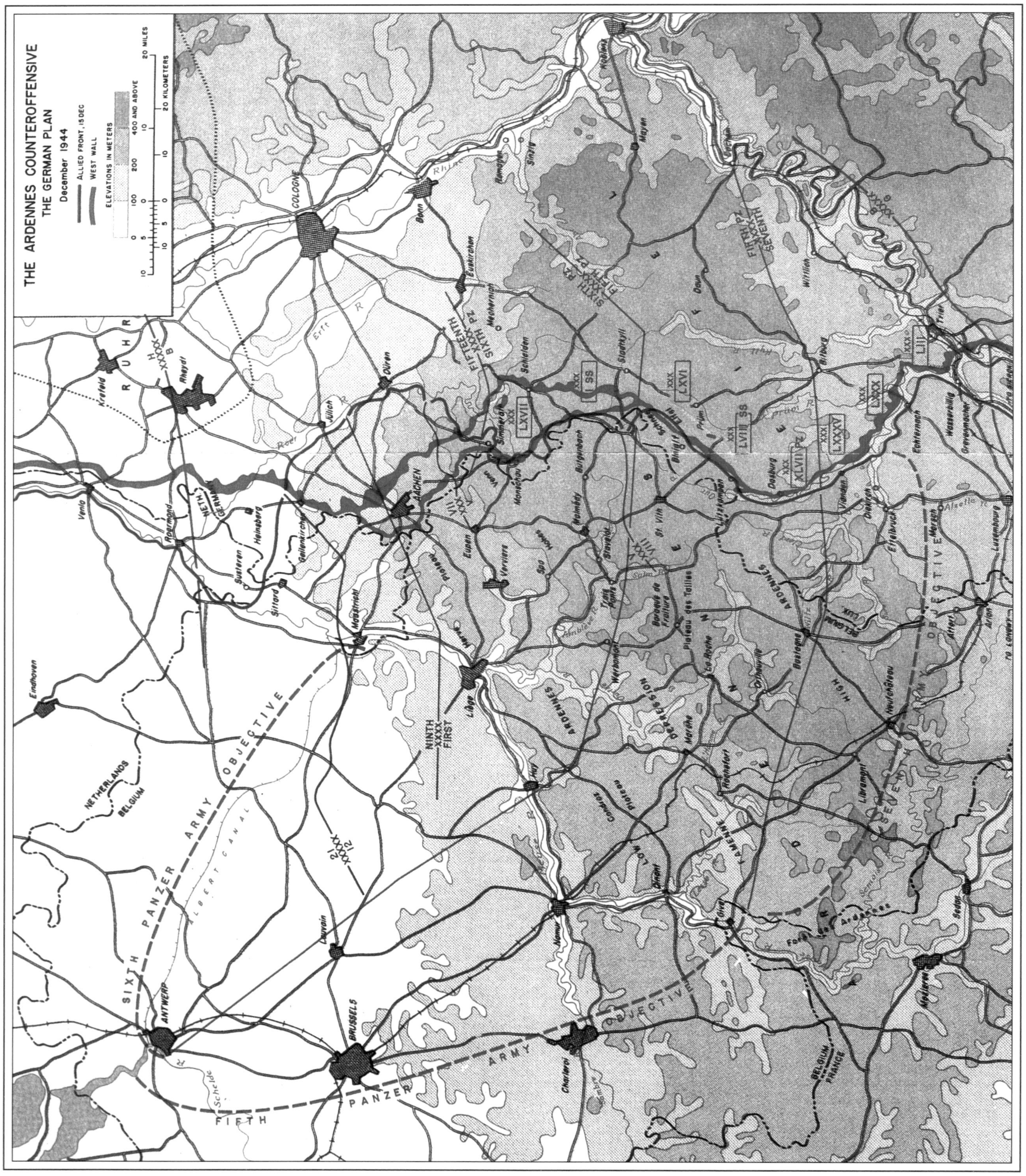
THE ARDENNES COUNTEROFFENSIVE
THE GERMAN PLAN
December 1944
ALLIED FRONT, 15 DEC
WEST WALL
ELEVATIONS IN METERS
0
100
200
400 AND ABOVE
MILES
KILOMETERS
COLOGNE
AACHEN
ANTWERP
BRUSSELS
SIXTH PANZER ARMY OBJECTIVE
FIFTH PANZER ARMY OBJECTIVE
NINTH
FIRST
Bonn
Düren
Liège
Namur
Charleroi
Louvain
Eindhoven
Venlo
Maastricht
St. Vith
Bastogne
NETHERLANDS
BELGIUM
FRANCE
ARDENNES
SIXTH
FIFTEENTH
SEVENTH
LXVII
LXVI
LVIII
XLVII
LXXXV
LXXX
LIII
Trier
Koblenz

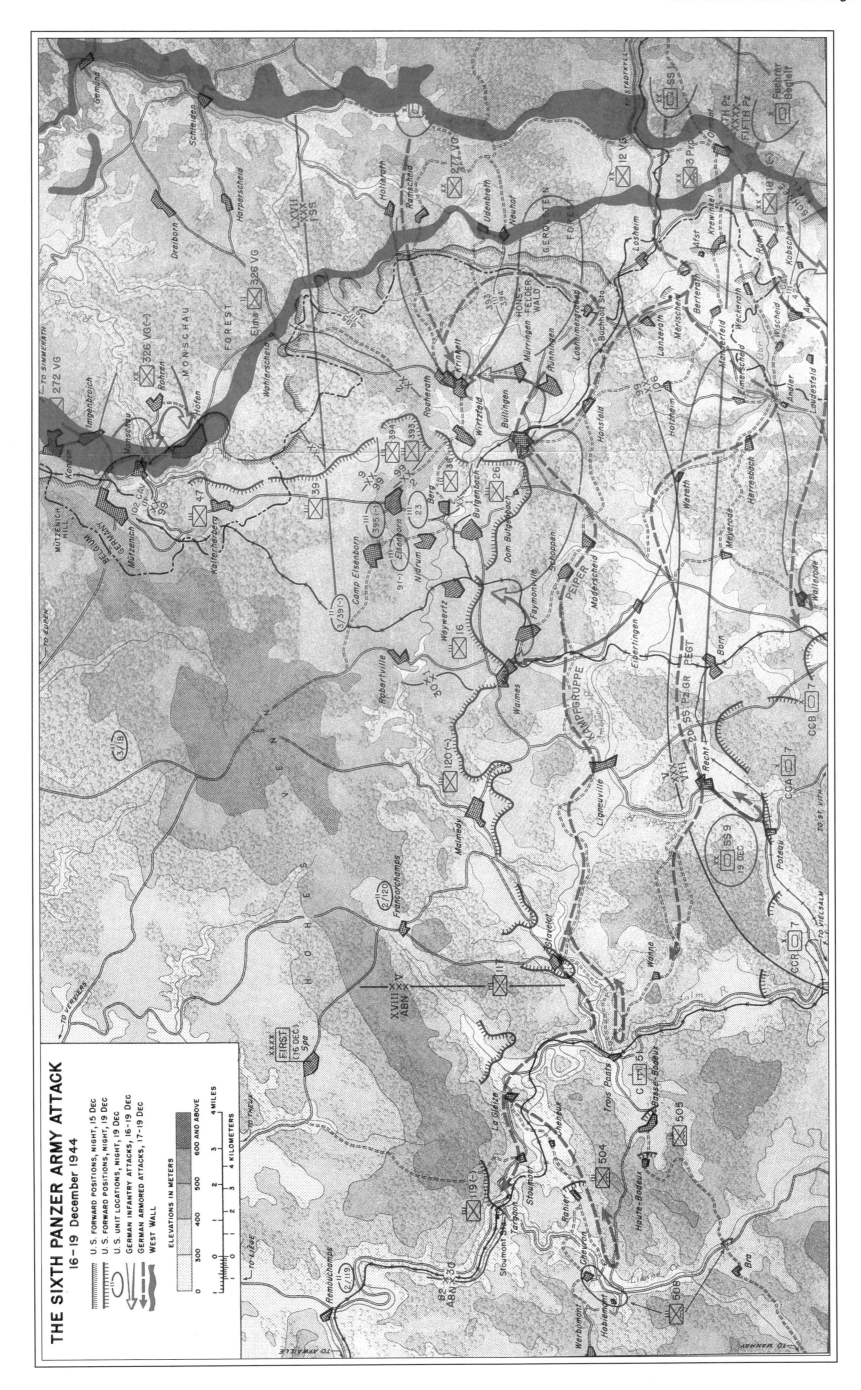

THE SIXTH PANZER ARMY ATTACK
16–19 December 1944

U.S. FORWARD POSITIONS, NIGHT, 15 DEC
U.S. FORWARD POSITIONS, NIGHT, 19 DEC
U.S. UNIT LOCATIONS, NIGHT, 19 DEC
GERMAN INFANTRY ATTACKS, 16–19 DEC
GERMAN ARMORED ATTACKS, 17–19 DEC
WEST WALL

ELEVATIONS IN METERS

| 0 | 300 | 400 | 500 | 600 AND ABOVE |

0   1   2   3   4 MILES
0   1   2   3   4 KILOMETERS

THE LXVI CORPS ATTACKS
THE 106TH INFANTRY DIVISION

16–19 December 1944

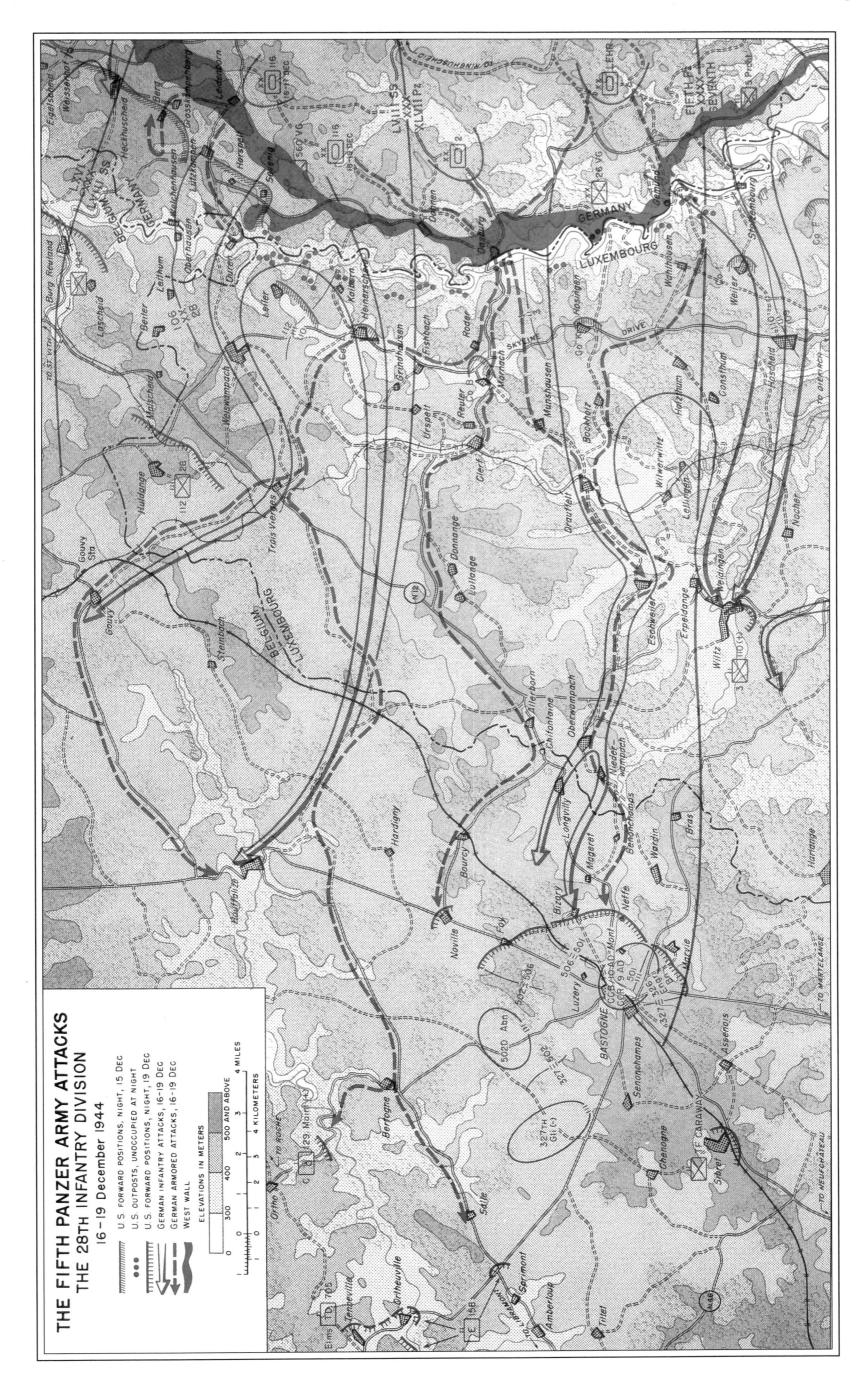

THE FIFTH PANZER ARMY ATTACKS
THE 28TH INFANTRY DIVISION
16–19 December 1944

U.S. FORWARD POSITIONS, NIGHT, 15 DEC
U.S. OUTPOSTS, UNOCCUPIED AT NIGHT
U.S. FORWARD POSITIONS, NIGHT, 19 DEC
GERMAN INFANTRY ATTACKS, 16-19 DEC
GERMAN ARMORED ATTACKS, 16-19 DEC
WEST WALL

ELEVATIONS IN METERS

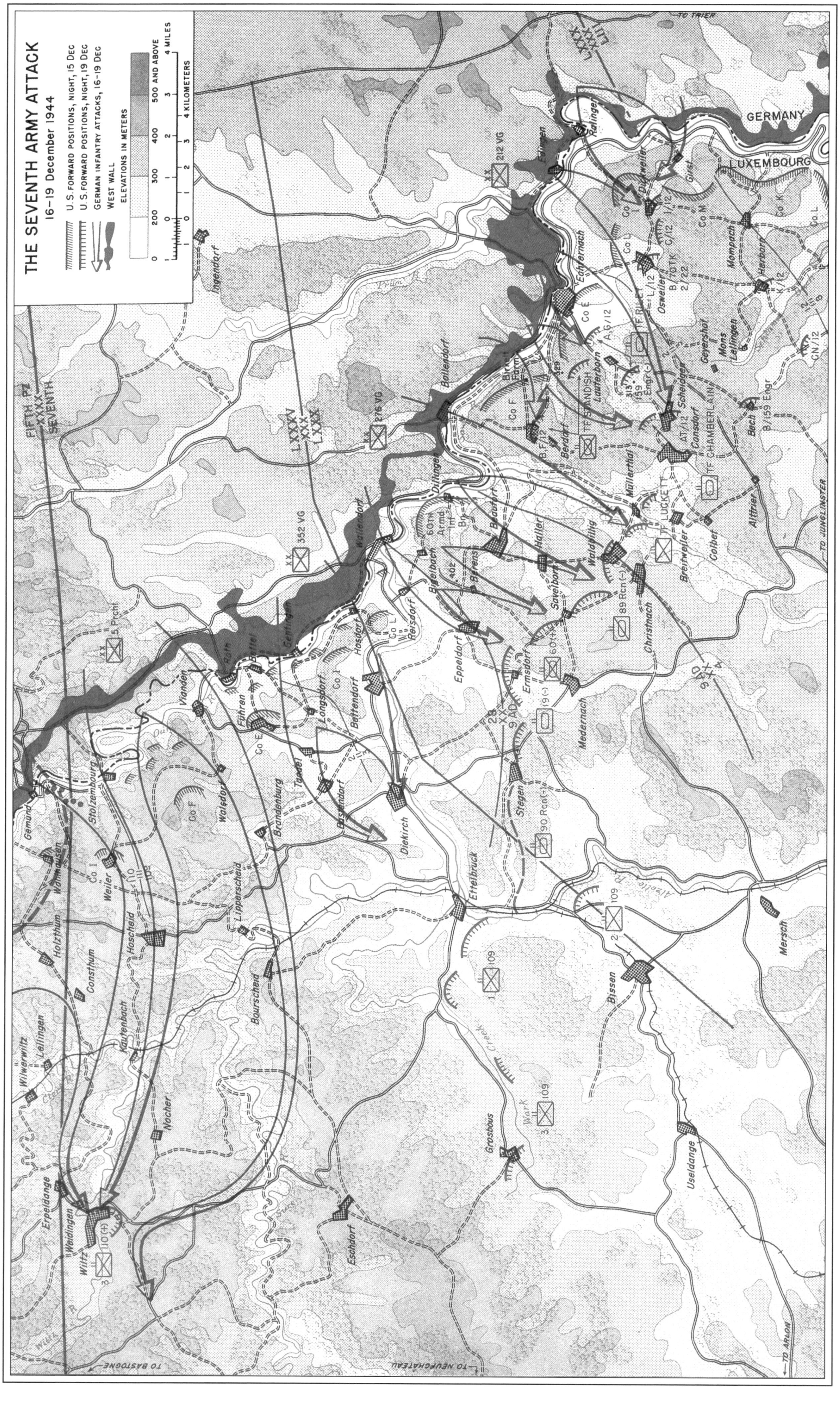

THE SEVENTH ARMY ATTACK
16–19 December 1944
U.S. FORWARD POSITIONS, NIGHT, 15 DEC
U.S. FORWARD POSITIONS, NIGHT, 19 DEC
GERMAN INFANTRY ATTACKS, 16–19 DEC
WEST WALL
ELEVATIONS IN METERS
0 200 300 400 500 AND ABOVE
0 1 2 3 4 MILES
0 1 2 3 4 KILOMETERS
GERMANY
LUXEMBOURG
TO TRIER
TO JUNGLINSTER
TO ARLON
TO NEUFCHATEAU
TO BASTOGNE
Echternach
Bollendorf
Wallendorf
Dillingen
Beaufort
Diekirch
Ettelbruck
Bissen
Mersch
Wiltz
Vianden
Eschdorf
Grosbous
Useldange
Christnach
Medernach
Eppeldorf
Ermsdorf
Stegen
Consdorf
Scheidgen
Lauterborn
Osweiler
Dickweiler
Girst
Herborn
Mompach
Bech
Altrier
Colbet
Breitweiler
Müllerthal
Waldbillig
Savelborn
Haller
Berdorf
Reisdorf
Bigelbach
Hoesdorf
Longsdorf
Bettendorf
Tandel
Fuhren
Brandenburg
Bastendorf
Walsdorf
Stolzembourg
Gemünd
Weiler
Hoscheid
Consthum
Holzthum
Lipperscheid
Bourscheid
Kautenbach
Lellingen
Wilwerwiltz
Nocher
Erpeldange
Weidingen
Ingendorf
Ralingen
Edingen
FIFTH PZ
SEVENTH
212 VG
276 VG
352 VG
5 Prcht
TF CHAMBERLAIN
TF LUCKETT
TF RILEY
TF STANDISH
89 Rcn (-)
60 (+)
19 (-)
90 Rcn (-)
109
110 (+)
9 AD

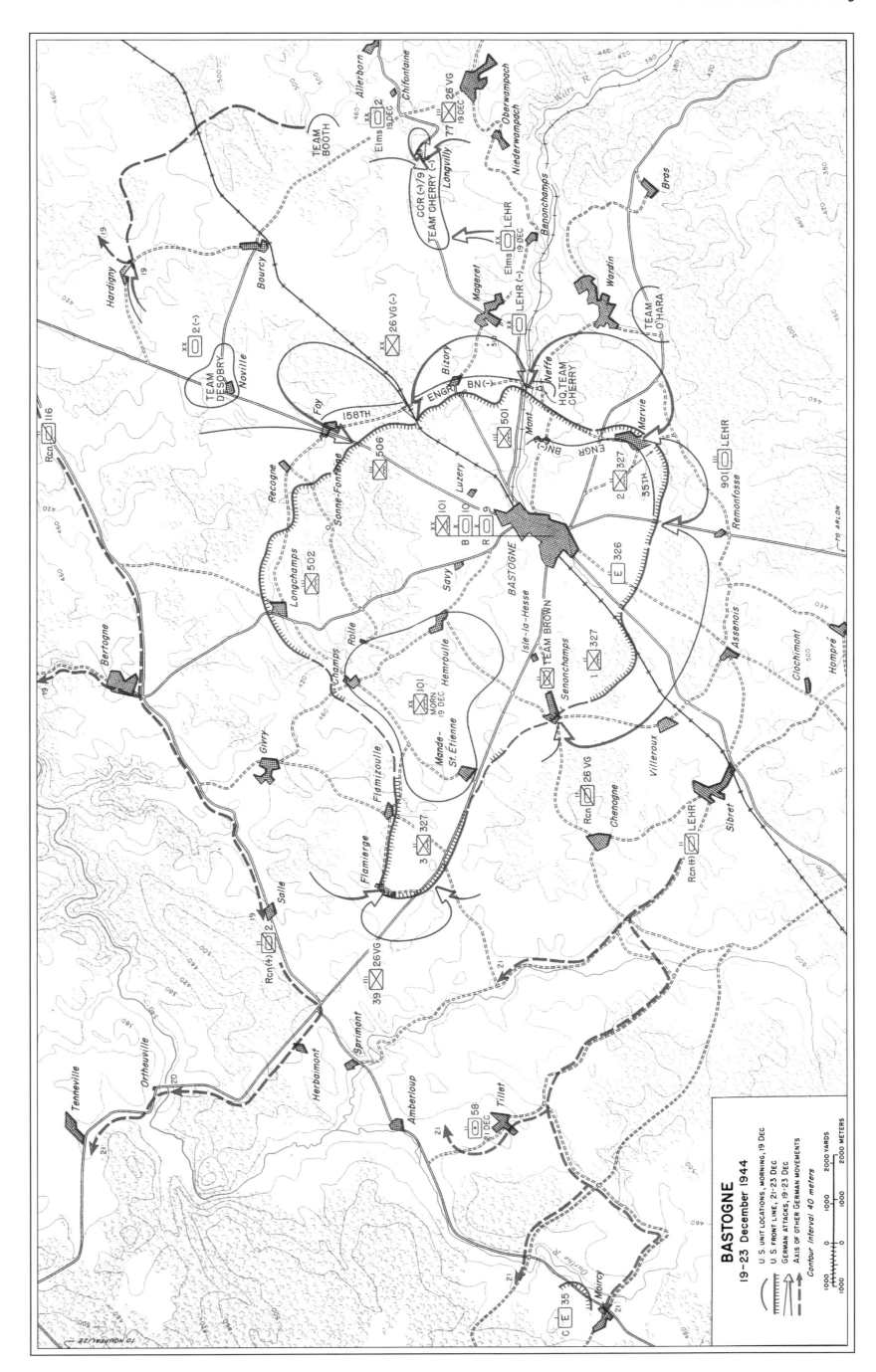

BASTOGNE

19–23 December 1944

U.S. UNIT LOCATIONS, MORNING, 19 DEC
U.S. FRONT LINE, 21–23 DEC
GERMAN ATTACKS, 19–23 DEC
AXIS OF OTHER GERMAN MOVEMENTS

Contour Interval 40 meters

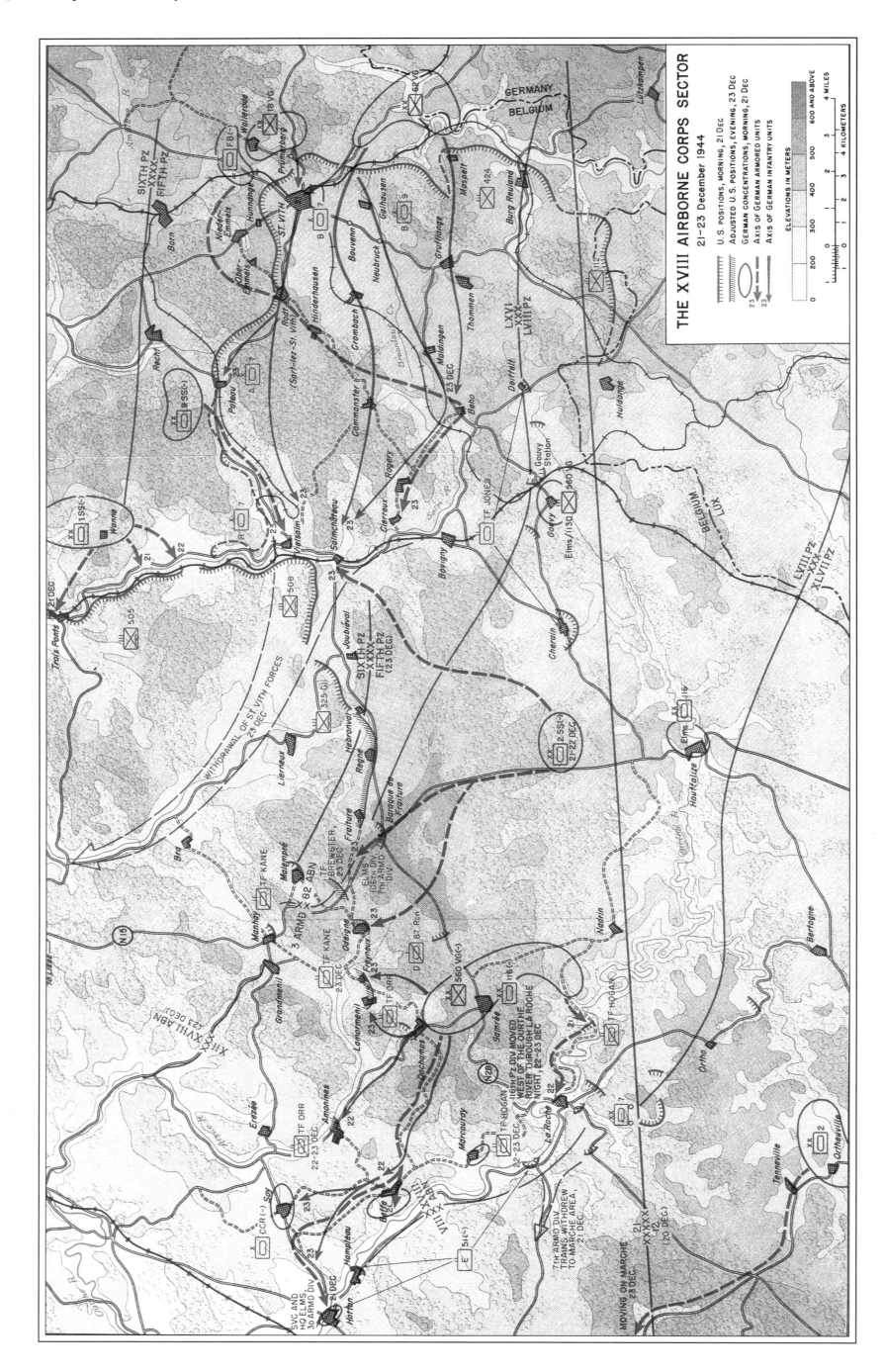

THE XVIII AIRBORNE CORPS SECTOR

21–23 December 1944

U.S. POSITIONS, MORNING, 21 DEC
ADJUSTED U.S. POSITIONS, EVENING, 23 DEC
GERMAN CONCENTRATIONS, MORNING, 21 DEC
AXIS OF GERMAN ARMORED UNITS
AXIS OF GERMAN INFANTRY UNITS

ELEVATIONS IN METERS

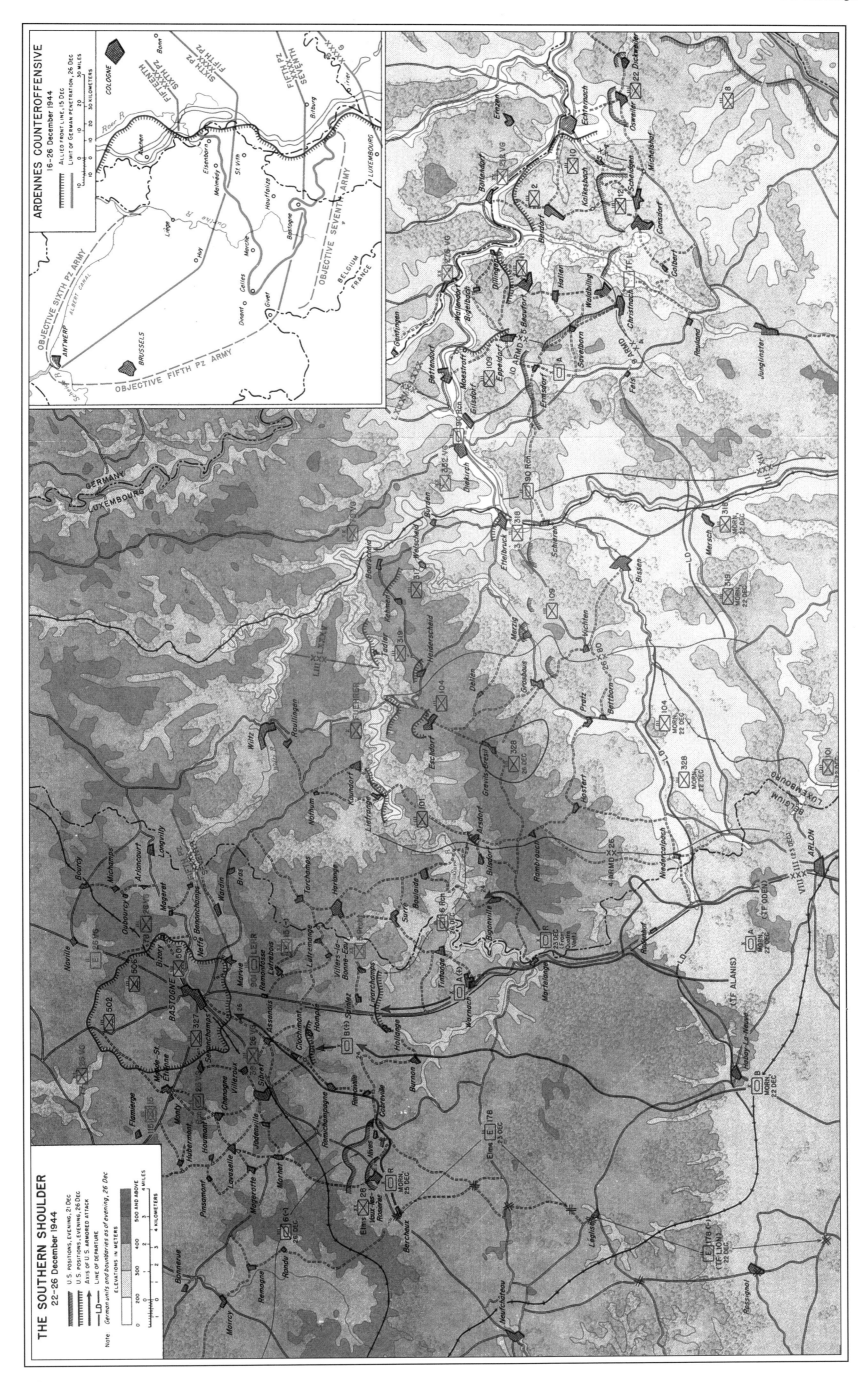

THE SOUTHERN SHOULDER
22–26 December 1944

ELEVATIONS IN METERS

ARDENNES COUNTEROFFENSIVE
16–26 December 1944

TO NAMUR
TO ANDENNE
TO HUY
TO LIÈGE
BR GUARDS
27 DEC
24 DEC
27 DEC
Moressée
B 2
Morn, 25 DEC
Ciney
N4
Pessoux
Baillonville
Achêne
Leignon
3 ROYAL
BR 29
24-27 DEC
82 Rcn(-)
Morn, 25 DEC
Dinant
Foy-Notre Dame
Bois de Geauvelant
Le Houisse
A 2
Morn, 24 DEC
2 ARMD
84
Haversin
24 4
Morn, 24 DEC
R(+) 2
25-26 DEC
Hogne
Conneux
Conjoux
Rcn 2
Haid
Boisselles
Celles
Petite Trisogne
Grande Trisogne
BR 53
27 DEC
Custinne
25-26
304(+) 2
Buissonville
Jamodenne
Marche
335
Meuse R.
Havrenne
Humain
Marloie
Hedree
9(-)
(Relieved forces at Hargimont and Humain, 25-26 DEC)
2(-)
24-25 DEC
Hargimont
Harsin
3(-) 2
(From Hargimont)
4 4
27 DEC
Ciergnon
Bois de Fomenne
T F A
T F B
A M E N N E
F A M E N N E
23 HUSSARS
BR 29
25-27 DEC
BELGIUM
FRANCE
Wanlin
Lesse R.
Rochefort
3(-) 335
Jemelle
LEHR(-)
XLVII Pz CORPS
Givet
21
XXXXX
12
FIRST
XXXX
THIRD
1 333
(Withdrew, 24-25 DEC)
VII
XXX
VIII
Beauraing
Wellin
Grupont
Lhomme
TO SEDAN
TO NEUFCHÂTEAU
TO BOUILLON
TO ST. HUBERT

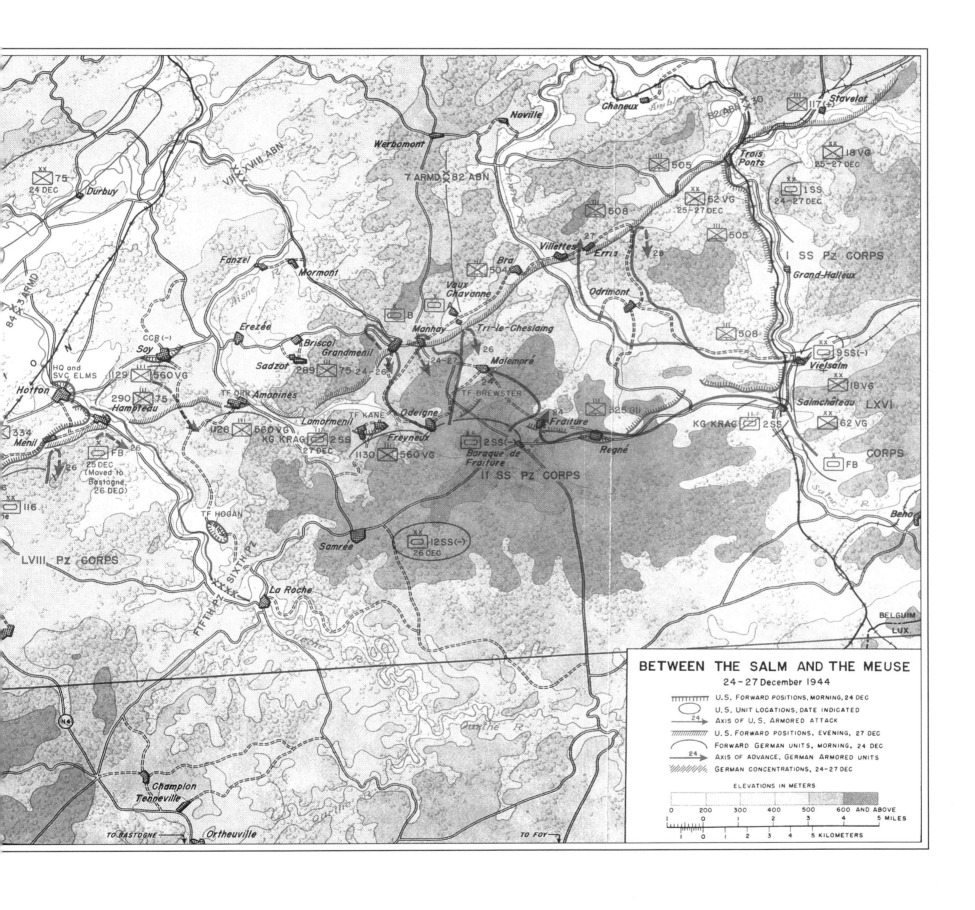

BETWEEN THE SALM AND THE MEUSE
24–27 December 1944

	U.S. FORWARD POSITIONS, MORNING, 24 DEC
	U.S. UNIT LOCATIONS, DATE INDICATED
24	AXIS OF U.S. ARMORED ATTACK
	U.S. FORWARD POSITIONS, EVENING, 27 DEC
	FORWARD GERMAN UNITS, MORNING, 24 DEC
24	AXIS OF ADVANCE, GERMAN ARMORED UNITS
	GERMAN CONCENTRATIONS, 24–27 DEC

ELEVATIONS IN METERS

0   200   300   400   500   600 AND ABOVE

5 MILES

5 KILOMETERS

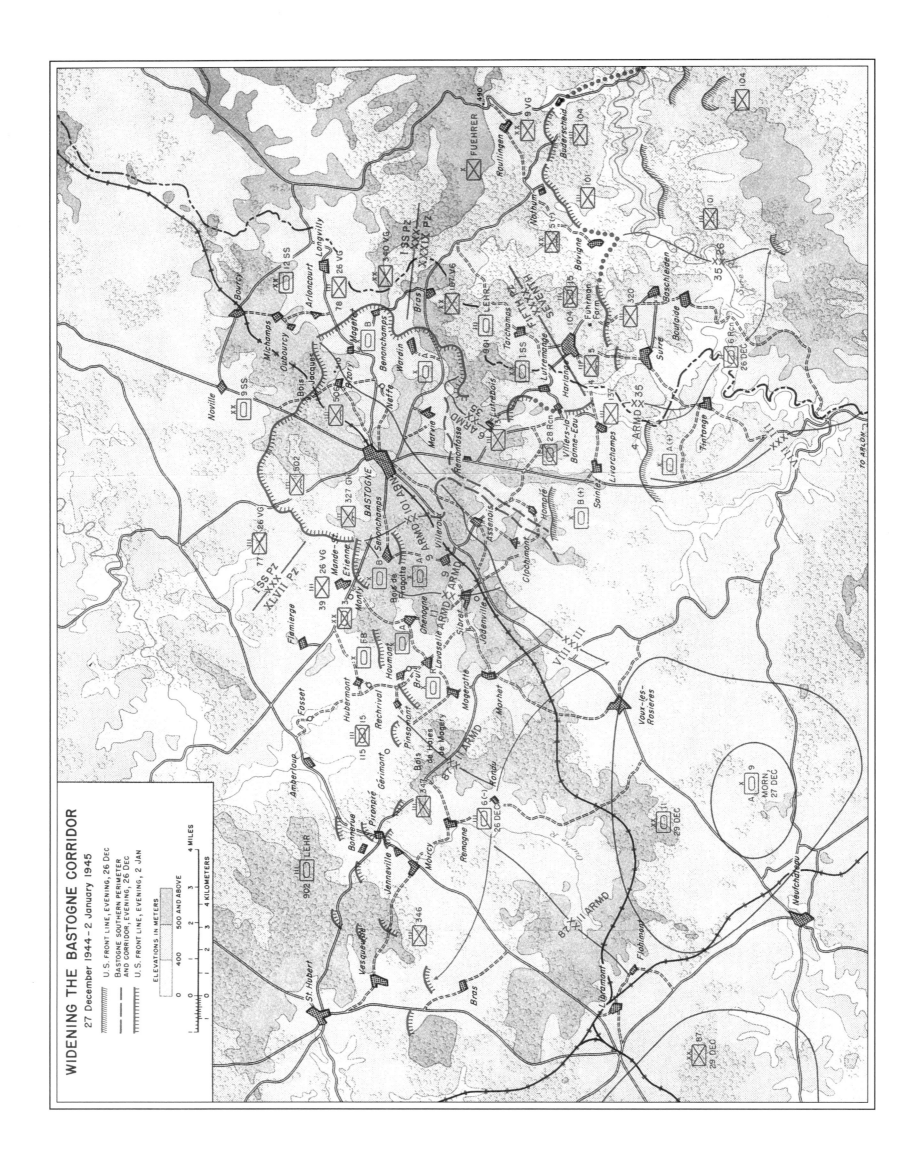

WIDENING THE BASTOGNE CORRIDOR
27 December 1944 – 2 January 1945

ⱭⱭⱭⱭⱭ U.S. FRONT LINE, EVENING, 26 DEC

– – – – BASTOGNE SOUTHERN PERIMETER
AND CORRIDOR, EVENING, 26 DEC

ⱮⱮⱮⱮ U.S. FRONT LINE, EVENING, 2 JAN

ELEVATIONS IN METERS

400   500 AND ABOVE

0   1   2   3   4 KILOMETERS

0   1   2   3   4 MILES

ABOVE LEFT: *U.S. infantrymen crouch in wet snow in the Ardennes Forest as they defend against German attack in the Battle of the Bulge. One of the defenders remarked, "Someday I'm going to live in Florida. I never want to see any more snow…. Try wading in it up to your knees, sleeping in it, eating it, and breathing it for a winter in the Ardennes and you'll know what I mean."* **ABOVE RIGHT:** *Germans advance past a burning American tank at the height of the Battle of the Bulge. An American soldier described the scene: "Then, wham, they hit us. Our line up there in the Ardennes was pretty thin, and the Jerries knew it. Old Von Rundstedt massed a lot of stuff behind the lines and let us have it…. We didn't have many supplies, and we didn't have many men."* **LEFT:** *American military vehicles fight through heavy traffic along a narrow, snow-banked road through the Ardennes Forest. At the other end of the battlefield were similar, backed-up convoys of German tanks and military vehicles carrying armaments, men, and supplies to the German front. General Carl von Clausewitz, an early nineteenth-century German military theorist, described the effects of these sort of ordinary, but sometimes unexpected, delays as the "friction" of war.*

The Riviera to the Rhine

August 15, 1944–February 5, 1945

ON AUGUST 15, 1944, THE ALLIES LAUNCHED AN amphibious attack in southern France along the Riviera near St. Tropez. The operation was code-named Operation Anvil (Dragoon) and was the most successful amphibious operation during the European War. The purpose of the invasion was to focus greater pressure on Germany by establishing a southern front.

Once an aggressive breakout was in full swing, Allied forces captured the French ports of Marseille and Toulon, and an invasion of the Rhone and Saone valleys carried the invaders all the way to Lyon. At that point, the First French Army, commanded by General Jean de Lattre de Tassigny, and the U.S. Seventh Army, led by Lieutenant General Alexander M. Patch, were combined into the 6th Army Group, directed by Lieutenant General Jacob L. Devers. The 6th became the potent southern wing of Eisenhower's Allied army in Europe.

The 6th Army Group was pitted against the German Nineteenth Army, commanded by General Friedrich Wiese. Soon, the 6th struggled its way through the Vosges Mountains, driving the Germans from the Saverne and Belfort gaps. In November, a well-orchestrated offensive brought 6th Army Group to the banks of the Rhine. Meanwhile, General Jacques Leclerc's 2d French Armored Division liberated Strasbourg.

When Patch's Seventh Army was ordered to reinforce the less successful Allied operations in Lorraine and in the Ardennes, however, Dever's army group lost much of its momentum, and the Germans established a stronghold in the city of Colmar and strengthened their resistance in Alsace.

During the Battle of the Bulge, 6th Army Group, in extending its lines northward to support 12th Army Group, had allowed the Germans to take advantage of the longer, weakened U.S. southern front to mount Operation Nordwind, in January 1945. By February, however, after bitter, prolonged fighting in the worst weather, Devers finally stemmed the German counteroffensive, eliminated the Colmar pocket, and destroyed the bulk of the German Nineteenth Army.

LEFT: *An Allied bomber passes over Berlin, Germany, on a bombing mission. One American airman wondered what it would be like when Allied infantrymen finally entered the city (which would at that point be in ruins, in his estimation, after so many onslaughts). The airman remembered taking part in a 1,000-plane assault on the city that lasted forty-five minutes and "dropped about 2,500 tons of incendiaries and high explosives." He also recalled the Allied losses: thirty-five Allied bombers and five fighters.* OPPOSITE INSET: *The city of Cologne, Germany, its famous cathedral in the foreground, looks battered and broken in the wake of the Allies' systematic aerial bombardment. Afterward, many of the city's buildings were mere shells, stark testimonials to the holocaust dropped from the sky. Such bombardments were not without cost to the Allied air forces, which lost a significant percentage of men and planes on each mission. Officers and crews, after flying a relatively small number of missions, were thereafter challenging the odds of remaining alive.* LEFT INSET: *An American flak unit watches a dogfight between German and Allied planes. Arcing contrails lace the sky above, a result of the violent aerial duels. Fighter aircraft generally accompanied Allied bombers on raids, protecting the slower, larger aircraft from the attacks of German fighter pilots who were, in turn, defending vital ground targets.*

WESTERN AND CENTRAL EUROPE
1 September 1939

0 _____ 500

MILES

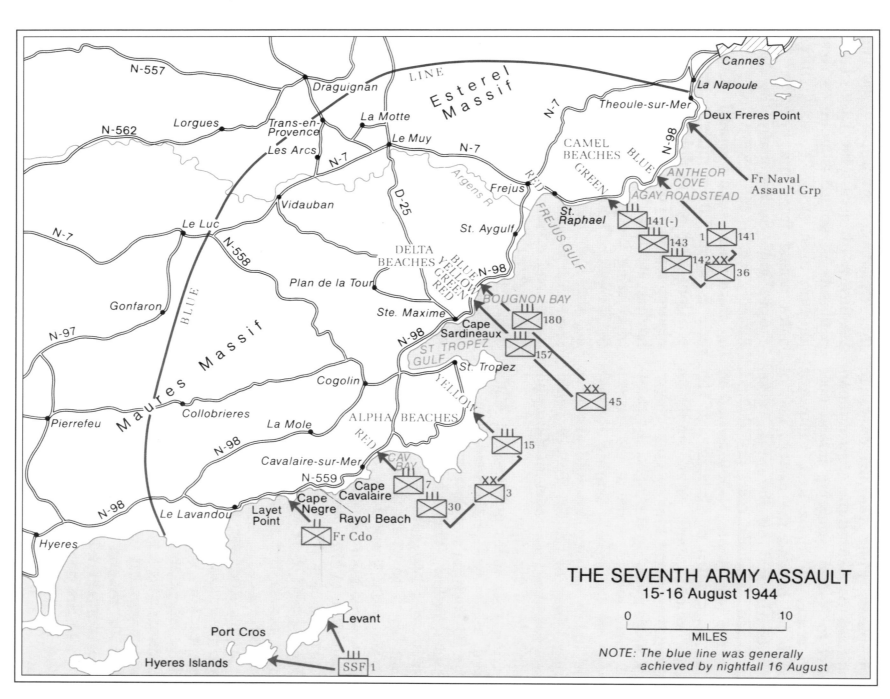

THE SEVENTH ARMY ASSAULT
15-16 August 1944

0 _____ 10

MILES

NOTE: The blue line was generally achieved by nightfall 16 August

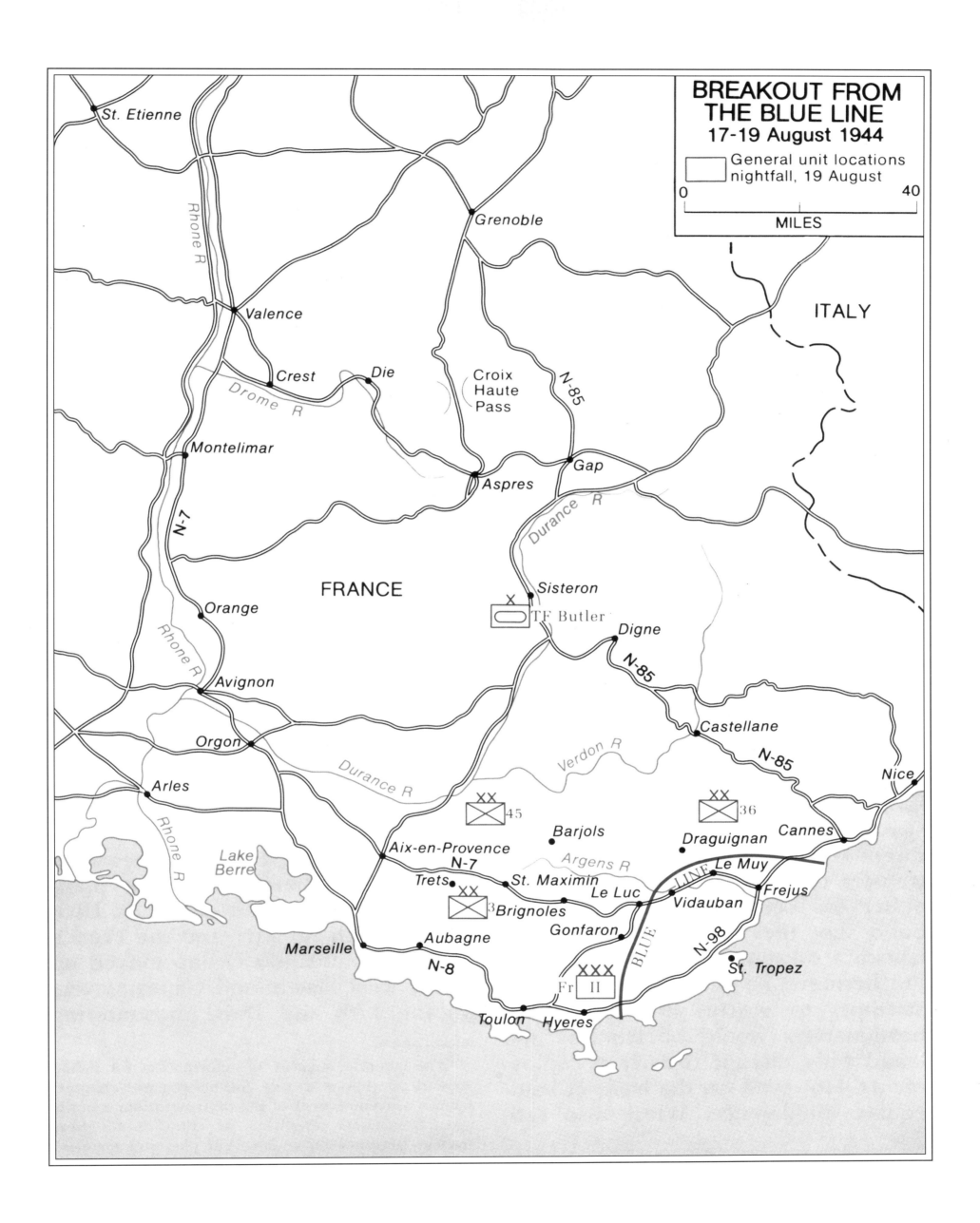

BREAKOUT FROM THE BLUE LINE
17-19 August 1944

General unit locations nightfall, 19 August

0   40

MILES

St. Etienne

Rhone R

Grenoble

Valence

Crest

Die

Croix
Haute
Pass

N-85

Drome R

Montelimar

Gap

Aspres

N-7

Durance R

FRANCE

Sisteron

Orange

TF Butler

Digne

N-85

Rhone R

Avignon

Castellane

N-85

Orgon

Verdon R

Nice

Durance R

Arles

45

36

Barjols

Draguignan

Cannes

Lake
Berre

Aix-en-Provence

Argens R

N-7

Rhone R

Trets

St. Maximin

Le Luc

Le Muy

Frejus

3 Brignoles

Vidauban

BLUE LINE

Gonfaron

Aubagne

N-98

Marseille

N-8

St. Tropez

Fr   II

Toulon

Hyeres

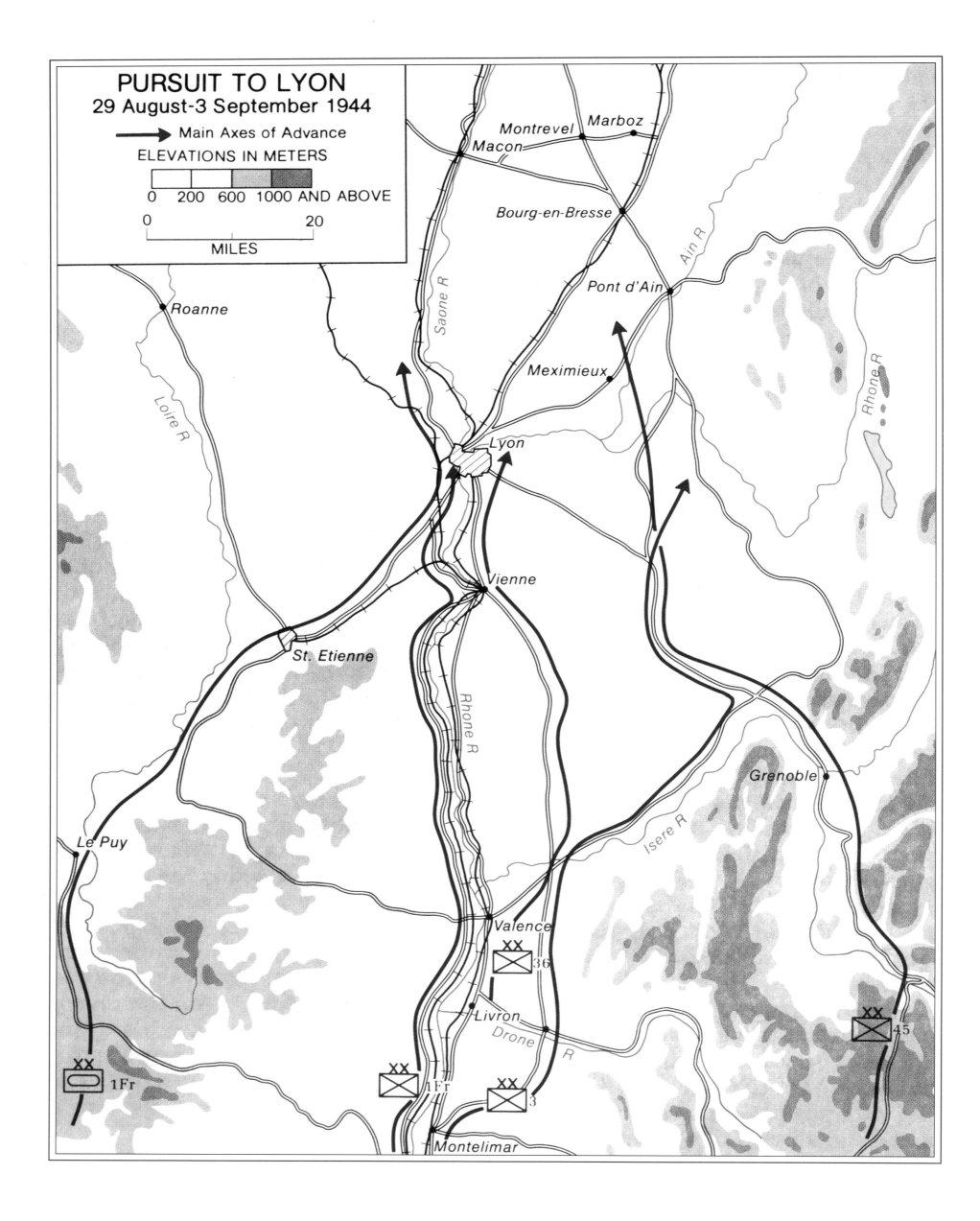

PURSUIT TO LYON
29 August-3 September 1944

→ Main Axes of Advance

ELEVATIONS IN METERS

0   200   600   1000 AND ABOVE

0   20
MILES

Roanne

Montrevel   Marboz
Macon
Saone R
Bourg-en-Bresse
Ain R
Pont d'Ain
Loire R
Meximieux
Rhone R
Lyon
Vienne
St. Etienne
Rhone R
Grenoble
Isere R
Le Puy
Valence
XX 36
Livron
Drone R
1Fr
XX 1Fr
XX 3
XX 45
Montelimar

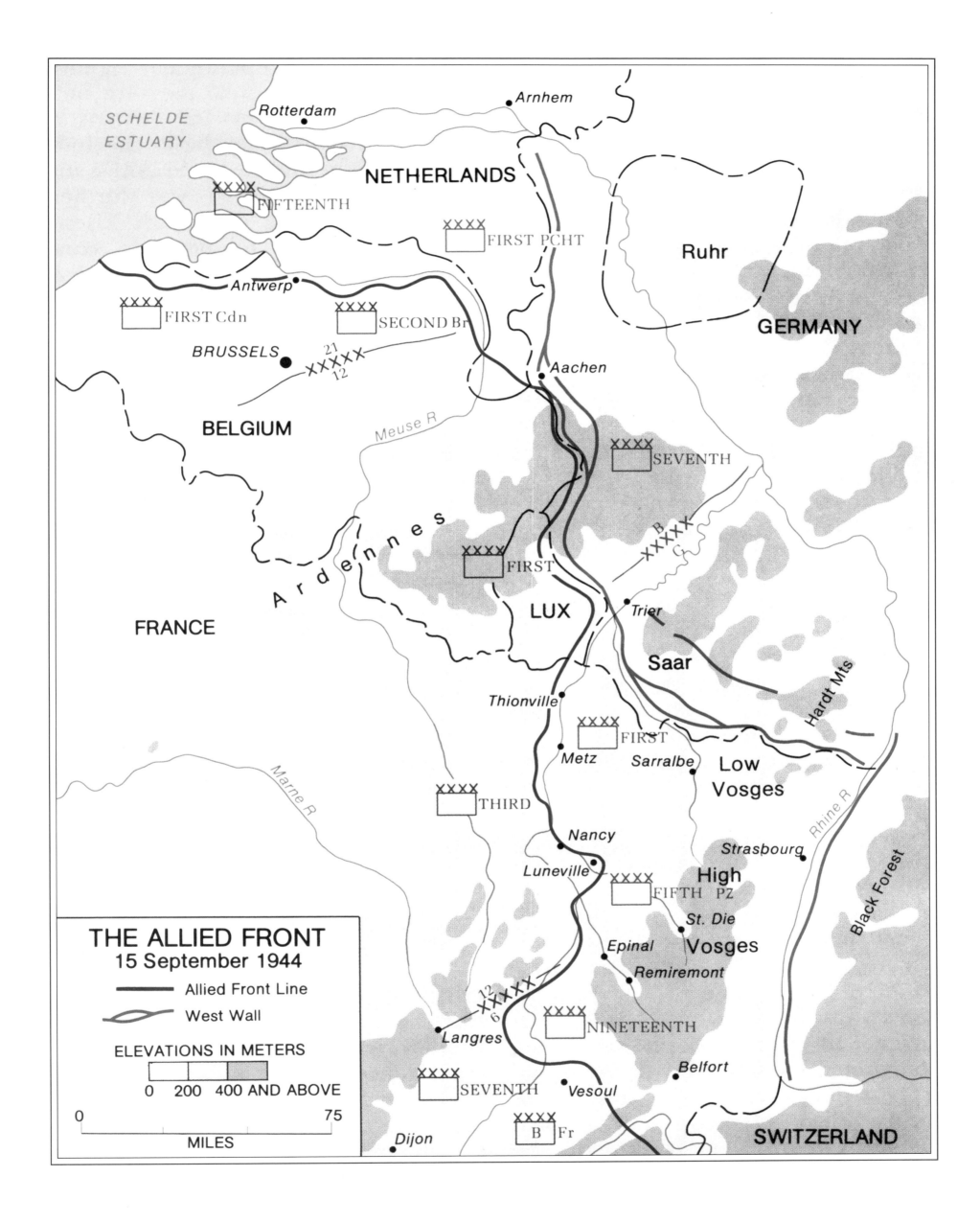

SCHELDE
ESTUARY

Rotterdam

Arnhem

NETHERLANDS

XXXX
FIFTEENTH

XXXX
FIRST PCHT

Ruhr

GERMANY

XXXX
FIRST Cdn

Antwerp

XXXX
SECOND Br

BRUSSELS

XXXXX 21
       12

BELGIUM

Meuse R

Aachen

XXXX
SEVENTH

FRANCE

A r d e n n e s

XXXX
FIRST

LUX

•Trier

B
XXXXX
C

Saar

Hardt Mts

Thionville

XXXX
FIRST

Marne R

•Metz

Sarralbe

Low
Vosges

Rhine R

XXXX
THIRD

Nancy

Strasbourg

Luneville

XXXX
FIFTH PZ

High

St. Die

Vosges

Epinal

Black Forest

Remiremont

THE ALLIED FRONT
15 September 1944

───── Allied Front Line

〜〜〜 West Wall

ELEVATIONS IN METERS

0   200 400 AND ABOVE

0 ──────────────── 75
      MILES

12
XXXXX
6

Langres

XXXX
NINETEENTH

XXXX
SEVENTH

Vesoul

Belfort

XXXX
B Fr

Dijon

SWITZERLAND

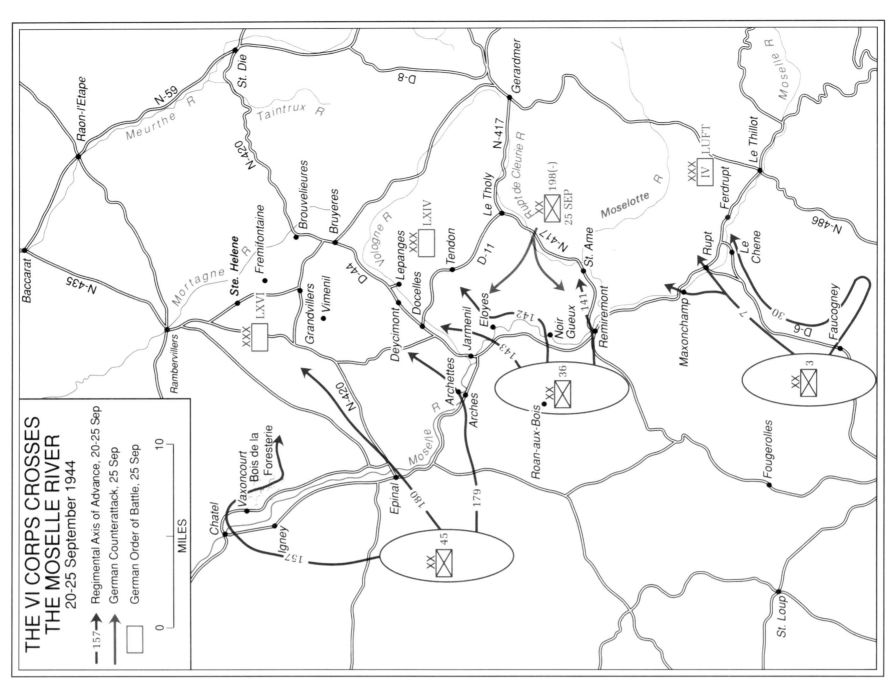

THE VI CORPS CROSSES
THE MOSELLE RIVER
20-25 September 1944

—157→ Regimental Axis of Advance, 20-25 Sep

German Counterattack, 25 Sep

German Order of Battle, 25 Sep

MILES

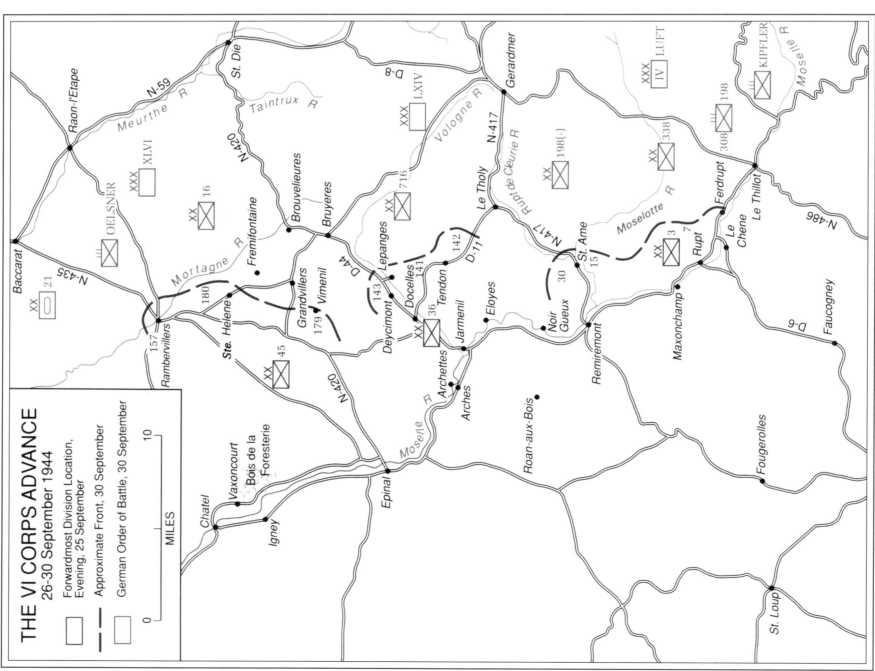

THE VI CORPS ADVANCE
26-30 September 1944

Forwardmost Division Location,
Evening, 25 September

Approximate Front, 30 September

German Order of Battle, 30 September

MILES

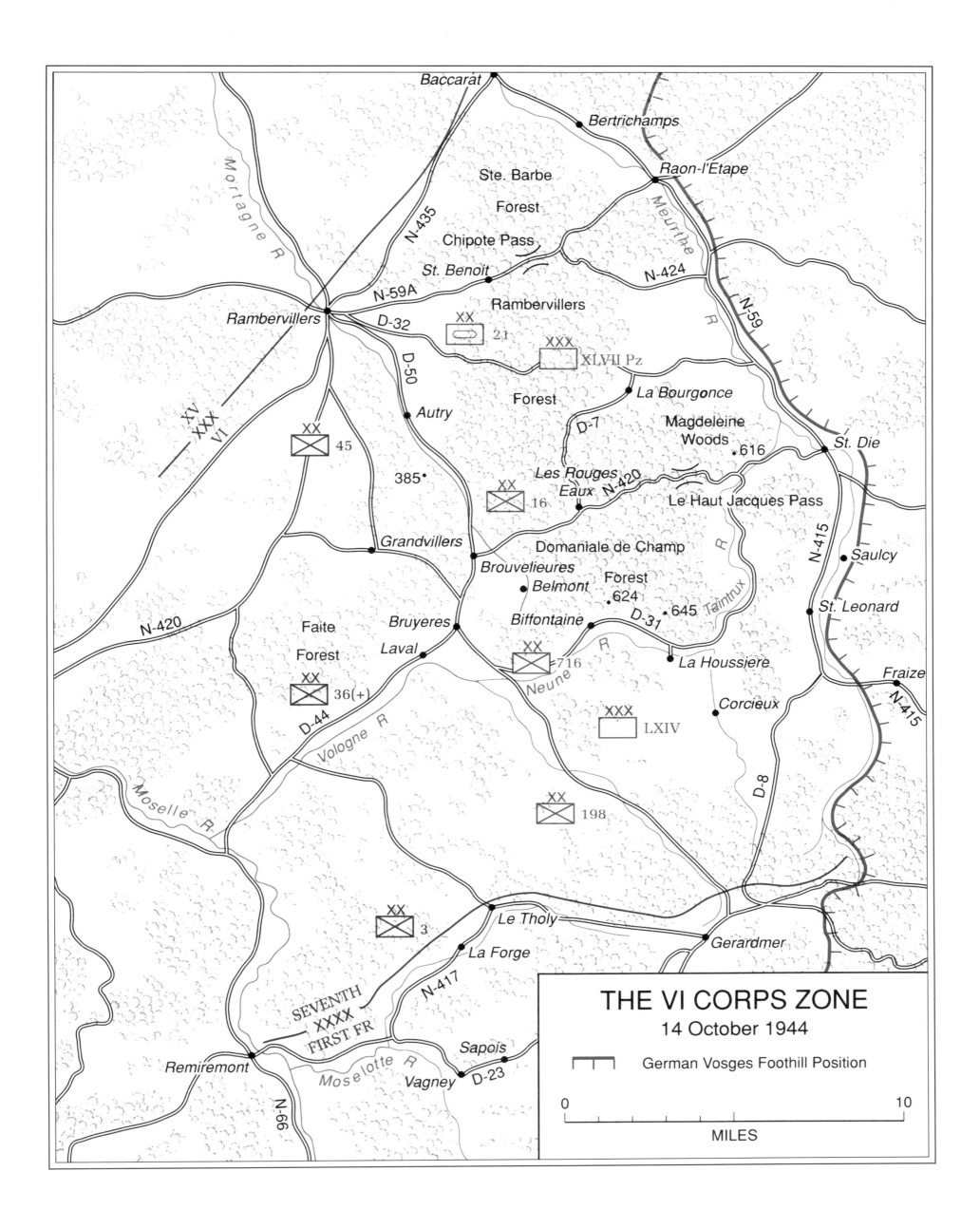

Baccarat

Bertrichamps

Raon-l'Etape

Ste. Barbe
Forest

Chipote Pass

St. Benoit

N-435

N-59A

Rambervillers

D-32

D-50

N-424

N-59

Meurthe R

XX 21

XXX XLVII Pz

La Bourgonce

D-7

Forest

Magdeleine Woods

.616

St. Die

Autry

XX 45

385.

Les Rouges Eaux

N-420

Le Haut Jacques Pass

N-415

Saulcy

XX 16

Grandvillers

Domaniale de Champ

Brouvelieures

Belmont

Forest
.624

.645

D-31

Taintrux

St. Leonard

Faite Forest

Bruyeres

Laval

Biffontaine

Corcieux

Fraize

N-415

N-420

XV XXX VI

XX 36(+)

D-44

Vologne R

XX 716

Neune R

La Houssiere

XXX LXIV

D-8

Moselle R

XX 198

XX 3

Le Tholy

Gerardmer

La Forge

N-417

SEVENTH XXXX FIRST FR

Sapois

D-23

Remiremont

N-66

Moselotte R

Vagney

THE VI CORPS ZONE
14 October 1944

German Vosges Foothill Position

0   10

MILES

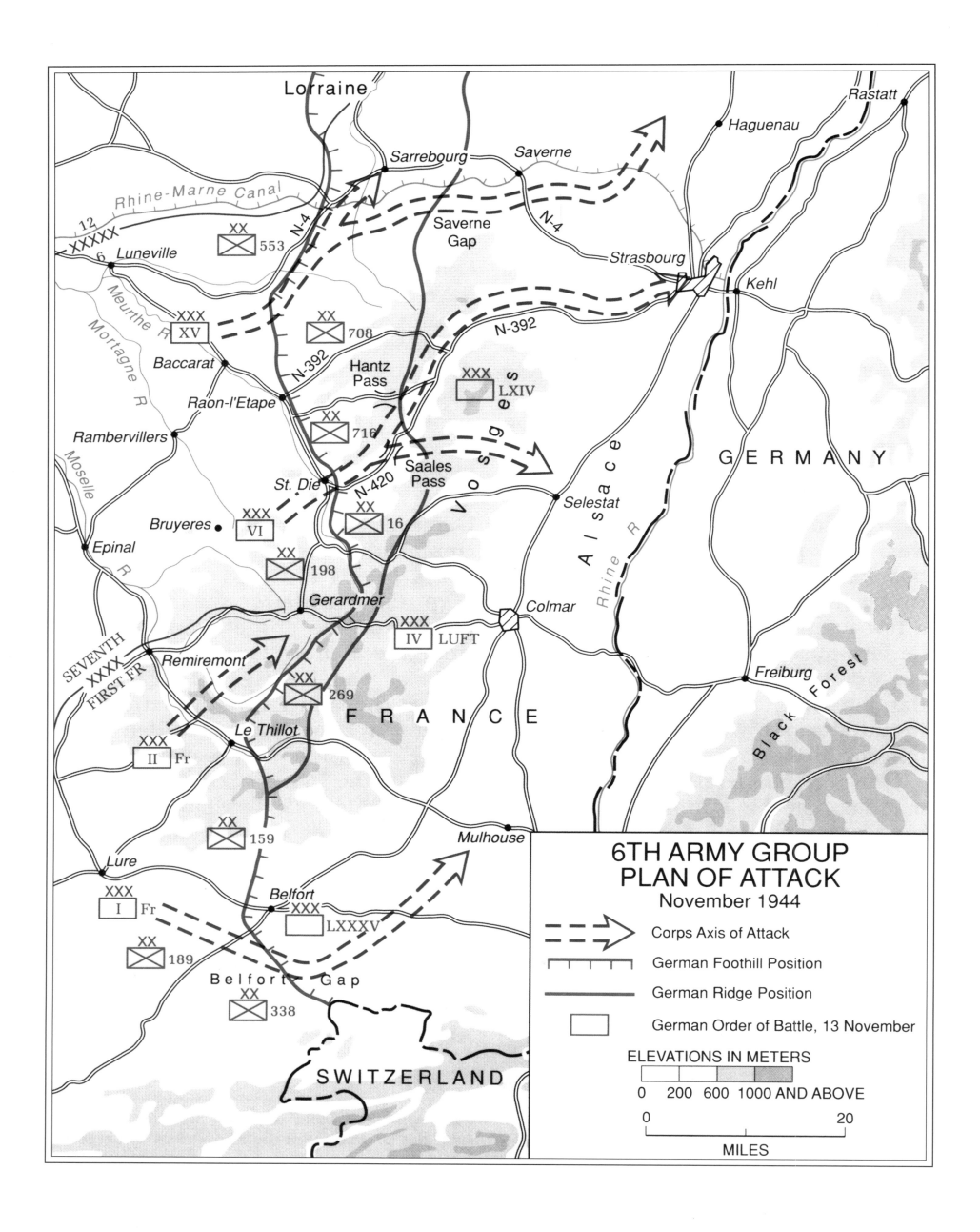

Lorraine

Rastatt

Haguenau

Sarrebourg *Saverne*

Rhine-Marne Canal

12

XXXXX

6 Luneville

XX 553

N-4

Saverne
Gap

N-4

Strasbourg

Kehl

XXX

XV

XX 708

N-392

Baccarat

N-392

Hantz
Pass

XXX

LXIV

Vosges

Raon-l'Etape

Rambervillers

Mortagne R

Meurthe R

XX 716

St. Die

N-420

Saales
Pass

GERMANY

Moselle R

Bruyeres

XXX VI

XX 16

Selestat

Alsace

Rhine R

Epinal

XX 198

Gerardmer

XXX

IV LUFT

Colmar

SEVENTH

XXXX

FIRST FR

Remiremont

XX 269

F R A N C E

Freiburg

Black Forest

Le Thillot

XXX

II Fr

XX 159

Mulhouse

Lure

XXX

I Fr

Belfort

XXX

LXXXV

XX 189

B e l f o r t   G a p

XX 338

S W I T Z E R L A N D

6TH ARMY GROUP
PLAN OF ATTACK
November 1944

⟶ Corps Axis of Attack

⊤⊤⊤⊤⊤ German Foothill Position

——— German Ridge Position

▭ German Order of Battle, 13 November

ELEVATIONS IN METERS

0   200 600 1000 AND ABOVE

0   20

MILES

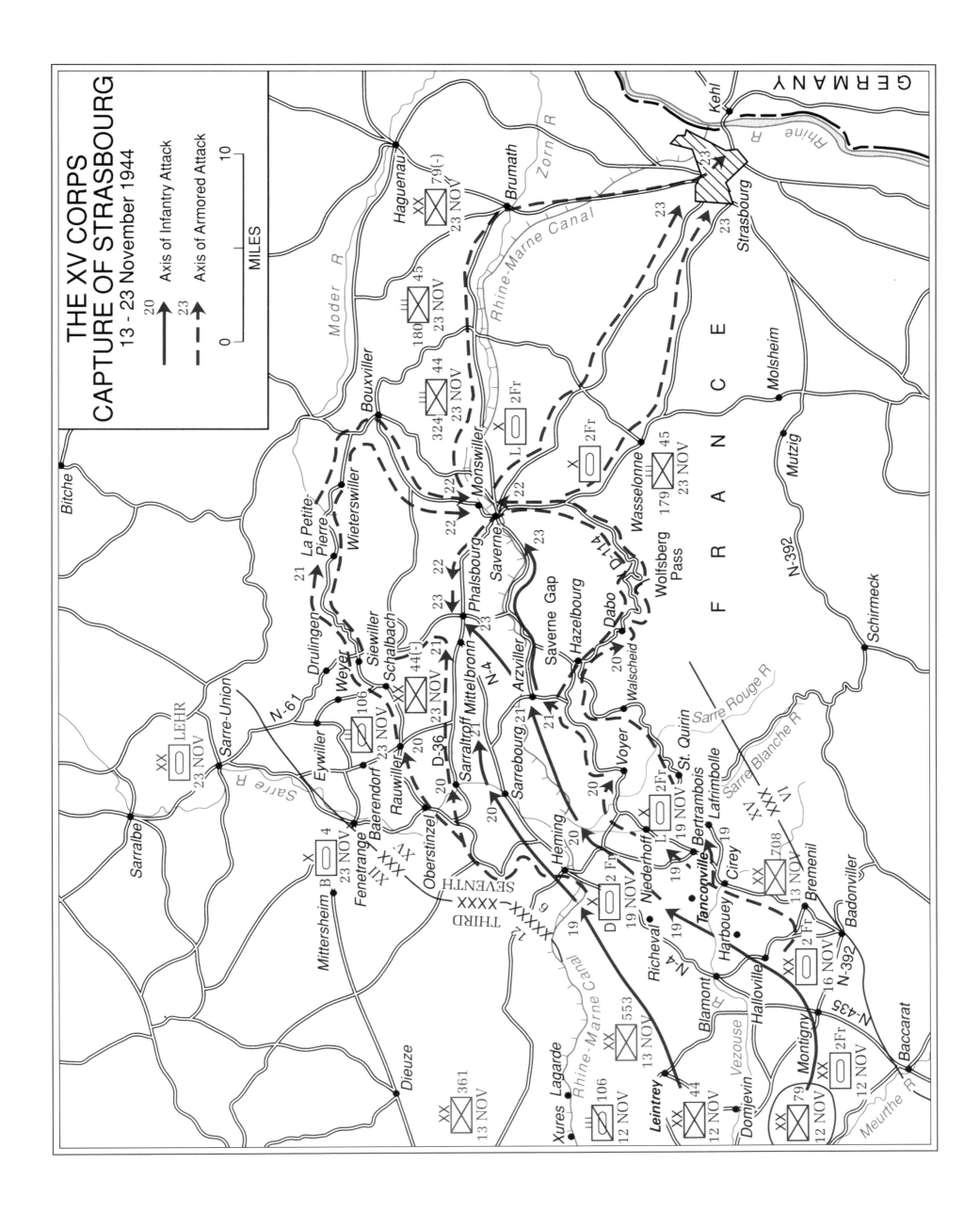

THE XV CORPS
CAPTURE OF STRASBOURG
13 - 23 November 1944

Axis of Infantry Attack

Axis of Armored Attack

MILES

0   10

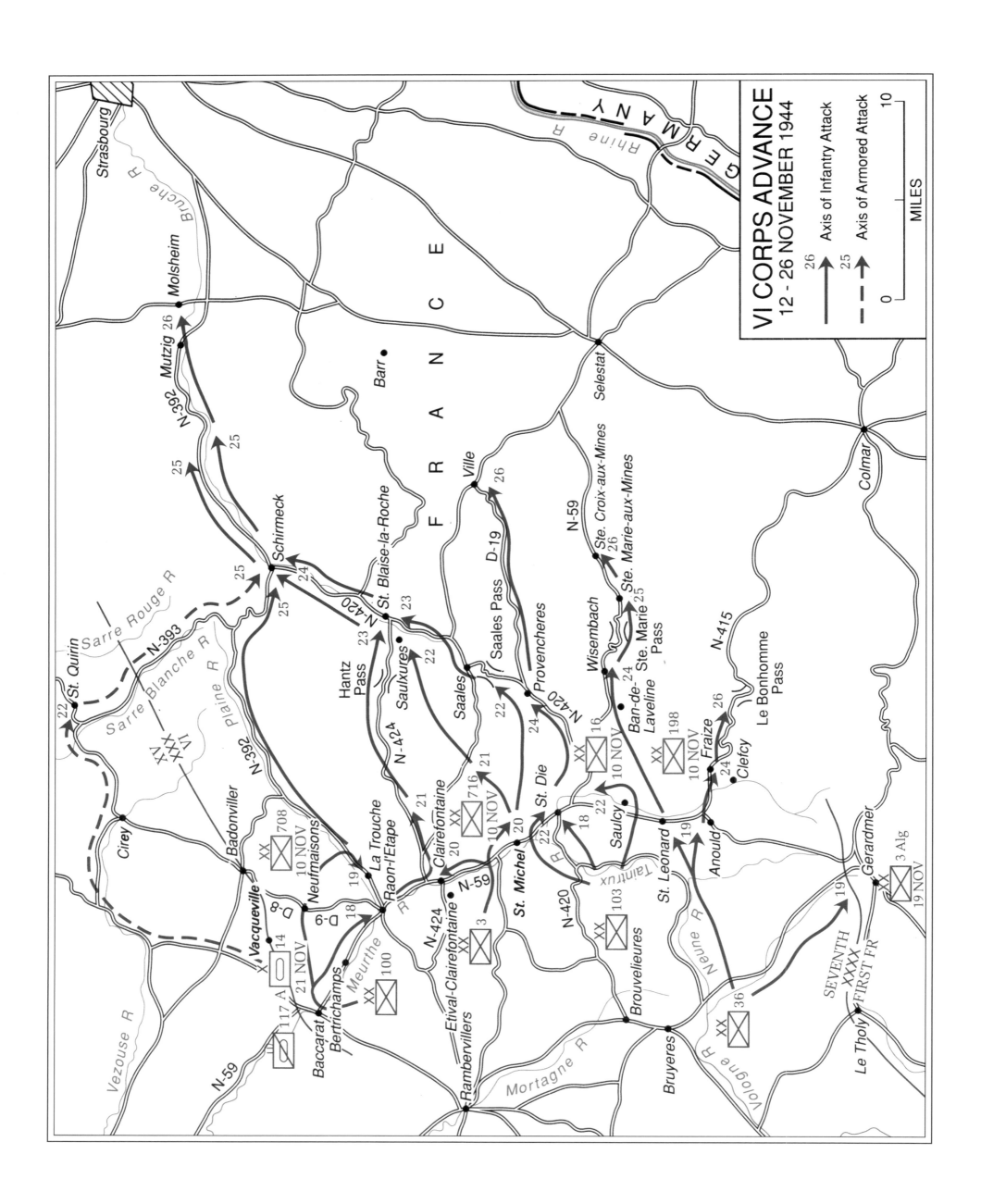

GERMANY

Rhine R

F R A N C E

Strasbourg

Bruche R

Molsheim

Mutzig 26

N-392

25

25

Barr

Schirmeck

25

25

24

St. Blaise-la-Roche

N-420

23

Ville

Selestat

Hantz
Pass

23

Saulxures

D-19

Saales Pass

Saales

26

N-59

Ste. Croix-aux-Mines

26

Sarre Rouge R

St. Quirin

22

N-393

Sarre Blanche R

N-393

Plaine R

XXX
IV

N-424

22

Provencheres

22

24

N-420

Wisembach

Ste. Marie 25

Ste. Marie-aux-Mines

Ste. Marie
Pass

XV
XXX

Badonviller

N-392

La Trouche

21

Clairefontaine

716
XX
10 NOV

21

XX
16
10 NOV

Ban-de-
Laveline

24

N-415

198
XX
10 NOV

Fraize

26

Le Bonhomme
Pass

Cirey

708
XX
10 NOV

Neufmaisons

18 19

Raon-l'Etape

20

20

21

St. Michel

20

St. Die

22

18 22

Saulcy

St. Leonard

19

Anould

24

Clefcy

Vacqueville

D-8

D-9

Meurthe R

N-424

N-59

3

Etival-Clairefontaine

XX
3

Taintrux

N-420

103
XX

Neune R

19 NOV

19

14
21 NOV
117 A

Baccarat
Bertrichamps

100
XX

Rambervillers

Brouvelieures

36
XX

Vologne R

Gerardmer

3 Alg
XX
19 NOV

Vezouse R

N-59

Mortagne R

Bruyeres

Le Tholy

SEVENTH
XXXX
FIRST FR

FIRST FRENCH ARMY ADVANCE THROUGH THE BELFORT GAP
14 - 25 November 1944

Axis of Infantry Attack

Axis of Armored Attack

Axis of German Counterattack

MILES

0   10

GERMANY

FRANCE

SWITZERLAND

Colmar

Rhine R

N-68

N-83

N-417

Schlucht Pass

Gerardmer

Le Tholy

Remiremont

SEVENTH FIRST FR

Moselotte R

La Bresse

Cornimont

N-417

3 Alg

198

269

N-66

Le Thillot N-66

Moselle R

N-486

N-66

Bussang Pass

Ballon d'Alsace

Masevaux

Sewen

Doller R

Cernay

N-66

Mulhouse

Burnhaupt

Rhone-Rhine Canal

Rhine R

III R

Rhone-Rhine Canal

Harth

Chalampe Forest

Huningue Canal

Ottmarsheim

Hombourg

Kembs

Colonnier

Loechle

Rosenau

Huningue

Basel

Bartenheim

Waldighofen

Moernach

Seppois

Largue R

RCN

N-463

N-19

Altkirch

Illfurth

Dannemarie

Largitzen

Suarce

Courtelevant

Rechesy

Pfetterhouse

Allaine R

Villescot

Brebotte

Delle

Villars-les-Blamont

Glay

Abbevillers

Herimoncourt

Doubs R

9 Col(+)

338

N-463

N-83

Bretigney

Montbeliard

Morvillars

Hericourt

Luze

Lisaine R

Valdoie

BELFORT

N-19

N-19A

N-19 Belfort

189

490

269

Champagney Res

Champagney

Chevestraye Pass

Ronchamp

MOLLE

Lure

2 Mor(+)

D-6

159

Plancher-les-Mines

Giromagny

Rougemont-le-Chateau

N-83

N-465

1

Doller R

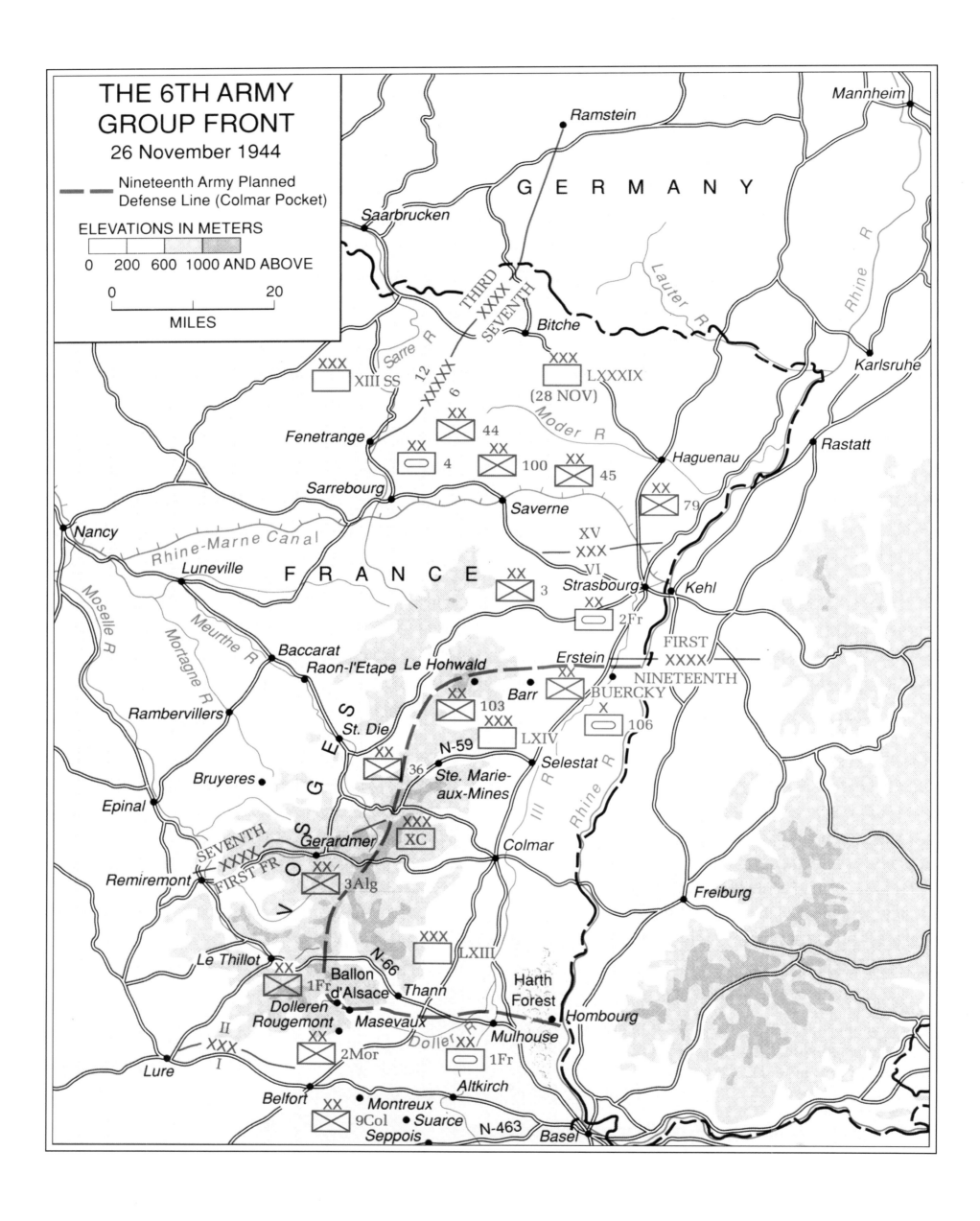

THE 6TH ARMY GROUP FRONT
26 November 1944

▬ ▬ ▬ Nineteenth Army Planned
          Defense Line (Colmar Pocket)

ELEVATIONS IN METERS

0   200   600   1000 AND ABOVE

0   20
            MILES

GERMANY

Mannheim

Ramstein

Saarbrucken

Bitche

Karlsruhe

THIRD XXXX SEVENTH

Sarre R.

XXX XIII SS

12

XXXX 6

XXX LXXXIX
(28 NOV)

Fenetrange

Moder R.

XX 44

XX 4

XX 100

XX 45

Haguenau

Rastatt

Sarrebourg

Saverne

XV XXX

XX 79

Nancy

Rhine-Marne Canal

Luneville

F R A N C E

XX 3

Strasbourg

Kehl

Moselle R.

Meurthe R.

Mortagne R.

Baccarat

Raon-l'Etape

Le Hohwald

Erstein

VI XXX 2Fr

FIRST XXXX
NINETEENTH

Rambervillers

St. Die

XX 103

Barr

XX BUERCKY

X 106

Bruyeres

XX 36

N-59

Ste. Marie-
aux-Mines

LXIV XXX

Selestat

Rhine R.

Ill R.

Epinal

V O S G E S

Gerardmer

XXX XC

Colmar

SEVENTH XXXX FIRST FR

XX 3Alg

Remiremont

Freiburg

Le Thillot

N-66

XXX LXIII

XX 1Fr

Ballon
d'Alsace

Thann

Harth
Forest

Dolleren

Rougemont

Masevaux

Doller R.

Hombourg

II XXX I

XX 2Mor

XX 1Fr

Mulhouse

Lure

Belfort

Altkirch

XX 9Col

Montreux

Suarce

N-463

Seppois

Basel

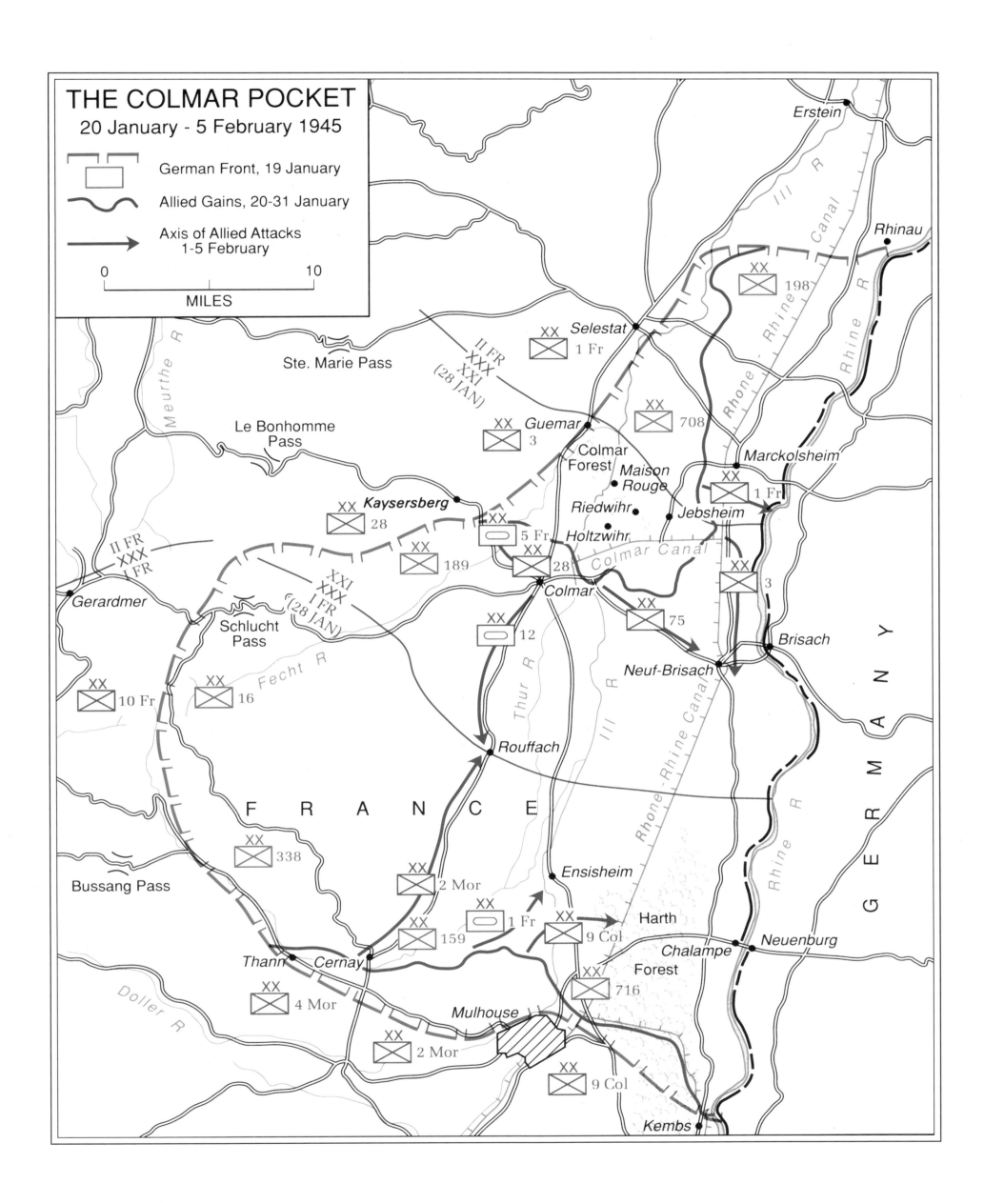

THE COLMAR POCKET
20 January - 5 February 1945

German Front, 19 January

Allied Gains, 20-31 January

Axis of Allied Attacks
1-5 February

0   10
MILES

Erstein

Rhinau

Selestat
1 Fr

XX 198

Ste. Marie Pass

II FR
XXX
XXI
(28 JAN)

Guemar
XX 3

Colmar
Forest

Maison
Rouge

XX 708

Marckolsheim

Le Bonhomme
Pass

Kaysersberg
XX 28

Riedwihr

Jebsheim

XX 1 Fr

II FR
XXX
1 FR

XX 189

5 Fr

Holtzwihr

XX 28

Colmar Canal

XX 3

Gerardmer

XXI
XXX
1 FR
(28 JAN)

Schlucht
Pass

Colmar

12

XX 75

Neuf-Brisach

Brisach

Fecht R

XX 10 Fr

XX 16

Thur R

III R

Rouffach

Rhone-Rhine Canal

Rhine R

G E R M A N Y

F R A N C E

XX 338

Bussang Pass

Ensisheim

Harth

XX 2 Mor

1 Fr

XX 9 Col

Chalampe
Forest

Neuenburg

XX 159

Thann   Cernay

XX 4 Mor

Mulhouse

XX 716

XX 2 Mor

XX 9 Col

Kembs

Meurthe R

Doller R

The Last Offensive

January 3–May 3, 1945

AFTER THE ALLIES PUSHED THE GERMAN FORCES out of the Ardennes, Eisenhower agreed to Montgomery's proposed northern attack on Germany. In the assault, Lieutenant General W.H. Simpson's Ninth Army would support Montgomery's 21st Army Group. These maps follow this operation and the subsequent ones that ultimately ended the war in Germany.

On February 22, 1945, Simpson's Ninth Army launched Operation Grenade, an assault across the Roer River in conjunction with the First Canadian Army. The goal was to push the Germans beyond the Rhine. The Germans, however, slowed the attack by flooding the Roer, which forced the Ninth, with Collins' VII Corps in support, to postpone their attack until the river level lowered. Nonetheless, by March 5, Collins had crossed the river and captured Cologne. In its sector, U.S. 9th Armored Division, on March 7, charged the Remagen Bridge over the Rhine, capturing it intact (before the Germans could destroy it). Within twenty-four hours after the crossing, the Americans had placed 8,000 men on the east side of the river. Germany was invaded.

By mid-March, Patton's Third Army had cut off German troops west of the Rhine and captured more than 100,000 prisoners. On March 23, the Third crossed the Rhine on two pontoon bridges, while Patch's Seventh Army seized another bridgehead at Worms.

On March 26, Hodge's First Army and Simpson's Ninth Army began encircling the Germans in the Ruhr industrial district in a bitter, hard-fought struggle that culminated on April 1 with the capture of 317,000 German prisoners. By April 24, Hodges, Patton, and Simpson had advanced across central Germany and forced a bridgehead on the Elbe River. Soon, Patton was on the Czechoslovakian border, where he was ordered to halt. A link-up was made afterward with Russian forces, and VE-Day was consummated. The end of World War II in Europe was declared.

LEFT: *American troops board a boat under heavy fire during the crossing of the Rhine River at St. Goar, March 1945. One soldier present described the harrowing scene: "I drew an assault boat to cross in—just my luck. We all tried to crawl under each other because the lead was flying around like hail."* **OPPOSITE INSET:** *Perched perilously, American GIs—some of them clutching their carbines—pose for a photograph atop an enormous railroad gun that is festooned with camouflaging material. Though they had been a staple in World War I, such large, rail-mounted guns had become largely irrelevant by World War II; nonetheless, both the Allies and the Germans made occasional use of them in the latter war.* **LEFT INSET:** *General Dwight David Eisenhower, Supreme Commander, Allied Expeditionary Forces, was the right man for the extremely difficult task of welding together French, English, and American commanders and troops into a unified fighting organization capable of defeating a highly trained and experienced enemy.*

RIGHT: *Antitank artillerymen aboard their motorized weapon move slowly forward as they feel their way warily in search of German panzers. At this point in the war, the German tanks had more-powerful, longer-range guns than American tanks. Only the steady supply of new tanks from the United States and the dauntless efforts of American and British tank crews allowed the Allied armor to remain competitive in the field.* **BELOW:** *American troops thread their way through tank obstacles and minefields along the Siegfried Line in early 1945. As formidable as the West Wall was, once it was breached, troops and equipment poured through the gaps, allowing the Allied armies to enter Germany in force and to attack the enemy on his own ground for the first time in the war.*

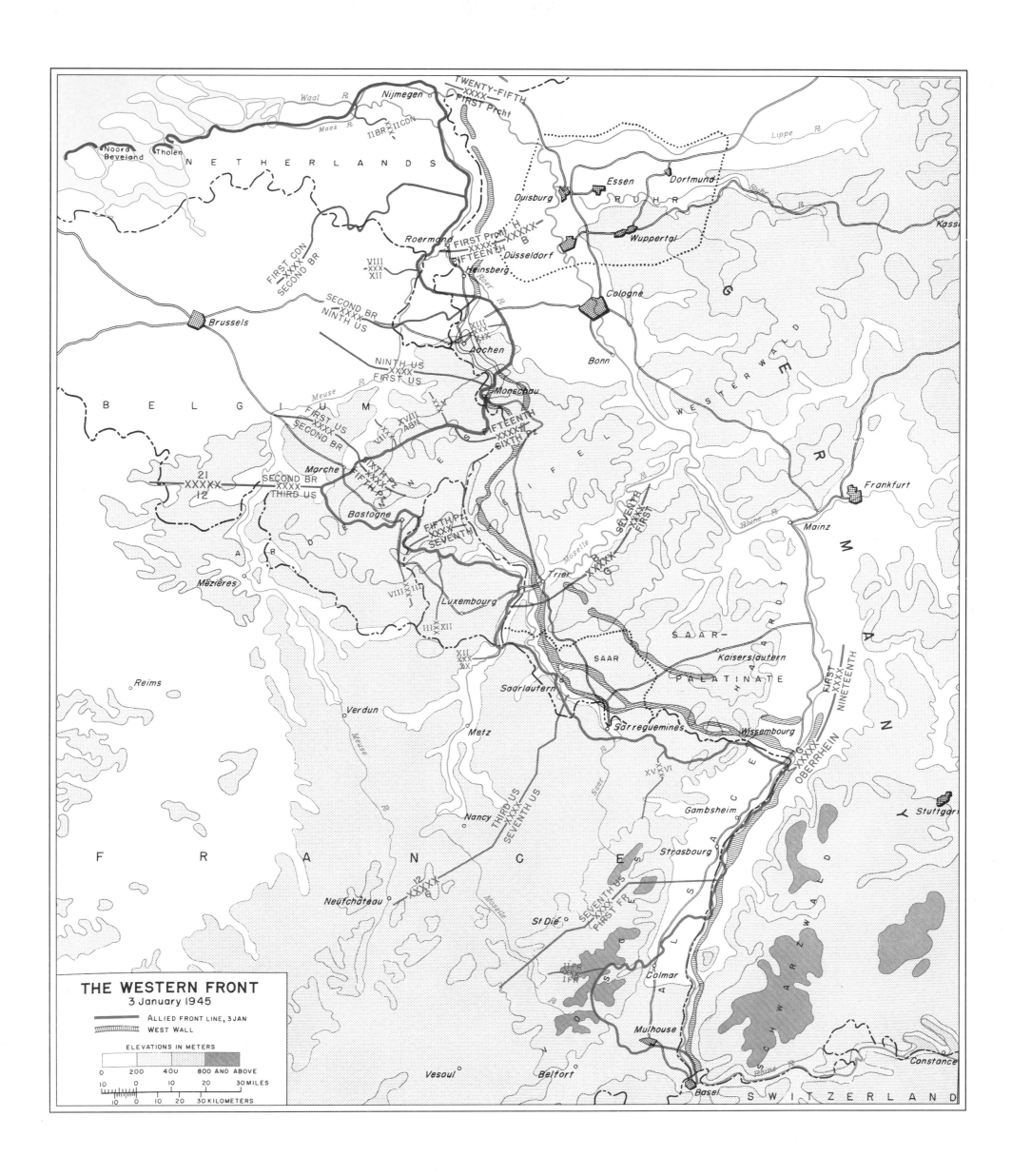

THE WESTERN FRONT
3 January 1945

▬▬▬ ALLIED FRONT LINE, 3 JAN
▥▥▥ WEST WALL

ELEVATIONS IN METERS

0   200   400   800 AND ABOVE

10   0   10   20   30 MILES

10   0   10   20   30 KILOMETERS

A R D E N N E S

L O W

Ourthe R.

VII
XXX
30 BR

Hotton

Marche

XX
53 Br

X
33 Br

XX
8 JAN 51 Br

SIXTH PZ
XXXXX
FIFTH PZ

La Roche

XX
11 JAN 51 Br

21
XXXXX
12

Plateau

XX
84

XX
3

XX
2

XX
29 Br

XX
6 Br

LVIII PZ
XXX
XLVII PZ

1 SS PZ
XXX
XLVII PZ

Longchamps

XX
101

Ourthe R.

St. Hubert

14

R
87

Tillet

XX
17

II

Bastogne

Mar

XX
35

A

N
N
E
N
E

THE ARDENNES COUNTEROFFENSIVE
3–28 January 1945

——————— FRONT LINE, MIDNIGHT, 3 JAN
•••••••••• FRONT LINE, MIDNIGHT, 16 JAN
◻◻◻ FRONT LINE, MIDNIGHT, 28 JAN
——— ➤ AXIS OF INFANTRY ADVANCE
———➤ AXIS OF ARMORED ADVANCE

ELEVATIONS IN METERS

0   200   300   400   500 AND ABOVE

1   0   1   2   3   4   5 MILES
1   0   1   2   3   4   5 KILOMETERS

THE DRIVE ON PRÜM
3–10 February 1945

⊥⊥⊥⊥⊥⊥⊥⊥	FRONT LINE, EVENING, 3 FEB
••••••••	FRONT LINE, EVENING, 6 FEB
————————	FRONT LINE, EVENING, 10 FEB
——→	AXIS OF ADVANCE
————————	GERMAN DEFENSIVE LINE, EVENING, 3 FEB
– – – – –	GERMAN DEFENSIVE LINE, EVENING, 6 FEB
⊓⊓⊓⊓	GERMAN DEFENSIVE LINE, EVENING, 10 FEB
▨▨▨	WEST WALL

Note: German divisions are approximate

Contour interval in meters

2 MILES
2 KILOMETERS

St. Vith

BELGIUM
GERMANY

345

1/8

3/8

2,3/22

1/12

2/1

Bleialf

3/12

4
XX
90

Br

2/359

1/359

FIFTH
XXXX
SEVENTH

3/359

XX
XIII

359

Habscheid

759
358

Heckhuscheid

1/358

3/358

11Armd
XX
90
3/A/B

5/A/B

BELGIUM
LUX

358
1/1
351

2/357

2/358

568

41Cav

Grosskampenberg

3/357

500

Lützkampen

400

Leidenborn

Irsen Cr

1/357

VIII
XXX
III

400

LUX
GERMANY

XX
276VG

Manner Cr

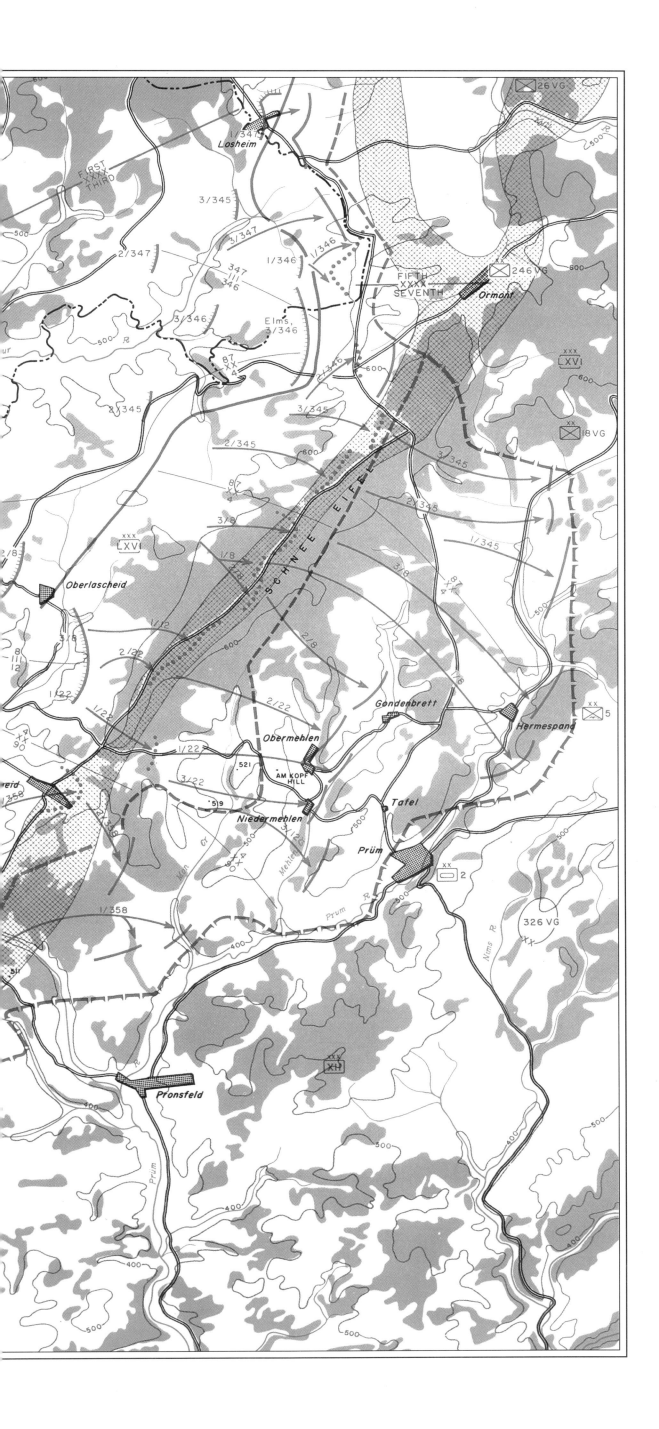

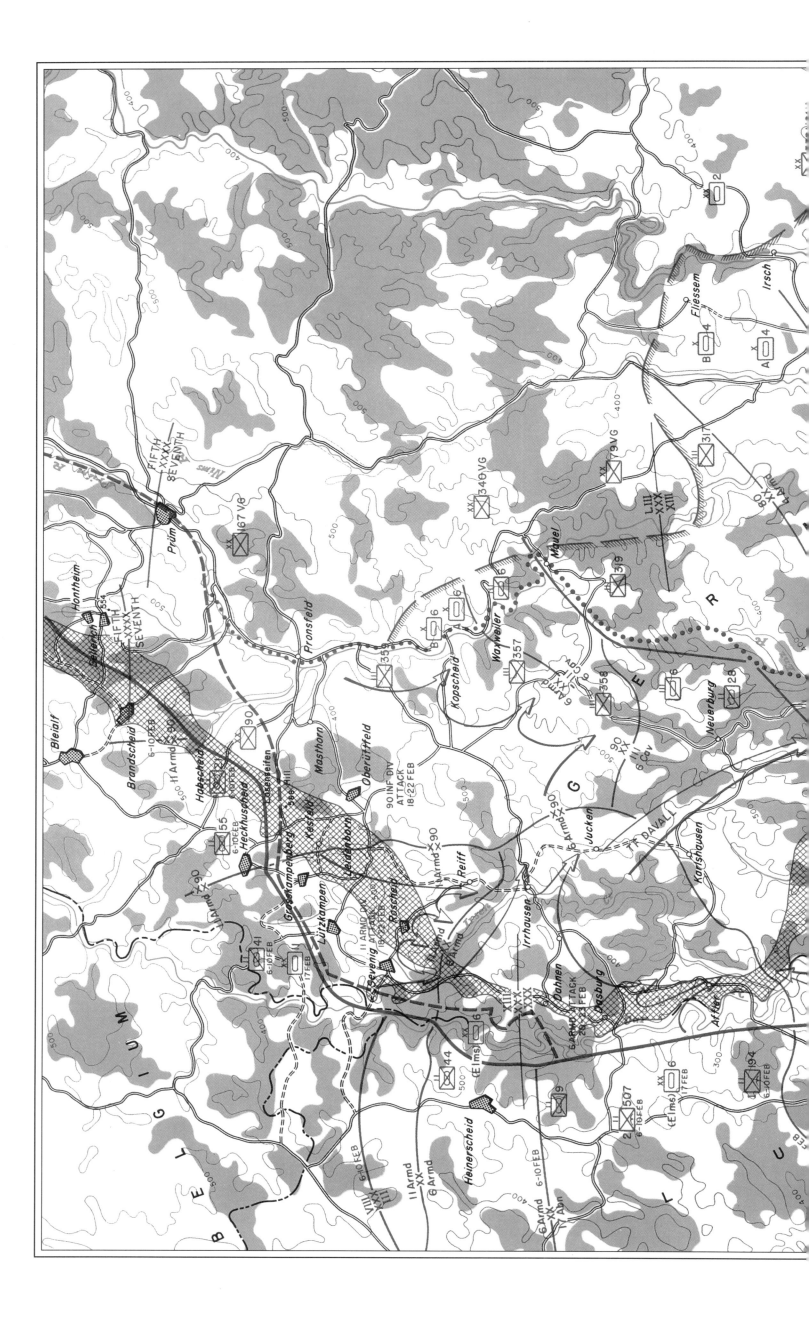

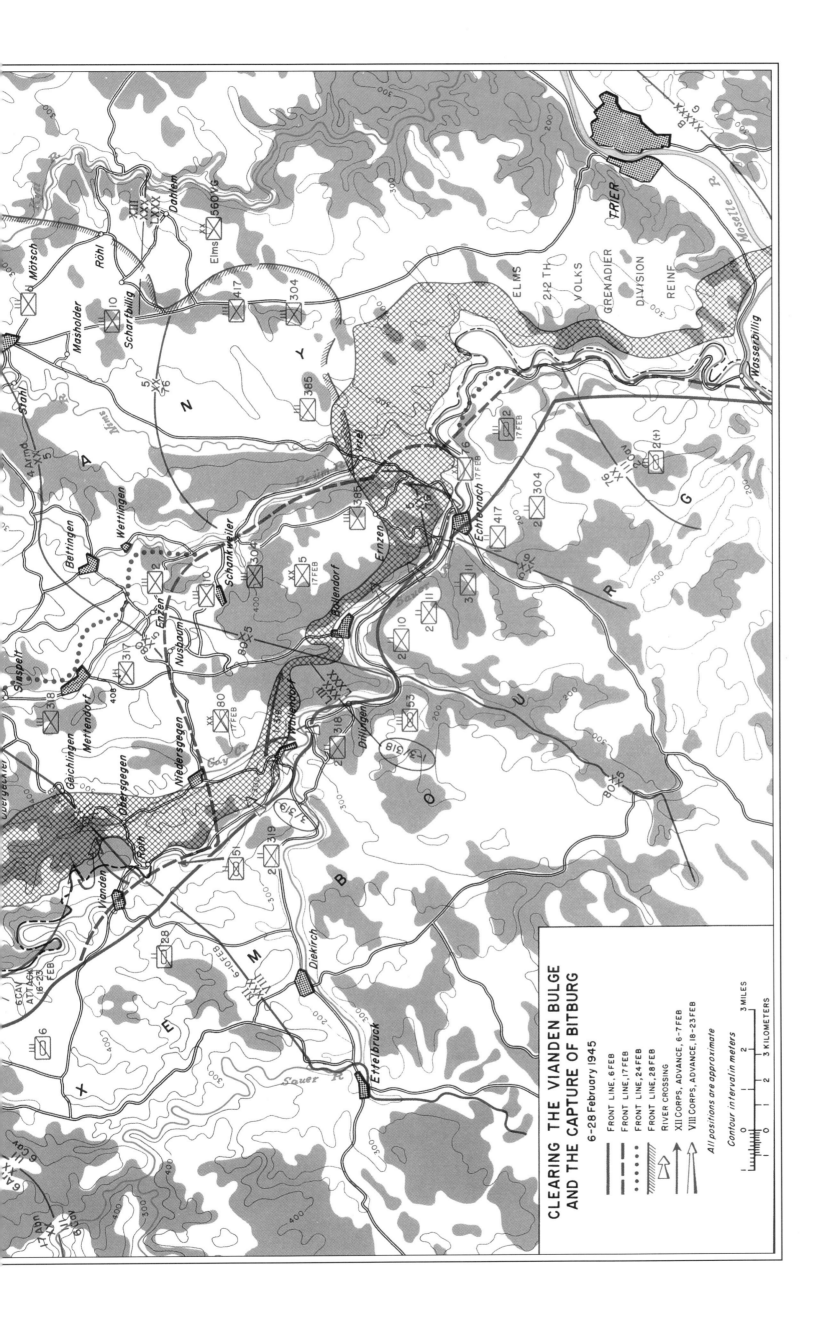

CLEARING THE VIANDEN BULGE
AND THE CAPTURE OF BITBURG

6–28 February 1945

FRONT LINE, 6 FEB
FRONT LINE, 17 FEB
FRONT LINE, 24 FEB
FRONT LINE, 28 FEB
RIVER CROSSING
XII CORPS, ADVANCE, 6–7 FEB
VIII CORPS, ADVANCE, 18–23 FEB

All positions are approximate

Contour interval in meters

3 MILES

3 KILOMETERS

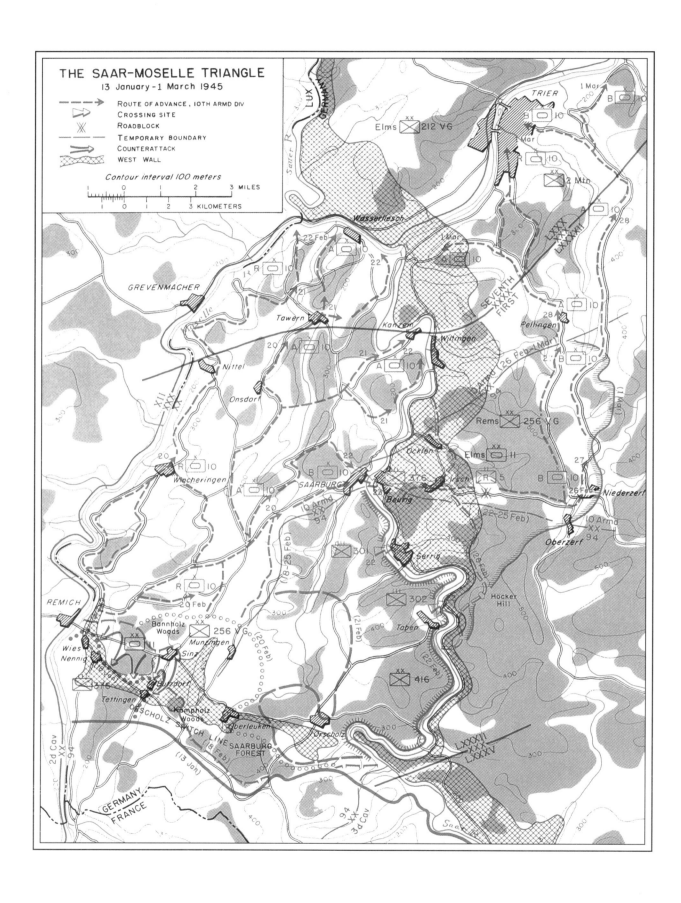

THE SAAR-MOSELLE TRIANGLE
13 January - 1 March 1945

- ▷→ ROUTE OF ADVANCE, 10TH ARMD DIV
- CROSSING SITE
- ✕ ROADBLOCK
- TEMPORARY BOUNDARY
- COUNTERATTACK
- WEST WALL

Contour interval 100 meters

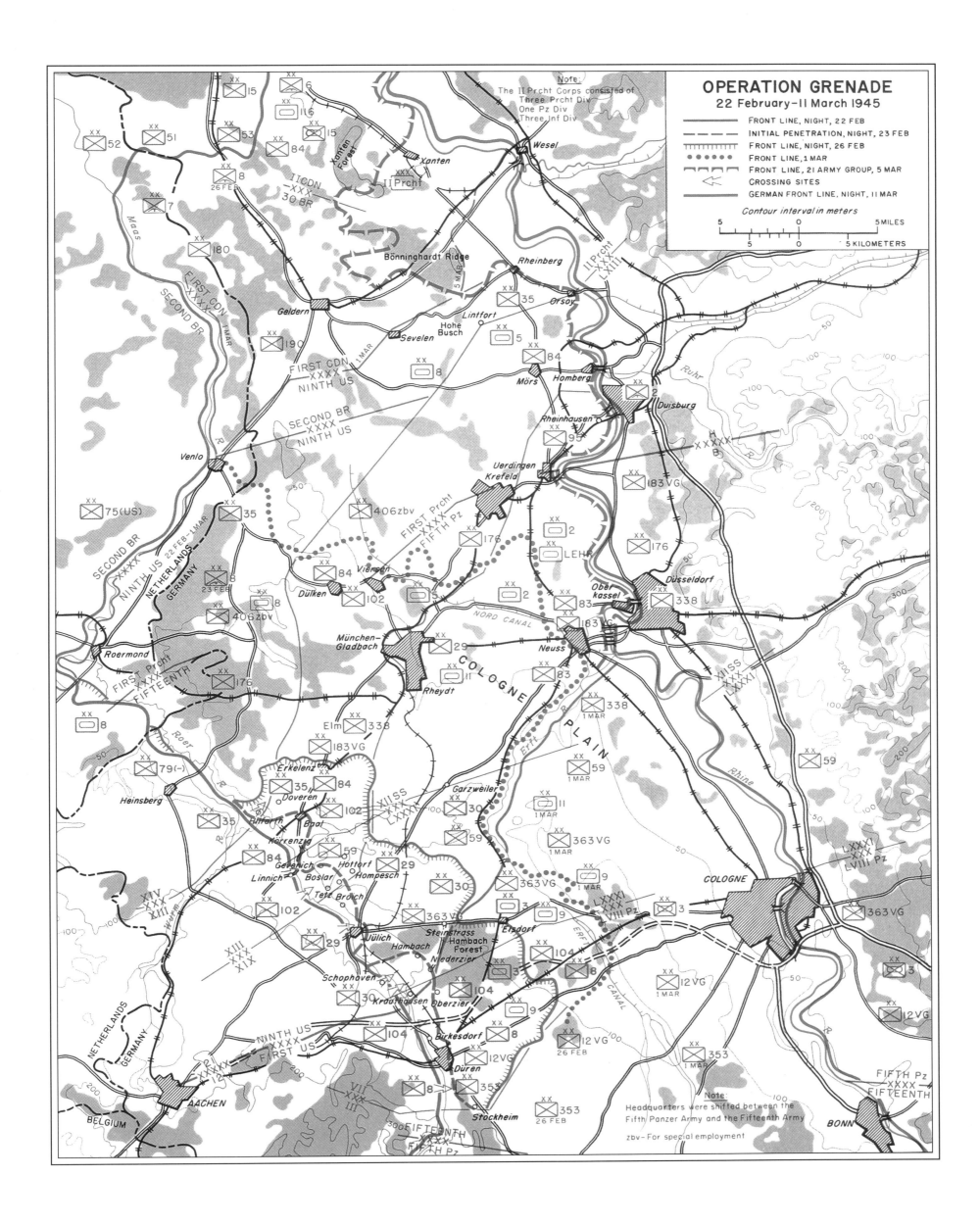

OPERATION GRENADE
22 February–11 March 1945

FRONT LINE, NIGHT, 22 FEB
INITIAL PENETRATION, NIGHT, 23 FEB
FRONT LINE, NIGHT, 26 FEB
FRONT LINE, 1 MAR
FRONT LINE, 21 ARMY GROUP, 5 MAR
CROSSING SITES
GERMAN FRONT LINE, NIGHT, 11 MAR

Contour interval in meters

5   5 MILES
5   0   5 KILOMETERS

Note:
The II Prcht Corps consisted of
Three Prcht Div
One Pz Div
Three Inf Div

Note:
Headquarters were shifted between the
Fifth Panzer Army and the Fifteenth Army

zbv–For special employment

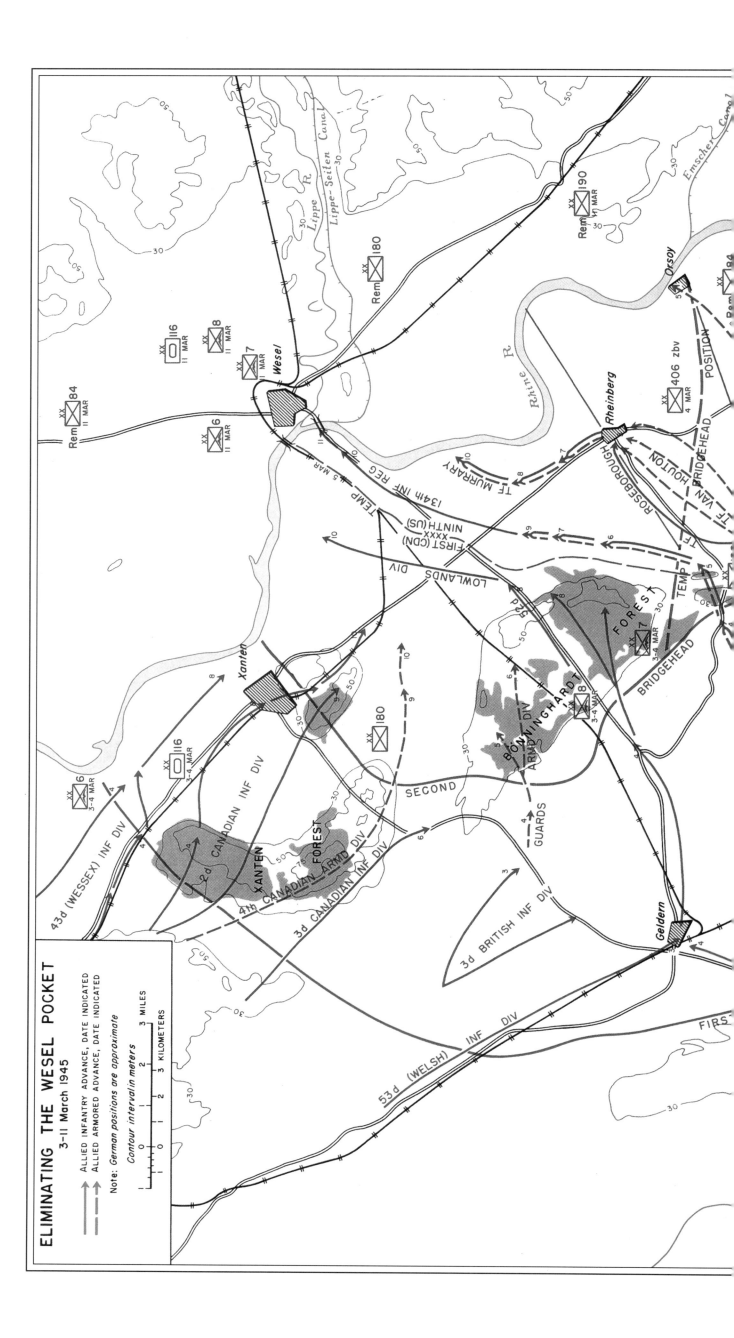

ELIMINATING THE WESEL POCKET
3-11 March 1945

ALLIED INFANTRY ADVANCE, DATE INDICATED
ALLIED ARMORED ADVANCE, DATE INDICATED

Note: *German positions are approximate*

Contour interval in meters

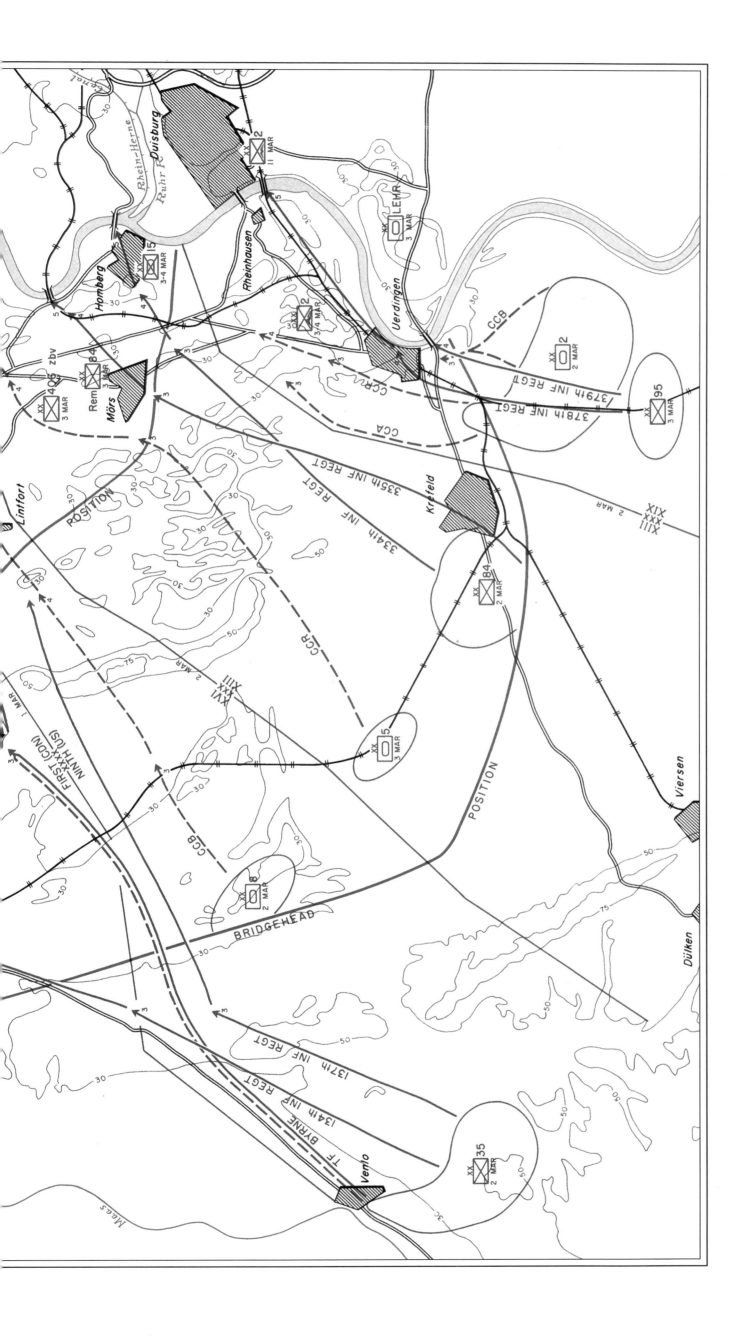

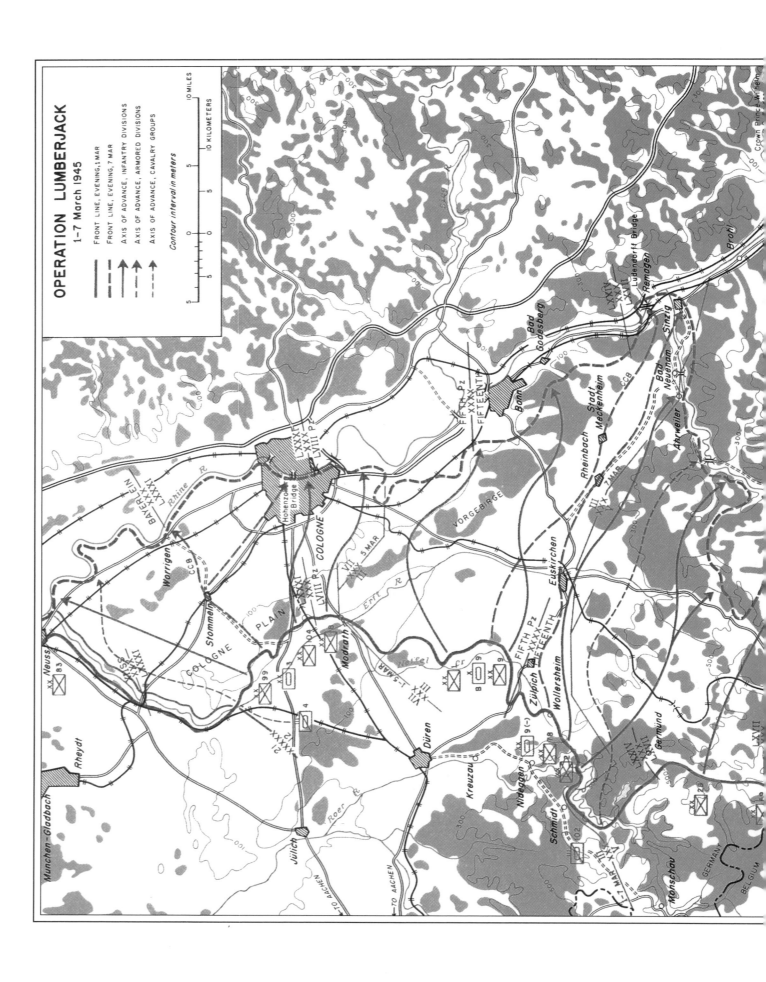

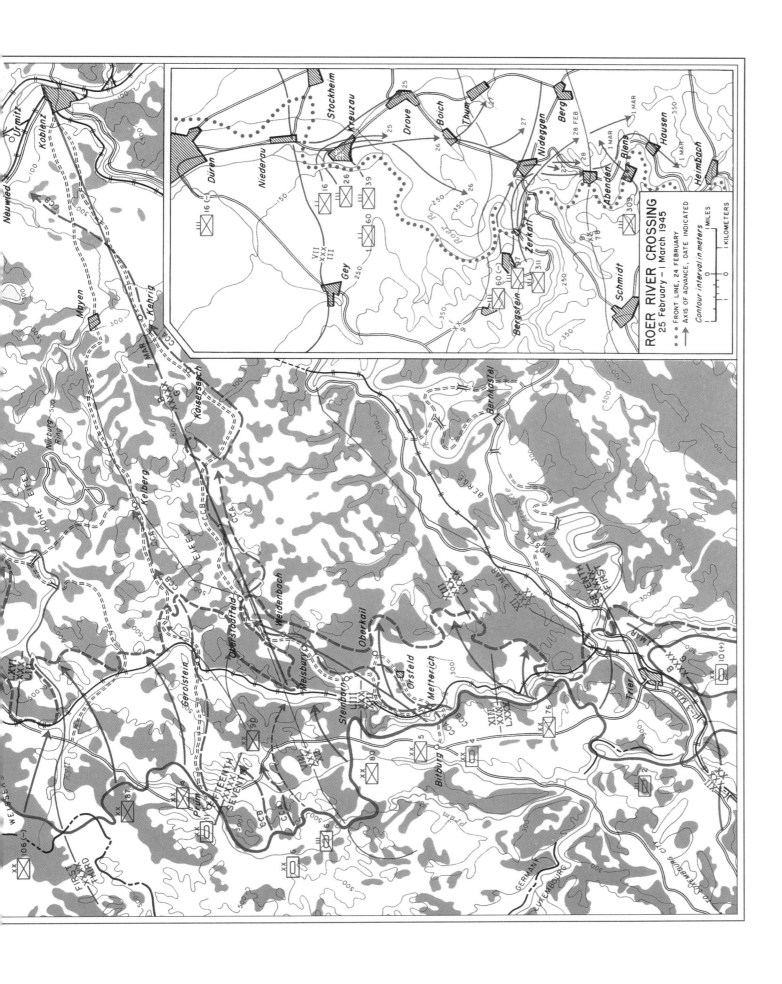

ROER RIVER CROSSING
25 February – 1 March 1945

• • • • FRONT LINE, 24 FEBRUARY
⟶ AXIS OF ADVANCE, DATE INDICATED

Contour interval in meters

0   1 MILES
0   1 KILOMETERS

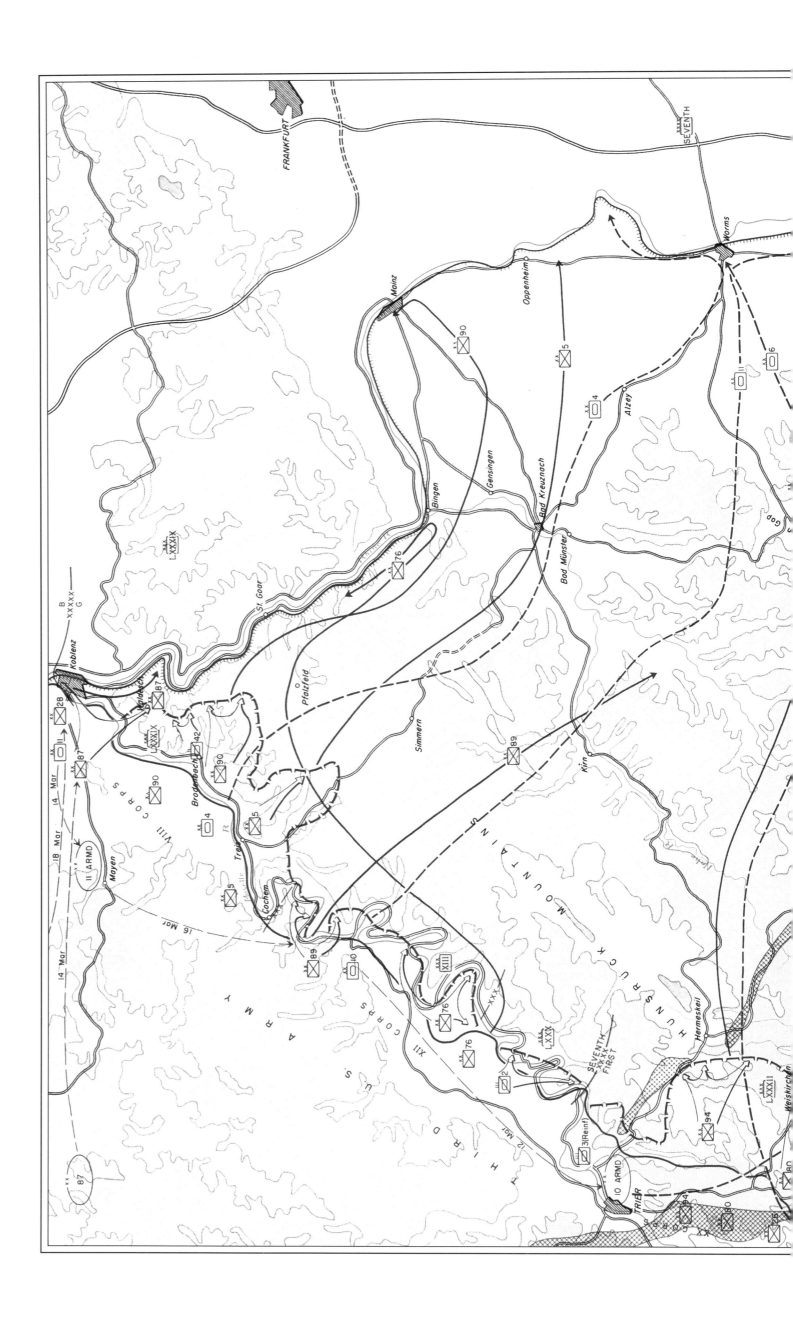

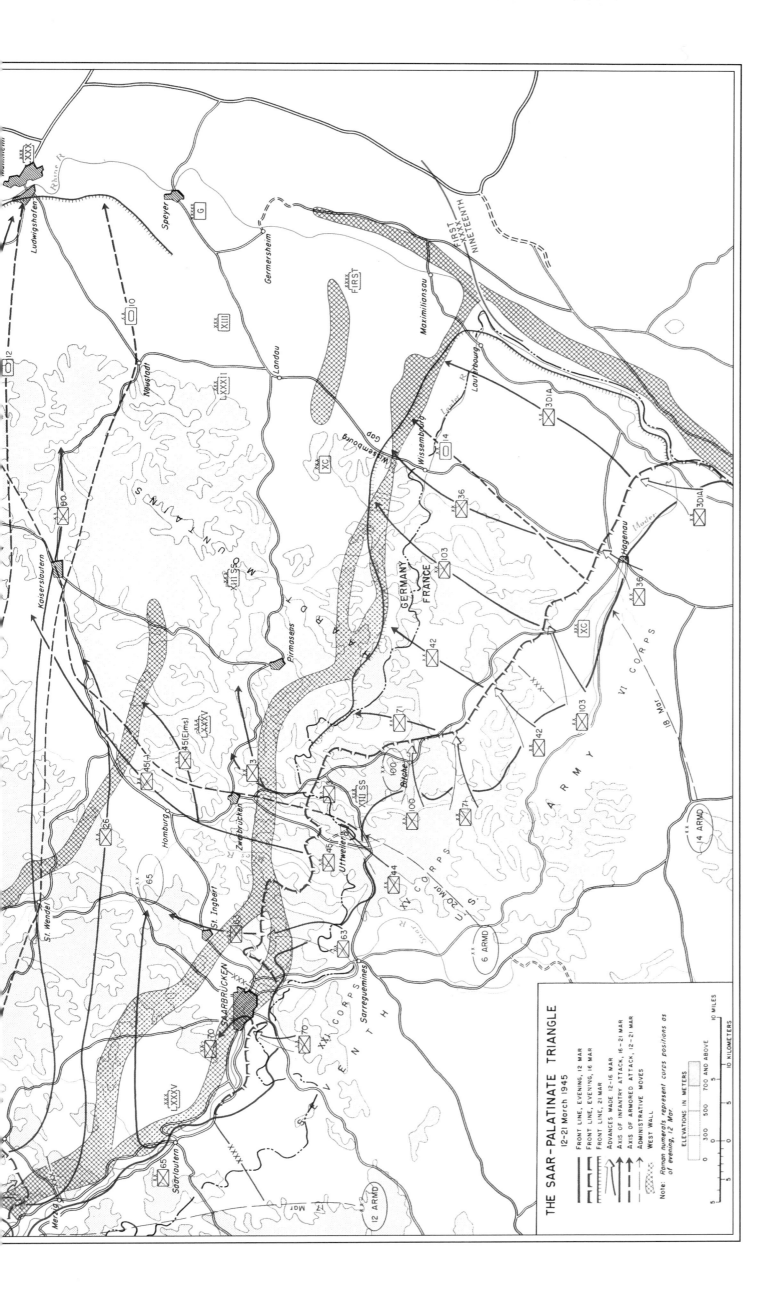

THE SAAR-PALATINATE TRIANGLE
12-21 March 1945

Koblenz

Limburg

R 9

276 VG

87

Contact: Elm Elm

Oberlahnstein

FIRST
XXXX
THIRD

Elms

Rhens
0001
25 MAR

Braubach

87

87

LXXXIX   Corps

6 SS

76

Contact

87

276 VG Div
St. Goarshausen

Mtn

St. Goar
0200
26 MAR

89

89

WIESBADEN

80

Oberwesel

Elms 6 SS
Mtn Div

Elms

Div

76

89

80

Rhine R.

90

16
26 MAR

Mainz

2

80

Bingen

Nierstei
2200
22 MAR

5

Bad Kreuznach

Nahe R.

THIRD
XXXX
SEVENTH
(26 MAR)

Alzey

12
XXXXX
6

26
XX

89

Glan R.

12 Armd(-)
XX

We

80(-)
XX

THE RHINE RIVER CROSSINGS
IN THE SOUTH
22–28 March 1945

FRONT LINE, EVENING, 22 MAR
BRIDGEHEAD, EVENING, 26 MAR
FRONT LINE, EVENING, 28 MAR
RHINE RIVER CROSSINGS
•••••••• PATROLLING
ARMD AXIS OF ATTACK

Contour interval in meters

5   0   5   10 MILES

5   0   5   10 KILOMETERS

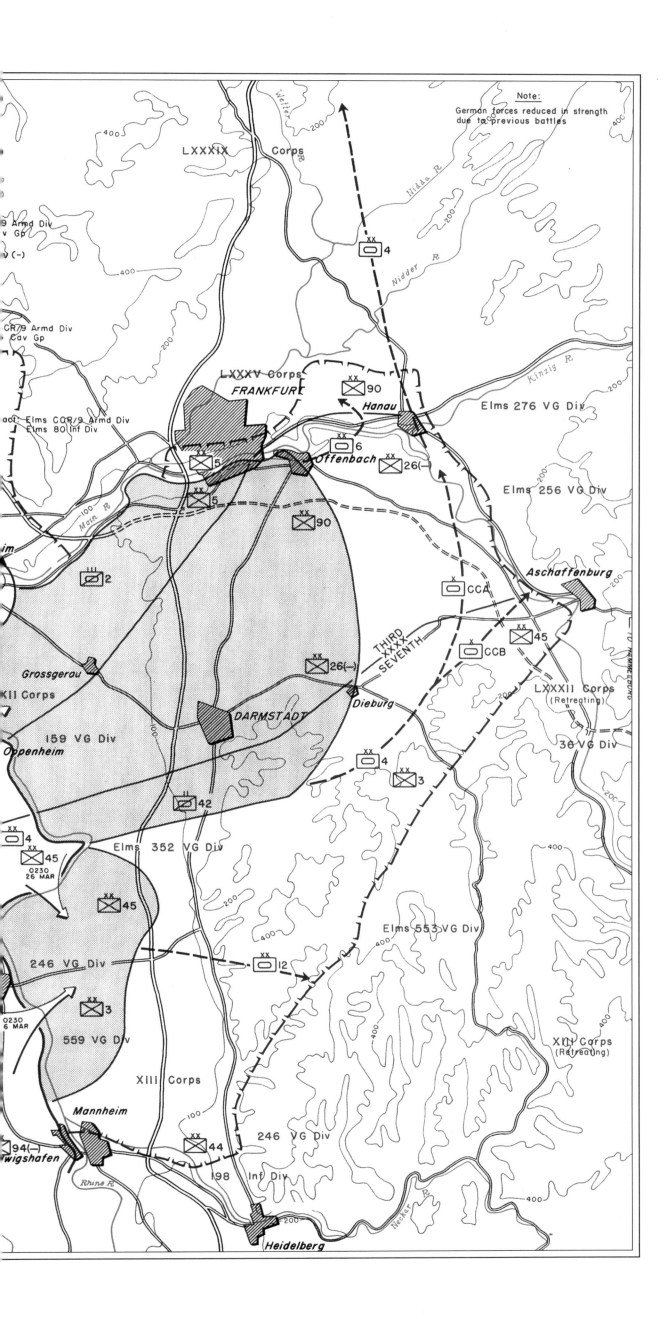

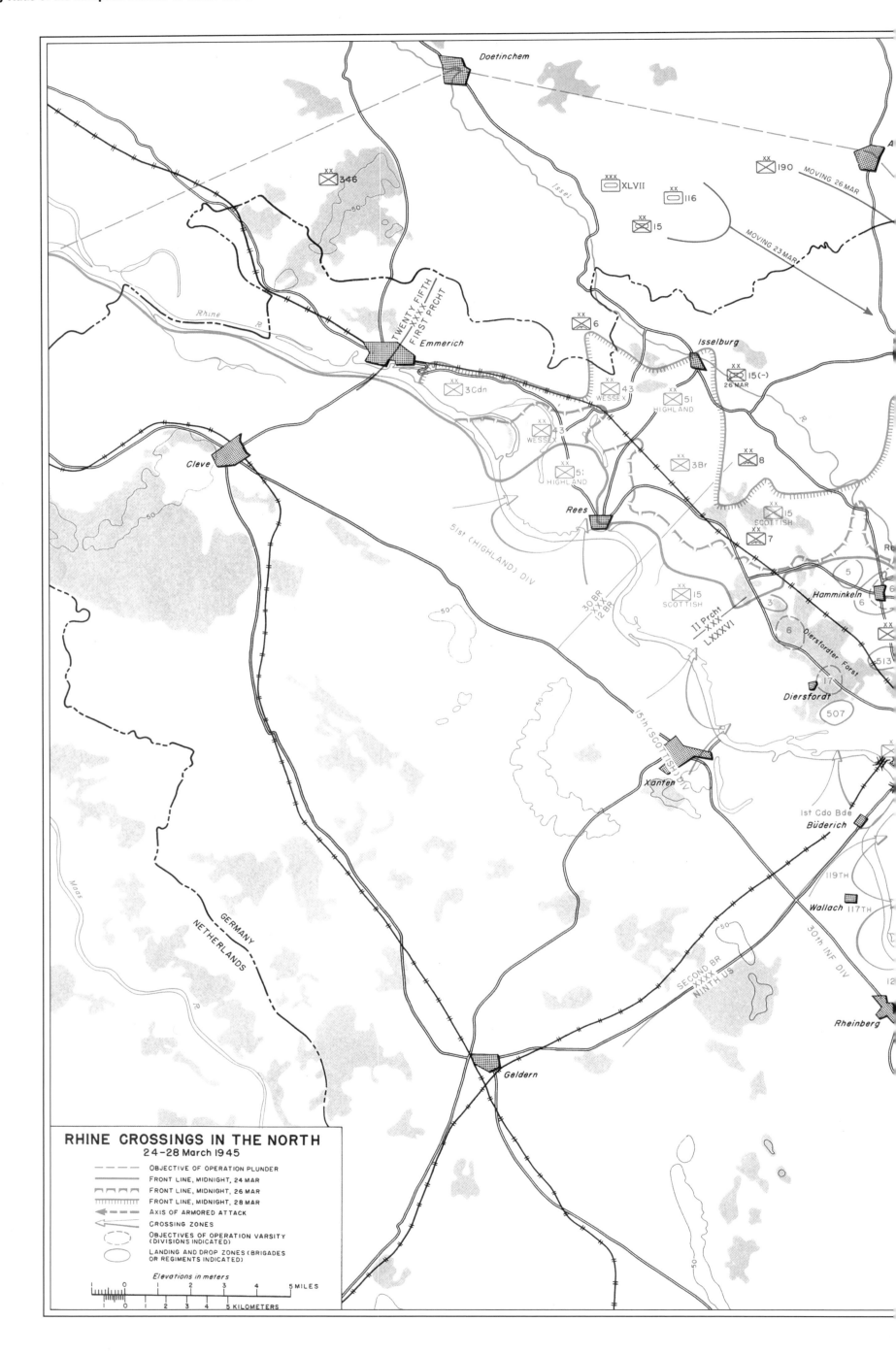

RHINE CROSSINGS IN THE NORTH
24–28 March 1945

--- OBJECTIVE OF OPERATION PLUNDER
——— FRONT LINE, MIDNIGHT, 24 MAR
———— FRONT LINE, MIDNIGHT, 26 MAR
⊔⊔⊔⊔ FRONT LINE, MIDNIGHT, 28 MAR
← AXIS OF ARMORED ATTACK
←- - AXIS OF ARMORED ATTACK
← CROSSING ZONES
⬭ OBJECTIVES OF OPERATION VARSITY (DIVISIONS INDICATED)
◯ LANDING AND DROP ZONES (BRIGADES OR REGIMENTS INDICATED)

Elevations in meters

5 MILES
5 KILOMETERS

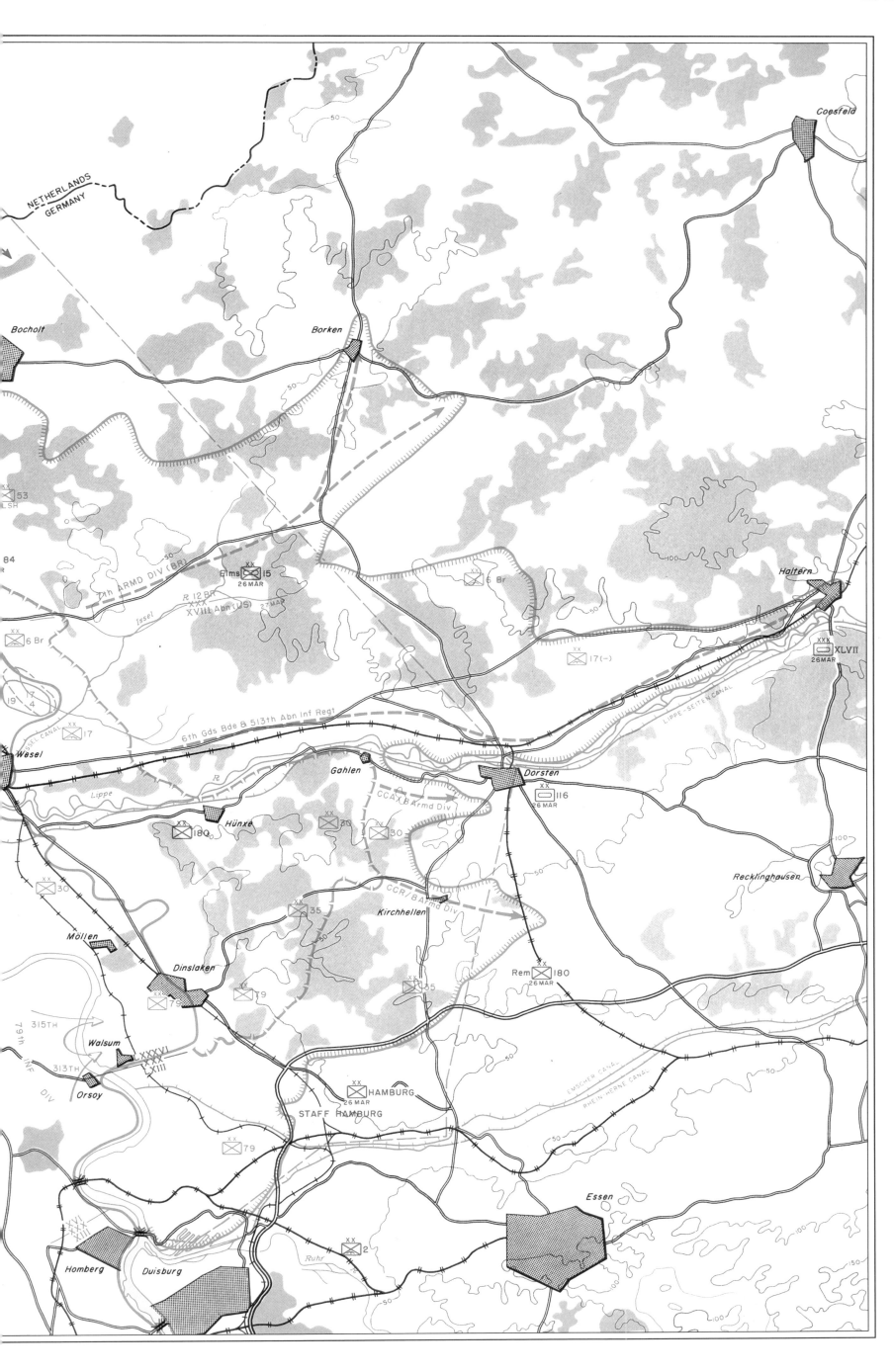

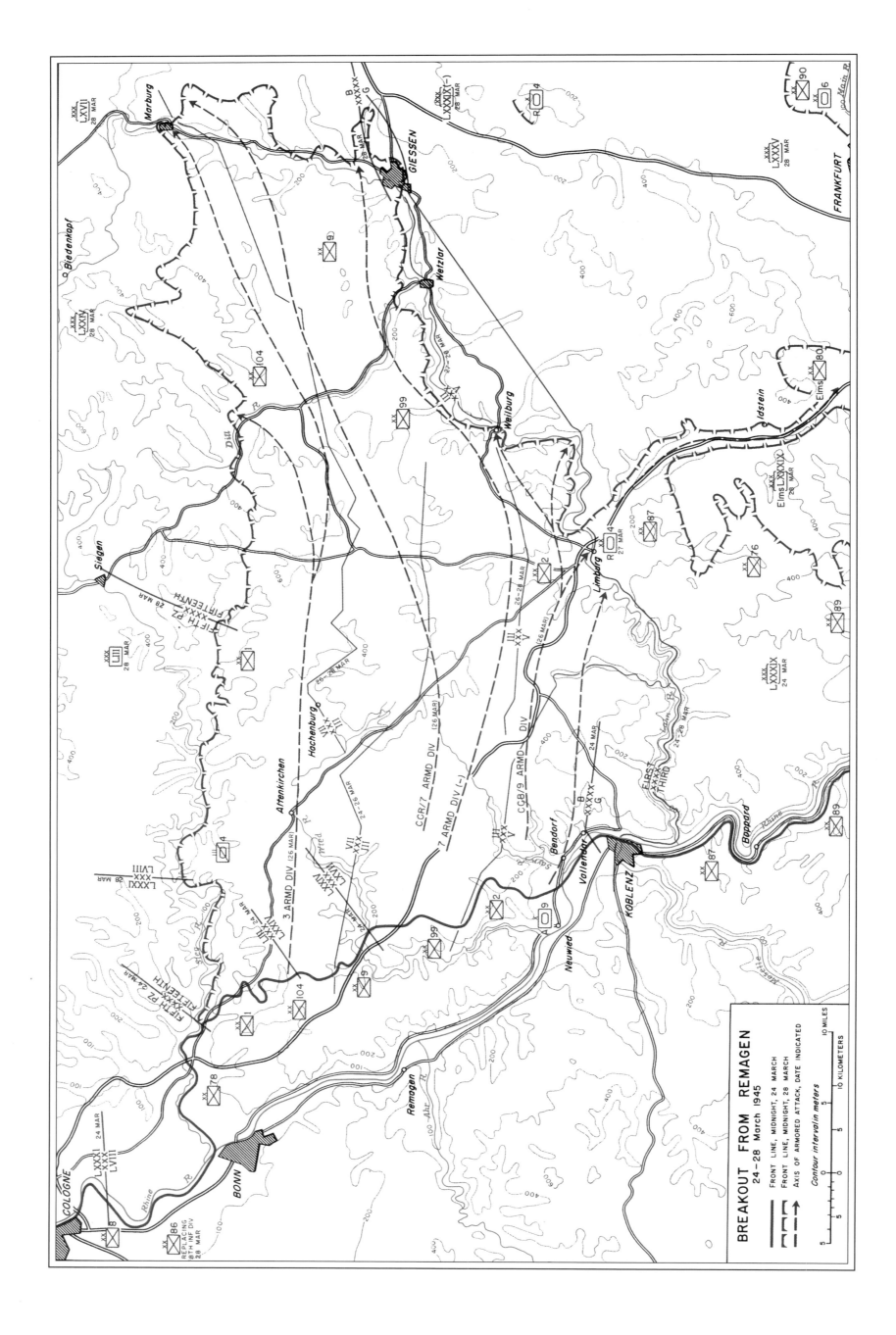

BREAKOUT FROM REMAGEN
24–28 March 1945

FRONT LINE, MIDNIGHT, 24 MARCH
FRONT LINE, MIDNIGHT, 28 MARCH
AXIS OF ARMORED ATTACK, DATE INDICATED

Contour interval in meters

10 MILES
10 KILOMETERS

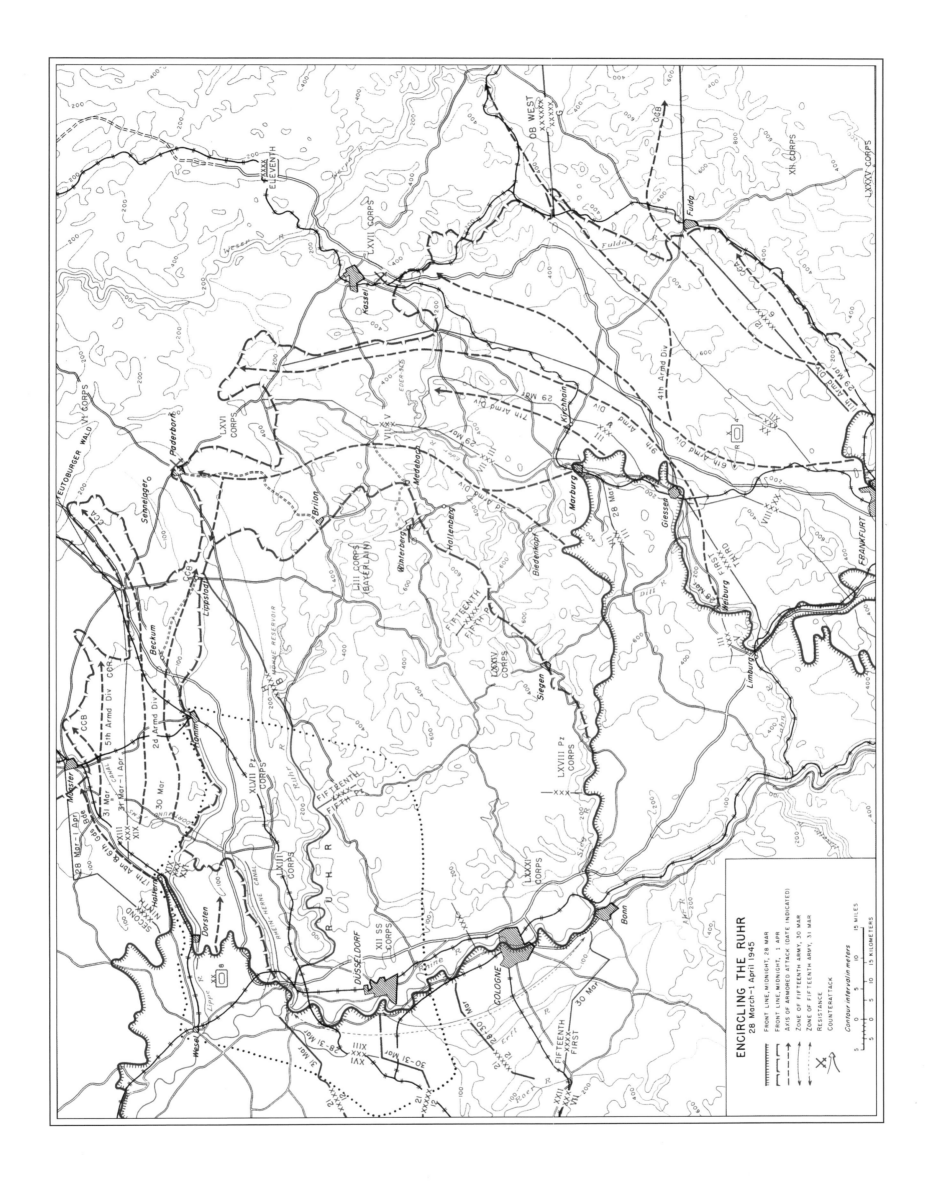

ENCIRCLING THE RUHR
28 March–1 April 1945

FRONT LINE, MIDNIGHT, 28 MAR
FRONT LINE, MIDNIGHT, 1 APR
AXIS OF ARMORED ATTACK (DATE INDICATED)
ZONE OF FIFTEENTH ARMY, 30 MAR
ZONE OF FIFTEENTH ARMY, 31 MAR
RESISTANCE
COUNTERATTACK

Contour interval in meters

5   0   5   10   15 MILES
5   0   5   10   15 KILOMETERS

COUNTERATTACK
ON THE ELBE
13–14 April 1945

U.S. POSITIONS, 13 APRIL.
U.S. ATTACK, NIGHT, 13 APRIL.
ARMORED INFANTRY REGIMENT
COUNTERATTACK, MORNING, 14 APRIL.

0   1   2   3   4   5 MILES
0   1   2   3   4   5 KILOMETERS

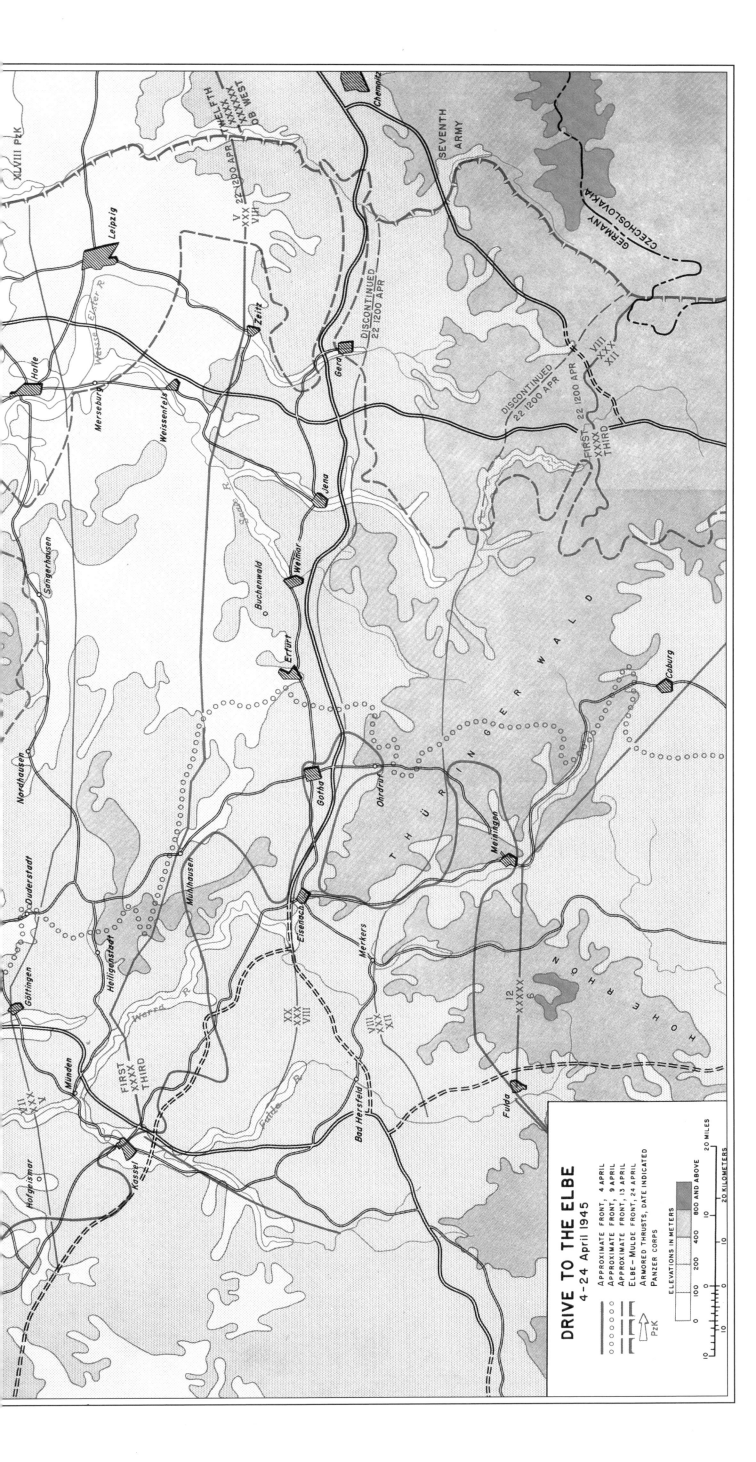

DRIVE TO THE ELBE
4–24 April 1945

	APPROXIMATE FRONT, 4 APRIL
	APPROXIMATE FRONT, 9 APRIL
	APPROXIMATE FRONT, 13 APRIL
	ELBE–MULDE FRONT, 24 APRIL
	ARMORED THRUSTS, DATE INDICATED
P2K	PANZER CORPS

ELEVATIONS IN METERS

0   100   200   400   800 AND ABOVE

20 MILES
20 KILOMETERS

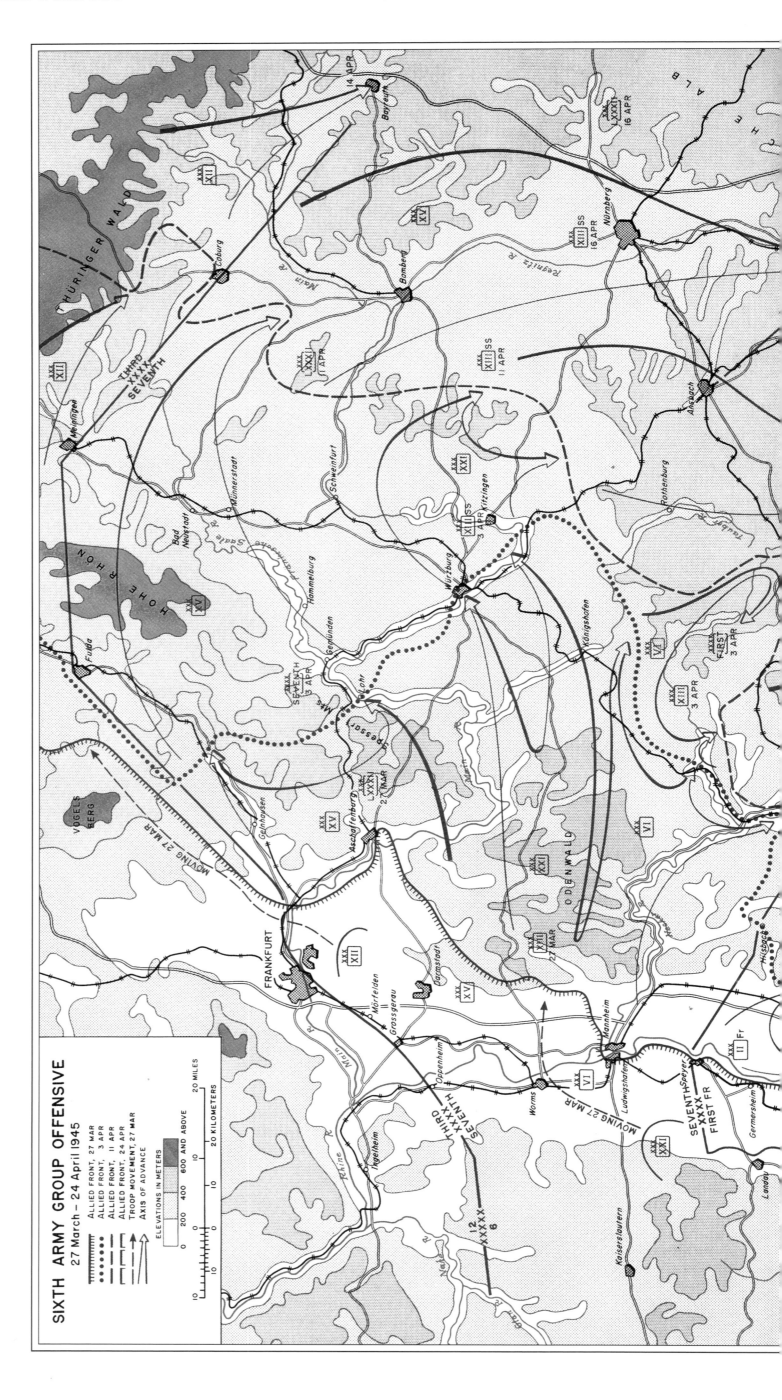

SIXTH ARMY GROUP OFFENSIVE
27 March – 24 April 1945

ALLIED FRONT, 27 MAR
ALLIED FRONT, 3 APR
ALLIED FRONT, 11 APR
ALLIED FRONT, 24 APR
TROOP MOVEMENT, 27 MAR
AXIS OF ADVANCE

ELEVATIONS IN METERS

0   200   400   600 AND ABOVE

0   10   20 MILES

0   10   20 KILOMETERS

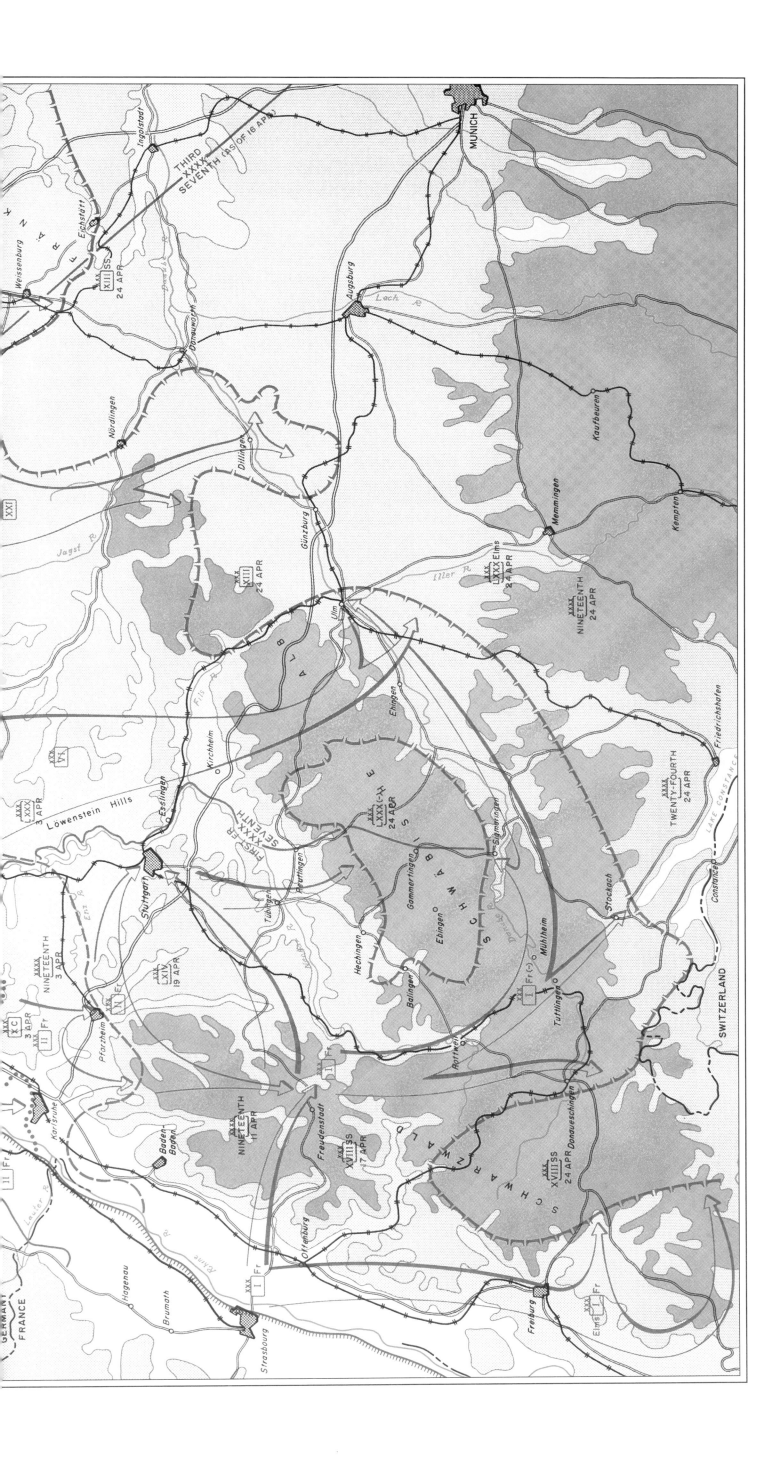

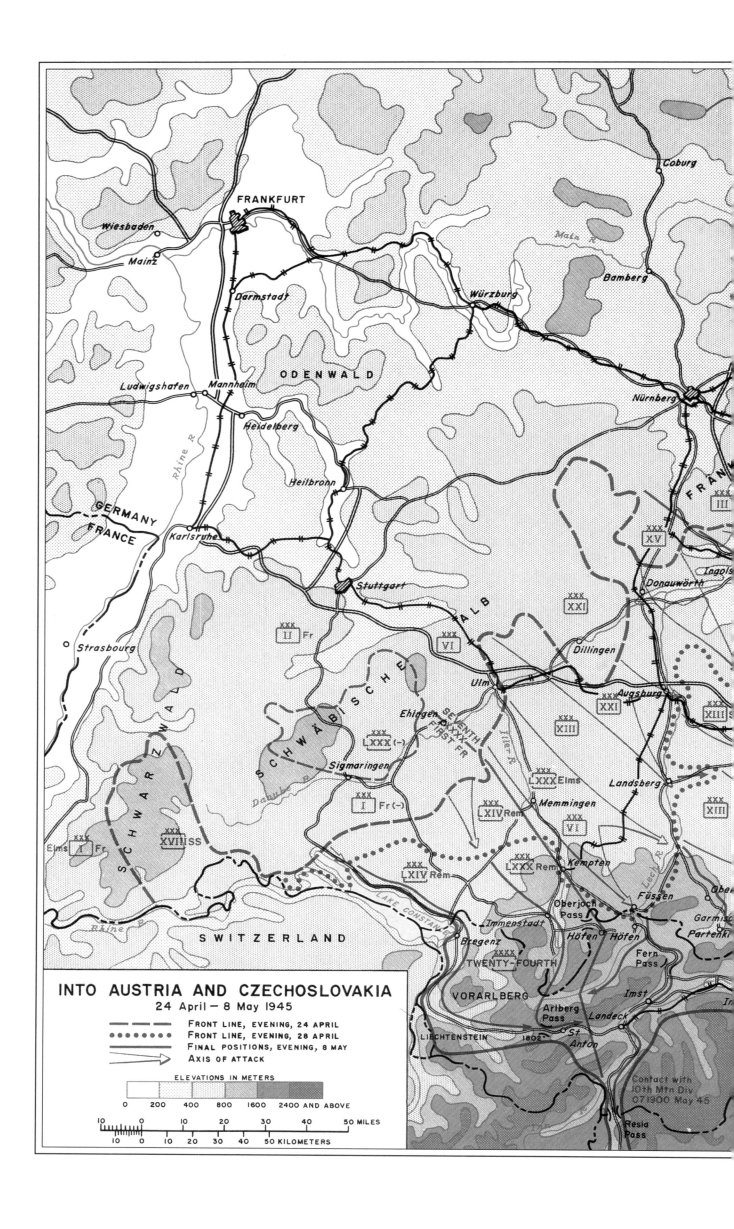

INTO AUSTRIA AND CZECHOSLOVAKIA
24 April – 8 May 1945

— — — — FRONT LINE, EVENING, 24 APRIL
••••••••• FRONT LINE, EVENING, 28 APRIL
━━━━━━ FINAL POSITIONS, EVENING, 8 MAY
━━━━▷ AXIS OF ATTACK

ELEVATIONS IN METERS

| 0 | 200 | 400 | 800 | 1600 | 2400 AND ABOVE |

10 0   10   20   30   40   50 MILES

10 0   10   20   30   40   50 KILOMETERS

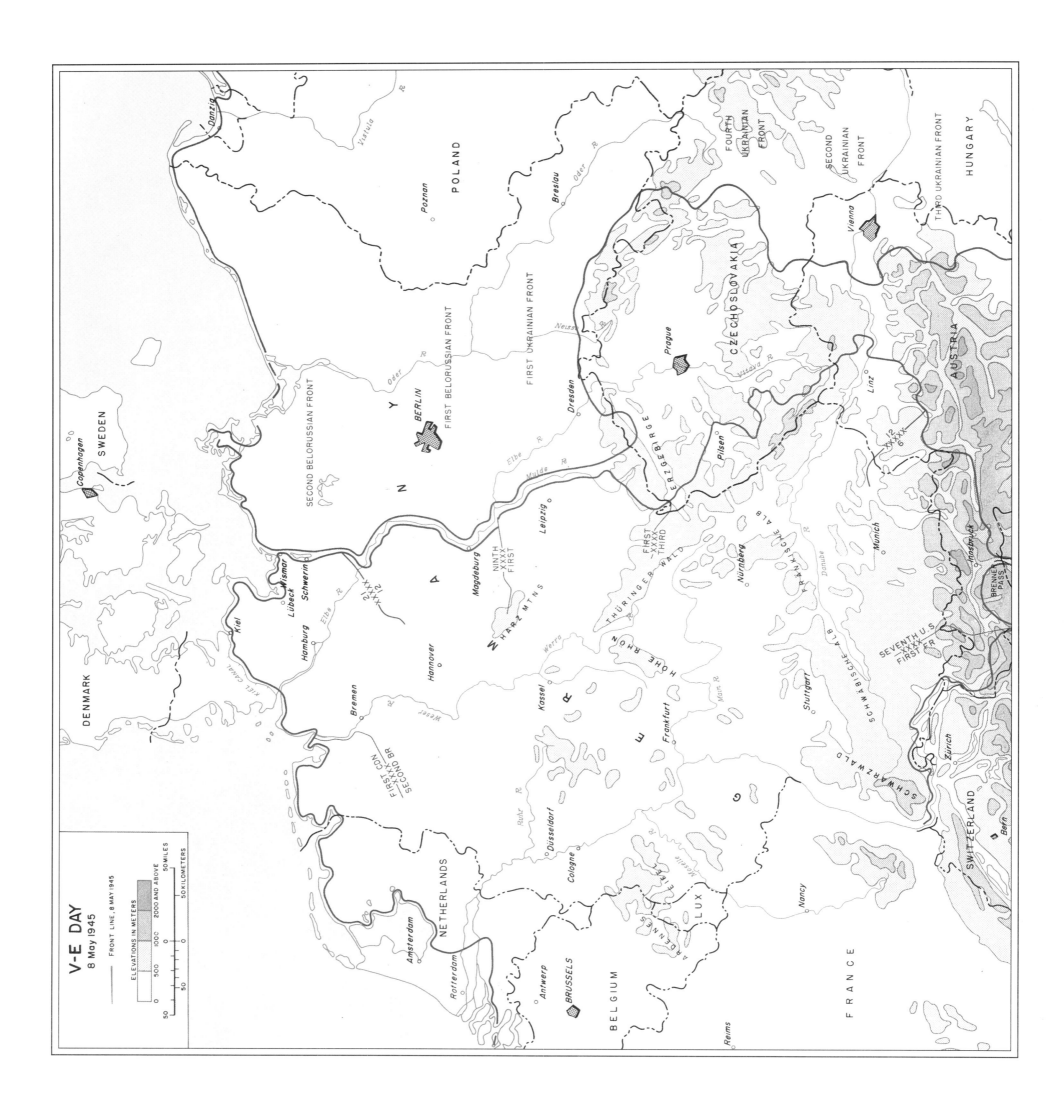

V-E DAY
8 May 1945

FRONT LINE, 8 MAY 1945

ELEVATIONS IN METERS

2000 AND ABOVE
1000
500
50
0

50 MILES
50 KILOMETERS